In Cold Fear

In Cold Fear

The Catcher in the Rye
Censorship Controversies and
Postwar American Character

Pamela Hunt Steinle

Ohio State University Press
Columbus

Library of Congress Cataloguing-in-Publication Data

Steinle, Pamela Hunt.
    In cold fear : the Catcher in the rye censorship controversies and
postwar American character / Pamela Hunt Steinle.
        p. cm.
Includes bibliographical references and index.
    ISBN 0-8142-5053-x (alk. paper)
        1. Salinger, J. D. (Jerome David), 1919– Catcher in the rye. 2.
National characteristics, American—History—20th century. 3. Salinger,
J. D. (Jerome David), 1919– —Censorship. 4. Censorship—United
States—History—20th century. 5. World War, 1939–1945—Literature and
the war. 6. Caulfield, Holden (Fictitious character) 7. Fiction—
Censorship—United States. 8. Runaway teenagers in literature.
9. Teenage boys in literature. 10. Cold War in literature. I. Title.
PS3537.A426 C395 2000
813´.54–dc21

                                            00-008777

Text design by John Delaine.
Jacket Design by Gore Studio.
Type set in Adobe Minion by BN Typographics West.
Printed by Thomson-Shore, Inc.

9 8 7 6 5 4 3 2

For Aurora Hunt Steinle,
in recognition of the fragile future that is her inheritance.

Contents

Acknowledgments

Given that the primary audience for this text is the intellectual community of scholars in American Studies as well as others living in neighboring environs of academia and engaged in the cultural analysis of American life and history, then the writing of these acknowledgments will surely be recognized as the academic ritual that, in one sense, it is. The danger here, as it is with all cultural rituals, is that the performance of the ritual becomes so familiar that it is attended to with a blind mind, absently reading through statements that in fact comprise, in the most important sense, a genealogy of intellectual identity and membership. As I write these acknowledgments, all of the following people are vivid in my mind for their contributions to this book and to my life.

This book began as my doctoral dissertation in Comparative Cultures at the University of California, Irvine under the direction of Professors Peter Clecak, Dickran Tashjian, and David Dickson Bruce. I was appreciative of their initial encouragement even as they doubted whether I would really be able to track down the participants from the early controversies over *The Catcher in the Rye* and feared for my success in getting any of the participants to talk openly. They offered their guidance without restricting my own intellectual curiosity, and I remain particularly grateful for their "light hand on the reins" as I conceptualized my arguments.

Professors Allan Axelrad, Paul Boyer, Peter Hales, Karen Lystra, and David Thelen read the manuscript in its earliest versions. Their insightful critiques and pointed questions as well as the spirited intellectual engagement that characterized each of their commentaries helped to make this a better book. Professors Al Stone, Cecelia Tichi, and Jay Mechling read the manuscript in its later version and I am indebted to them for their strong support for its publication. Each made a number of helpful suggestions for final revision: many of those suggestions were incorporated, while others caused me to at least think again about my reasons for constructing my arguments as I have. I am also indebted to Barbara Hanrahan for her enthusiastic support of this book during her tenure as director of Ohio State University Press, and to all the members of the press staff for seeing it through.

Throughout this project, I have had the honor of teaching with the extraordinary faculty of the Department of American Studies at California State University at Fullerton: Allan Axelrad, Jesse Battan, Wayne Hobson, John Ibson, Karen Lystra, Terri Snyder, Michael Steiner, Jim Weaver, and Leila Zenderland. I have learned from them as I have admired their wide-ranging scholarly interests and their wholehearted commitment to the teaching of American Studies, and I have richly enjoyed and benefited from our departmental culture of collegial support and deep friendship. I would also like to thank Barbara Campbell, a graduate student in our program who became my very necessary "computer guru" in the preparation of this manuscript, as well as my friend. American studies students Jonathan Menjivar and Justine Pas were my invaluable assistants in preparing the index.

Finally, few people outside of academia understand how lengthy and consuming the researching and writing of a book can be. For their unquestioning support throughout this undertaking—including endless patience with a project that on occasion took much of my time and self away from them—I would like to thank my family: Vernon Hunt, Jr., Grace Hunt, Deby Hunt, Vernon Hunt III, Melissa Hunt, and Elizabeth Hunt; Tom and Eleanor Steinle; Glenn and Donna Steinle; and most of all, my husband, Larry, and my daughter, Aurora. For the same reasons, I would also like to thank true friends: Patricia Thomas Crane, Shirley Dornin, Leslie Elliott, Dee Gessner, and (sadly too late) Ruby Valadez.

As to the necessities of funding and time, I benefited from the support I received from both the University of California at Irvine (UCI) and California State University at Fullerton (CSUF). The initial research phase of this study was supported by a grant from the UCI Chancellor's Patent Fund, while continuing research and writing were supported by CSUF with an award of course-release time in the spring of 1991, a summer stipend in 1991, and a spring sabbatical in 1995.

Introduction

Believing, with Max Weber, that man is an animal suspended in
webs of significance he himself has spun, I take culture to be those
webs and the analysis of it to be therefore not an experimental
science in search of a law but an interpretive one in search of
meaning.

— Clifford Geertz, *The Interpretation of Cultures*

In the fall of 1982, approximately fifty Baptist ministers, with the support of school officials and other community leaders, banned seven books from the school libraries of Calhoun County, Alabama: *A Clockwork Orange* by Anthony Burgess (1963), *The Way of Love* by John Cunningham and Frances Hanckel (1979), *Doris Day: Her Own Story* (1975), *No Place to Run* by Barbara Beasley Murphy (1977), J. D. Salinger's *The Catcher in the Rye* (1951), and two of John Steinbeck's novels: *East of Eden* (1952) and *The Grapes of Wrath* (1939).[1] To those unfamiliar with American book censorship in the period following World War II, this may appear to be a rather odd collection of titles — the autobiography of Hollywood's perennial Cold War sweetheart, Doris Day, paired with the gritty realism of John Steinbeck's fictionalized tales of labor and personal strife; an early 1950s "contemporary classic" *about* an adolescent, *The Catcher in the Rye,* and a late 1970s bestseller in popular paperback fiction *written for* adolescents, *No Place to Run.* One might find it strange that of those involved in the Calhoun County incident, only the librarian had actually read the majority of the books cited and some of the "censors" had not read one — or even a portion of one — of the books in question. Stranger still might seem the later discovery that one of the books, Steinbeck's *East of Eden,* had never been on the shelves of the challenged libraries in the first place.[2]

As one becomes acquainted with American censorship in the postwar period, however, these oddities form a recognizable pattern. Book lists

1

that appear almost random in their selection of titles, a lack of familiarity with the texts among those attempting to remove or restrict them, the "banning" of books already absent from libraries, the focus on adolescent or "young adult" reading materials, and the engagement of religious leaders, educators and school administrators, parents and other community members in censorship action and debate: each of these is among the defining characteristics of contemporary American censorship. Furthermore, it is an experience that was repeated with increasing frequency over the first thirty years following the end of World War II and continues today. Attempts to censor high school literature and the often heated controversies that surround them have occurred in every region of the United States, averaging nearly forty reported incidents per year, and leaving few school boards and communities untouched.[3]

Those who study censorship — primarily historians, librarians, and lawyers — have generally treated these incidents as isolated case studies, reflecting a tendency to explain censorship as a problem caused by narrow-minded "others" and to be resolved by the scholar's commitment to the First Amendment.[4] In this framework, censorship is a cultural problem only as it tests the boundaries of the freedom of speech. This focus directs attention away from the actual content or meaning of the texts themselves. The question quickly becomes whether or not one has the right to read a "filthy" or "un-American" book such as *The Catcher in the Rye,* not why the book is believed to be filthy or un-American in the first place.

My suggestion of *The Catcher in the Rye* at this point is intentional. One of the most salient characteristics of postwar American censorship has been the repeated inclusion of particular books on the censor's lists, and J. D. Salinger's novel stands out as a premier example. Selected in 1963 by the U.S. Information Service as "one of the twelve post–World War II American novels most likely to last," by 1981 *Catcher* had the dubious distinction of being at once the most frequently censored book across the country and the second most frequently taught novel in the public schools.[5] Indeed, beginning in the mid-1950s and continuing throughout the 1960s, even as *Catcher* was at the center of literary censorship across the nation and coming to epitomize the "controversial novel" for young adults, it repeatedly appeared on the American Library Association's annual list of "Outstanding Books for the College Bound" and would continue to do so into the 1990s.[6] After a slight drop in censorship activities in the early 1970s, *The Catcher in the Rye* has continued to receive public attention on "book-burning" and banning lists, recommendation lists, through direct references in popular literature and television, and even as implied justification for the fatal shooting of ex-Beatle John Lennon in 1980.[7] As he was arrested, Lennon's assassin read silently from *Catcher,* and at his court sentencing he read aloud the following passage:

> Anyway, I keep picturing these little kids playing some game in this big field of rye and all. Thousands of little kids, and nobody's around—nobody big, I mean—except me. And I'm standing on the edge of some crazy cliff. What I have to do, I have to catch everybody if they start to go over the cliff—I mean if they're running and they don't look where they're going I have to come out from somewhere and catch them. That's all I'd do all day. I'd just be the catcher in the rye and all.[8]

The debate over *The Catcher in the Rye*—a book with a lasting grip, if an uneasy one, on the public imagination—frequently begins with complaints about the use of "foul" language in the book ("237 goddams, 58 bastards, 31 Chrissakes, and 1 fart," according to one complaint).[9] On a strictly rational level, this is curious inasmuch as the protagonist, Holden Caulfield, spends a fair amount of his time trying to *erase* the obscenities he finds written by others. In this sense, the apparent focus of the debate may not be the actual center: offensive language may be an easier issue for complainants to address than, for instance, the offensive sentiments of Holden's idealistic if adolescent critique of the alienating ways and means of achieving status and identity in contemporary adult society.[10]

In either case, *Catcher*'s offensive nature is not sufficient in itself to explain the apparently endless nature of the debate. Its lengthy continuation is actually fed by an avoidance of deeper issues and an inability of the participants, for and against *Catcher,* to understand or articulate exactly what it is that is at stake. Here, anthropologist Raymond Firth's discussion of what he terms "disjunction" is helpful: "On the surface, a person is saying or doing something which our observations or inferences tell us should not be taken at face value—it stands for something else, of greater significance to him."[11]

I have found the debate surrounding *The Catcher in the Rye* to be indicative of a deepening cultural crisis in post–World War II America: a conflict or at the very least a lack of clarity as to what is believed about American adolescents—who they are, how childhood should be portrayed, and what nature of "world" adolescents should read about and study. The enculturation of children—the teaching (tacitly and explic-itly) of values, beliefs, and ideals, as well as explanations as to how to negotiate one's world—is perhaps the greatest charge and responsibility of any society. It is important that what a child is taught "fits" with cul-tural behavior and expectations, yet this task has become increasingly difficult in the latter half of the twentieth century.

The sheer pace of social change and relative ease of individual mobil-ity (geographic if not social) have long challenged American parents as they prepare their children for an adulthood of unclear definition. The greater difficulty in the post–World War II period, however, lies in the ever-widening distance between traditionally held American ideals and values (democracy, freedom, individualism, equality, voluntary social re-sponsibility) and the actual behaviors and expressions of Americans— as individuals, as a people. In exactly this sense, the narrator of *The Catcher in the Rye* sees his own adolescence as a precipitous jump from the cherished ideals and beliefs of childhood to the inauthentic and cyn-ical social reality of adulthood. Metaphorically, *Catcher* reads as a recog-nition of America's own process of maturity, from innocent and idealis-tic "childhood" to the "adult" pursuit of status and power in both our private lives and as a nation. Hence, *Catcher* and the surrounding debate can be said to point out a disjunctive gap of moral ambiguity in Ameri-can culture—for the adult as well as the child.

Until recently, scholarly work on mid-twentieth-century American culture has tended to reflect this moral ambiguity in a reliance on "objec-tive" historical and sociological description and a reluctance to interpret or evaluate moral values and beliefs in conjunction with the described behaviors. While some Cold War–era writers and scholars do offer inter-pretive arguments and explanations, they tend to follow one of two lim-ited approaches. The first has been to establish an overriding framework of explanation (such as David Riesman's thrice-directed Americans or Christopher Lasch's singular American self) to which the evidence is then fitted into place. The other approach has been to sustain a general con-tention that by or with the end of World War II, American culture was significantly different from its past—yet what exactly the "significant difference" is remains unclear, often taking the form of "felt" arguments tending toward vagueness.

A third course in the treatment of post–World War II American cul-ture has been to select a segment of the culture for study and to evaluate what one sees as the underlying problem or meaning of this specific behavior, with little consideration of the broader cultural context. In *The*

Feminine Mystique, for example, Betty Friedan generalized her study of middle-class suburban housewives in the 1950s to the experiences of all American women; in doing so, she largely put aside questions of class and subculture and ignored the restrictive requirements of the male role. Friedan did hint at broader considerations, however, in her eloquent and telling statement that the suburban pursuit in the 1950s of "the comforting reality of home and children" was primarily a cultural reaction shared by women and men alike to "the loneliness of war and the unspeakableness of the bomb, against the frightening uncertainty, the cold immensity of the changing world."[12]

"Immensity" of change, yes, but "unspeakableness"? In fact, middle-class Americans were speaking to issues of change in general and peace or security in particular, albeit addressing the issues symbolically. In both public and private spheres of American life, the pursuit and exhibition of an image of control and security is evident.[13] One has only to think of the American public's fascination with "candid" picture taking. Kodak's "Brownie" camera (and Polaroid's later "Swinger") combined postwar technology and marketing to make Everyman a photographer, producing increased volumes of family snapshot albums that nevertheless reflected the photographer's last-minute command: "Everybody smile."

The subsequent attempt of the counterculture movement of the late 1960s–early 1970s to challenge dominant beliefs and institutions relied heavily upon symbolic address in the form of "cultural reversals." Years later, when ex-Yippie Abbie Hoffman published his autobiographical documentary of the counterculture movement, *Soon to be a Major Motion Picture,* he subverted both the photographer's and the subject's control over "appearances." Juxtaposing a photograph from his own family album with an accompanying text of brief but grim biographies for each of the featured individuals, Hoffman then asked his reader in the caption, "Why is everyone smiling?"[14]

If such subversions were understood by countercultural activists of the 1960s to be necessary consciousness-raising tactics intended to confront postwar middle-class complacency and acritical rationalism, in retrospect they appear to have been an early theatrical frontline of what has more recently been referred to as the "culture wars." Taking place on shifting grounds of time and place and issue, these late-twentieth-century conflicts have been argued out between conservatives and liberals (the "voices of orthodoxy" and the "voices of progressivism") engaged in what has been recognized as a cultural contest over the sources as well as the symbols of individual control and cultural authority in postwar America.[15]

In point of fact, the evidence that the post–World War II period is "significantly different" from American experience of the past is abundant; the task lies in comprehending the complex and interwoven discourse of cultural response, which is not easily apprehended within the narrow boundaries of traditional scholarly disciplines. Interdisciplinary efforts meet with greater success in grasping the nature and variety of cultural expression but then face the problem of the sheer breadth of contemporary American experience. Even as the quarterly *Newsletter of the American Studies Association* featured a 1985 essay promoting "the thought of undertaking a twentieth century cultural history," the author of the piece openly acknowledged the difficulties inherent in writing such a history, from conceptualization to "the needed audacity" required in interpreting one's own historical moment.[16]

The year 1985 also saw the publication of historian Paul Boyer's *By the Bomb's Early Light: American Thought and Culture at the Dawn of the Atomic Age*, a study limited to the five years immediately following America's dropping of the atomic bomb(s), yet capturing through interdisciplinary research and analysis both the "unspeakability" and "immensity" of cultural change that would continue for the rest of the century. If a five-year period of evidence (however broad-reaching, densely compiled, and under however thoughtful scrutiny) does not in a literal sense stand as a twentieth-century cultural history, in a philosophical sense Boyer's book is exactly that. Writing in his introduction that "it is as though the Bomb has become one of those categories of Being, like Space and Time, that, according to Kant, are built into the very structure of our minds, giving shape and meaning to all our perceptions," Boyer highlighted his own subjectivity as participant in this historical moment and that of his reader as well, by asking—and answering—"Am I alone in this feeling? I think not."[17]

If a certain mix of intellectual curiosity, academic training, self-reflexivity, and attempted objectivity as well as simple perseverance at the tasks of research and writing is necessary to the production of any historical account, Boyer's words point out that a cultural history of the *second half* of the twentieth century requires not only the additional courage to study a historical crisis that continues to the present moment (unlike the moods of celebration and victory at the close of World War I or cautious relief following the Depression, the anxious fallout from World War II's atomic conclusion has only escalated to greater nuclear fears) but also a willingness to risk one's personal credibility as historian and as cultural participant. Only recently have these challenges begun to be met through the work of cultural critics such as Tom Engelhardt in *The End of Victory Culture: Cold War America and the Disillusioning of a Generation* and Alan Nadel in *Containment Culture: American Narratives, Postmodernism, and the Atomic Age*.[18]

Engelhardt's study opens with his tracing of the narrative of America as "victory culture" from its origination in the seventeenth-century Puritan errand into the wilderness with its Pequot wars and captivity narratives to the faltering narrative of what he terms "triumphalist despair" born of post–World War II nuclear fear. Sketching the landscape of postwar American childhood and adolescence through his survey of popular culture and analysis of commercially successful films and children's toys from 1945 to 1994, Engelhardt echoes Paul Boyer when he finds what has become "now practically a cliché that, with the end of the Cold War and the 'loss of the enemy,' American culture has entered a period of crisis that raises profound questions about national purpose and identity." Pinpointing the inception of this crisis to America's use of atomic bombs against Japan, Engelhardt follows the "slow-motion collapse of a heroic war ethos thereafter" to its eventual "decomposition through those years of generational loss and societal disillusionment to Vietnam, which was its graveyard for all to see."[19]

While *The Catcher in the Rye* lies outside the evidence examined by Boyer and Engelhardt, Alan Nadel devotes an entire chapter to the rhetoric of *Catcher*'s protagonist, Holden Caulfield, in his survey of Cold War narratives intended to "contain" democratic values within the nuclear family against the dual threats of communism and nuclear power. For Nadel, narratives are a way of bridging the gap between specific events and a larger sense of history, forging a link between action and meaning. Arguing that although personal narratives usually "oscillate, situationally, between identification with and alienation from a historical order," Nadel concludes that cultural attempts "to reconcile the cult of domesticity with the demand for domestic security" during the Cold War were so thoroughgoing as to result in a "rampant performance of narratives (of containment), in such a variety of sites and forms as to create the illusion that national narratives were knowable and unquestionable realities."[20]

Yet Americans have individually questioned the reality of these narratives, independently interpreting their own culture, and on occasion have spoken out with an astounding audacity that post–World War II scholars should particularly appreciate. Bald observations and impassioned statements of opinion usually reserved for the private company of friends and family go public when local citizens engage in a community debate—for example, in censorship controversies. In these discourses, participant dialogue offers comparative insights into individual understandings of community mores. In arguing out their differences, in making further attempts to be understood by (and perchance to convince) their fellow citizens, participants in public controversies necessarily find themselves articulating private beliefs that they not only hold to be significant but had previously assumed to be shared—in effect, an attempt to define if not to close the disjunctive gap between explicit community values (i.e., democracy, liberty, and education) and their tacit meanings for individual citizens.[21]

While local controversies usually revolve around the identity of a specific community, they also constitute a wider cultural debate when they occur across boundaries of place. The controversy generated by *The Catcher in the Rye* is just such a contemporary American debate: in public meetings and personal conversations, opinion letters and position papers, participants across America defend and criticize the text based on their individual and local assumptions about cultural truths. Laden with value judgments, character assessments, and philosophical polemics, public controversy over *Catcher* is essentially a Geertzian "note in a bottle": a cultural debate about what constitutes moral and ethical conduct in mid-twentieth-century American life.

Indeed, the participants in this debate are self-consciously aware that they are involved in "something larger than themselves." Drawn into the debate as citizens of geographic communities, participants almost always identify themselves in terms of their membership in broader communities of cultural practice: as literary critics, as educators, as librarians, as parents, and as members of the "Moral Majority" or what has been termed the New Right. And as the individual voices ring out in the local communities, standing for or against *Catcher,* it is their initial cries of "un-American" and "very American" that direct attention to the question of national character, the question of "what is the American," raised so long ago by Alexis de Tocqueville. Arguing ostensibly about whether or not *Catcher* is an appropriate reading for adolescents, participants often find themselves engaged in a gut-wrenching controversy over the definition and viability of our national character. This study tracks the *Catcher* debate across time and region, through letters, newspaper accounts, and interviews; makes explicit the discrepant assumptions and common concerns of participants; and seeks an understanding of some of the aspirations, fears, and tensions of post–World War II middle-class Americans in their own words.

Throughout the research process, I engaged in countless discussions of *The Catcher in the Rye* with students and colleagues, among friends, and occasionally with strangers. I was repeatedly struck by the avid interest expressed simply because *Catcher* was the focal text of the study. More revealing was the actual nature of these responses: everyone, it seems, has either a *Catcher* story of their own to tell (their individual experience in reading the book) or a favored or provocative segment of the novel that they believe to be *the key* to understanding what the story *really* means.

In all cases, the book was remembered with personal affection and remained vivid in memory and detail. Again and again, people of disparate ages and backgrounds would express how and why the book was important to them, and then continue on to volunteer "helpful hints" and sources to me. All of this interest and voluntarism was generated not by a searching question or in the reflective mood of an interview but in each case by my simplified answer to the polite (and sometimes tiresome) conversational question, "So what are you writing on?" While not formally collected as research data, these responses offer reasonable, if impressionistic, evidence that *Catcher* is a widely shared cultural text and as such does indeed engage the imaginations of many.

The "order of things" in this book in some sense replicates my own experience in seeking out and attempting to come to terms with this debate. I first read *Catcher* in the spring of 1964: the previously "banned" book had just been returned to the shelves of my California junior high school library on a restricted basis and I was a thirteen year old eagerly anticipating some "racy" reading material. While I found Holden Caulfield to be wholly credible and in some ways admirable, my more prurient adolescent interests were disappointed, and I was left curious as to why the book had ever been banned in the first place. In belated answer, this book begins with *The Catcher in the Rye:* the text itself and the immediate context of its publication. The chapters that follow explore the worldview and requirements of membership in the five relevant participant communities of cultural practice before entering the actual discourse of the debate over the book as it occurred within boundaries of time and place. The final chapter and the last-chance "afterword" offer interpretive conclusions on the "whys" of contemporary censorship of fiction for adolescents as well as speculations on the significance of *Catcher* as a cultural Rorschach symbol.

The original version of this study was written as my 1987 doctoral dissertation in the "Star Wars/evil empire" atmosphere of the Reagan administration. By the time the first round of revisions toward a book manuscript were completed in 1995, President Clinton and Soviet leader Boris Yeltsin were shaking hands and smiling before the cameras recording their agreement to "stand down" nuclear missiles, signifying the end of the Cold War. There was a moment's pause for reflection upon the wishful possibility of peace in our time—and then I was reeling with the rest of America over the bombing of the Federal building in Oklahoma City.

America's Heartland, already exhausted as an advertising metaphor, had been blown apart in one massive spasm of cardiac arrest, spurring various voices of public disappointment and disaffection into mass-mediated discourse alongside the more somber palliatives of swift and decisive punishment for the terrorists offered by President Clinton (and Hillary) to soothe adults via primetime news and children via a "special message" broadcast across the Saturday morning universe of children's television. Oklahoma City demonstrated that terror can strike at the heart of America and in the form of a bomb, with or without Communists or nuclear weapons. For many, part of the heartbreak, the inescapable heartsickness, was that the terrorists responsible were homegrown (school, church, and military) "patriots" after all. Considering some of the participant discourse in the censorship controversies, foreshadowing the internal terrorism that results from growing up in a culture of fear and deindividuation, I was somewhat less surprised—and all the more saddened.

The 1990s also saw the introduction of a new ritual of terror that gave equally new meaning to any consideration of "troubled teens" in America: the school shooting. Springing from adolescent fantasies of nihilistic revenge—given sound and weight in alternative rock music, popular literature, and film; given dimension in interactive video games; given connection through Internet Web sites and chat rooms—the shootings appeared at first (1993–95) to be isolated acts of "fledgling psychopaths."[22] But in 1996, when fourteen-year-old Barry Loukaitis walked into his eighth-grade algebra class at Frontier Junior High in Moses Lake, Washington, dressed in black from his boots to the long overcoat concealing his rifle, and began firing (killing the teacher and two students and wounding a third student), his individual actions were the first complete enactment of an emergent deadly ritual.[23]

With his stride and costuming mimicking Leonardo DiCaprio's "dream sequence" depiction of an adolescent boy's cool execution of his priest-teacher and classmates in the 1995 film *Basketball Diaries,* and as if following the stage directions for the classroom rampages in both that film and Pearl Jam's award-winning 1993 music video "Jeremy" (of which Loukaitis had his own personal copy), Loukaitis's murderous expression of his adolescent rage was as culturally scripted as it was personally motivated. This is *not* to say that popular culture is causal but rather that we should not be surprised when members of a culture, however alienated, act in ways that reflect their enculturation. Once Loukaitis acted, we should have seen Paducah and Springfield and Littleton coming.[24]

"Now the spectacle ... has come to Colorado, a place much closer to the nation's geographic and emotional center," wrote one reporter for the *Los Angeles Times.*[25] It took the "massacre" at Columbine for many Americans, and perhaps especially those living in suburbs of privilege, to realize that "it *can* happen here." However alienated and isolated the individual teenagers who did the shooting might have been, causing them to "cross the line," their actions took expressive forms that many American teenagers—and particularly suburban white adolescent males—are (on imaginary levels) familiar with in the narratives of popular culture. If the shooters' immediate sense of desperation, their "breaking point," hinged in each case to date on personal circumstances, the bleakness of their outlook is more commonplace among advantaged teens than we might wish to acknowledge. Their actions may well be more comprehensible if we frame them in the somewhat broader historical context of the nuclear fears and Cold War comforts of the past forty years.

All this is to say that this study came about in a context of cold fear generated at the end of World War II and was born of the systemically chilling experience of living in America in the second half of the twentieth century but that it is written with heat. In 2000, we may (hope upon hope, denial upon denial of nuclear "accidents," nuclear interests, and the nuclear potentialities of nations other than the "superpowers") be past the nuclear threat but we (troubled adults as well as troubled teens) are a long way from slumbering with peaceful consciences. The explosive reverberations of the terrorist's bomb or the adolescent's classroom barrage resonate within a still-familiar nuclear imagination in which our past and present as well as our hopes and dreams for the future can all come to naught in one annihilatory blast.

So it is that I share Robert Bellah's interest "in those cultural traditions and practices that, without destroying individuality, serve to limit
and restrain the destructive side of individualism." I believe I have found
at least one expression of them in the cultural debate over *The Catcher
in the Rye*.[26]

On Ethnographic Study

This study was initially inspired by an ongoing argument among my
cohorts at the University of California, Irvine in a 1981 graduate seminar
on the theory and methods of interdisciplinary research into expressive
forms of culture. Reading Stanley Fish's 1980 *Is There a Text in This Class?*
for that seminar was a radicalizing experience that made particular sense
to me in light of my preceding embrace of the works of Thomas Kuhn
and Clifford Geertz. My initial interest in processes of social change
expanded to incorporate a new fascination with understanding cultural
participation and, eventually, to a fascination with the construction of
cultural knowledge.[27]

Arguing at that time with my classmates, I used my recollections of
Catcher (as a text valued both critically and popularly, as a controversial
text, and as a text to which I could speak as a one-time reader) as we
debated the relative merits of auteur theory, traditional literary criticism,
and reader interpretation. Ethnography seemed the obvious method for
gaining understanding of the cultural significance of a text. The difficulty, it seemed to me then, lay in accessing an audience of readers as
they determined themselves rather than as constructed by the would-be
ethnographer. *Catcher* appeared to be a text with a self-identified and
multifaceted audience, and I knew I had found my dissertation topic.

I began my research by identifying my case study readers/participants
as they were named in newspaper accounts and civic meeting minutes.
I searched telephone directories and was able to convince all but one
person to agree to an interview—and even that person eventually called
me and then talked quite freely on the telephone. While in no way a random sample, they were all "just regular citizens," as one interviewee
referred to himself and his fellow participants, and except for one school
administrator, none of them had been involved in any other controversy
over books.

I met my participants in school classrooms and administrative offices,
in hotel lobbies and restaurants, and at their workplaces: libraries, a hospital, and a newspaper office. In one case, my research took on a rather

cloak-and-dagger feel when one participant, fearful of repercussions for her son (who was still in high school) or from her husband (who opposed her involvement in the censorship controversies although he agreed with her pro-*Catcher* sentiments), agreed to meet with me only if she could come directly to my motel room and I would already have all the draperies pulled closed. Imagine my surprise when she "snuck by," carrying two large cardboard boxes of newspaper clippings and debate-related documents!

The research process at this point was more oral history than interview. Starting my tape recorder and asking them to state their name, I then simply asked the participants to tell me how they had become involved in the local controversy over *Catcher,* what they thought about the book, and if they could tell me "their story" of what had happened: how they understood it and what they thought was important for me to know. In doing so, I was intentionally encouraging a narrative form that I believed would give clearest voice to their own interpretations of the text and of the controversy itself. Most "interviews" lasted from forty-five minutes to nearly two hours, with only occasional interjections of encouragement to continue or questions of clarification from me. If, for example, interviewees referred to *Catcher* as "very American" or "un-American" and did not follow with a voluntary explanation of what they meant, I would ask them if they could elaborate. Otherwise, I refrained from any direct questioning: the interview commentary in this study is a representative selection of what my readers/participants thought was important to tell.[28]

What I failed to appreciate before entering the debate discourse was *how much* of audience interpretation lies outside of the text and how difficult it was going to be to *re-present* the voices of my interviewees in the immediate context in which their responses occurred—and somehow fill in the larger contexts of reference and assumption within which their words had further meaning. Their compiled narratives presented a sometimes complicated, sometimes straightforward discourse about their beliefs and concerns as participants in postwar American culture, both defining what they considered to be heroic character and evaluating our contemporary historical moment.

I have tried to resist a traditional historical narrative tracing "main lines of response" or presenting condensed representative types. Rather than relying on a reductive narrative of my own telling, I chose to give print voice to the participants themselves whenever possible—as nuanced by the phrasing of their "everyday language" and contextualized by the

connections and frameworks they put forward. While such "thick description" cannot wholly escape reification of cultural participation and
also requires from the reader a patient immersion "in the trenches" of,
in this case, the *Catcher* controversies, I believe that the more complicated understandings revealed through ethnographic study are their
own reward.

There is one unique participant whose "voice" in this book bears
some explanation. In J. D. Salinger's strategic choice to give first-person
voice to Holden Caulfield as the fictional narrator of the tale, he also
(and perhaps unwittingly) gave him *fictional life*. From the earliest reviews by literary critics to the responses of more general readership to
references in popular culture, Holden Caulfield is very often referred to
as if he is a real person. Hence, instead of discussing Holden as might be
expected in a scholarly manuscript—as a fictional representation carrying out the author's narrative strategies as understood from the scholar's
perspective—I take my cue from the discourse of the controversies themselves and for the most part address Holden Caulfield as someone as
alive as he is to the debate participants. Sensitive to and interested in
understanding the contexts in which Holden is constructed by different
readers, I have tried to keep my own discussions in the same frame of reference as those readers rather than superimposing an analysis of Salinger's literary strategies. For better or worse, Holden Caulfield *is* incarnate
for most readers of *The Catcher in the Rye*.

1

The Catcher in the Rye as Postwar American Fable

Here's for the plain old Adam, the simple genuine self against the whole world.

—Ralph Waldo Emerson, *Journals*

J. D. Salinger's novel *The Catcher in the Rye* is one of the most significant books in American literature to appear since World War II. The center of heated censorship debates for the past forty years and the cause of some confusion and consternation to American literary critics, *The Catcher in the Rye* has held the attention of popular American readership with a force that can perhaps be best appreciated by a brief review of its publishing history. First published in mid-July 1951 by Little, Brown and Company, *The Catcher in the Rye* was simultaneously published as a Book-of-the-Month Club selection. By the end of July, Little, Brown and Company was reprinting the novel for the fifth time, and by late August *Catcher* had reached fourth place on the *New York Times* best-seller list. Signet Books brought out the first paperback edition in 1953, selling over three million copies in the next ten years. Grosset and Dunlap brought out an edition of their own in 1952, Modern Library in 1958, and Franklin Watts Publishers in 1967. In January of 1960, *Catcher* reappeared on the *New York Times* best-seller list, this time placing fifth among paperback books. All the while, Little, Brown and Company continued reprinting their original edition—completing thirty-five printings by 1981. In 1964, Bantam Books brought out their paperback edition and by 1981 had reprinted it fifty-two times. All in all, the total number of copies in print by 1997 was estimated at over ten million, with sustained sales of nearly two hundred thousand copies per year.[1]

Clearly *The Catcher in the Rye* is a landmark book for the post–World War II period in its immediate and sustained popularity. However, publication and printing records alone do not necessarily indicate that a literary work has engaged or become a significant part of the cultural imagination. One might argue that *Catcher* has been so frequently printed in response to its classroom usage — reflecting an appreciation of the novel by English teachers but not necessarily the choice or interest of a voluntary readership. Another interpretation is that sales of *Catcher* have been spurred by its very presence on various censorship lists. While these perspectives certainly bear some truth, the materials of popular culture provide evidence that the success of *Catcher* is broader and of deeper significance than these explanations acknowledge.

Continuing references to *Catcher* in commercial television series and several novels illustrate that the producers of popular media assume a broad base of audience familiarity with the novel.[2] A 1977 novel by Erich Segal, *Oliver's Story,* as well as 1982 episodes of the television series *Sixty Minutes* and *Archie Bunker's Place* all referred to *Catcher* in terms of its status as a controversial text. In another television series, the long-time favorite game show *Family Feud,* as the host reviewed the "correct" answers to an audience-survey question about types of bread, he called out, "Rye," and then quipped, "As in catcher."[3]

Revealing their own esteem for Salinger's work, three authors of contemporary novels have used *Catcher* to move their plot lines forward. In his 1987 teen novel *Can't Miss,* author Michael Bowen assumed and relied on the adolescent reader's familiarity with Holden Caulfield's critique of the "phoniness" of postwar American life to enhance his development of the teenage main character.[4] In the award-winning 1982 novel *Shoeless Joe,* not only did the author, W. P. Kinsella, assume reader familiarity with *Catcher* but the tale itself was written to facilitate an imaginary dialogue with J. D. Salinger. Given the same name as one of Salinger's fictional characters, the novel's protagonist, Ray Kinsella, is a baseball fan who has a vision of a game being played in his cornfields by a literal "dream team" that includes deceased baseball legends — and the very much alive if reclusive J. D. Salinger.

Transforming his cornfields into a ballfield based on the mysterious instructions given by an imaginary ballpark announcer in Ray's vision, the second command requires the real-life presence of Salinger to "ease his pain." Convincing the fictional Salinger that he should leave New Hampshire and come to Iowa with him, Ray tells Salinger, "I've thought about you and baseball.... You've captured the experience of growing up in America, the same way Freddy Patek corners a ground ball. *The Catcher in the Rye* is the definitive novel of a young man's growing pains, of growing up in pain. . . . But baseball can soothe even those pains, for it is stable and permanent, steady as a grandfather dozing in a wicker chair on a verandah."[5]

Yet it is Salinger's snug capture of adolescent angst in *Catcher* that is used to soothe the growing pains of a thirteen-year-old girl in popular writer Julie Smith's 1994 detective novel *New Orleans Beat*. At a crucial point in this story, an adult "friend of the family" named Darryl attempts to reach out to a recently returned adolescent "runaway" named Sheila by giving her a book as a gift at a "welcome home" gathering. At first, the title of the book is not disclosed to Sheila—nor to the reader—and she is clearly disappointed that her special adult friend has brought her something that she sees as an impersonal and typical adult-to-adolescent present.

Begrudgingly responding, "I'm not mad. I could . . . read a book," Sheila's disappointment deepens when Darryl tells her the novel is about a boy: "'A boy?' Her (inner) voice said, What on Earth are you thinking of?" Asking her to trust him, "even though it's a book and even though it's about a boy," Darryl then tells Sheila that this book is different, that "it's going to change your life. You're going to read this and think, 'There's somebody out there who understands.'" At this moment the book's title is finally revealed, not by Darryl nor by the unwrapping of the package, but by the larger gathering of adult family members and friends who exclaim in unison before they even see the book: "Catcher in the Rye."[6]

Everyone, it seems, is assumed to understand something about *Catcher.* Exactly what or how much the reader is required to understand is more vague, ranging from the brevity of the first few examples—requiring a "household familiarity" with at least the title *The Catcher in the Rye*—to the complexity of the latter three: to fully enjoy Kinsella's novel, the reader must have some knowledge of both the basic story of *Catcher* and the questions and problems that interested Salinger himself. As both the novels and the television series are geared toward a widespread "middle-American" audience, these references reveal an assumption about *Catcher*'s place in the culture: if people haven't read it for themselves, they are at least familiar with the book's title, its status, and some sense of the story line.[7]

For many of those who have read it, *Catcher* holds an enduring appeal that some readers believe can transcend the cultural gap between generations. When critic Sanford Pinsker sought to define the characteristics of a "formative book" for his literary peers, he chose *Catcher* as his post–World War II exemplar of fiction capable of leading "double lives as cultural statements, fastened as firmly to the here and now as they are to fiction's universals." Noting that formative books have their greatest impact among adolescents, engaging these readers "at a point when options loom larger than certainties, when an admonition to 'change your life' can still have teeth," Pinsker recalled his own youthful response to *Catcher* as a reader "hooked" on Holden Caulfield's "talking" voice.[8]

Similarly, critic Adam Moss, reflecting upon his early reading of *Catcher,* wrote in 1981 that it had become "one of those rare books that influence one generation after another, causing each to claim it as its own."[9] Five years later, the casual remarks of a department store cosmetician in her mid-thirties confirmed and further personalized Moss's point when she commented to me that "*The Catcher in the Rye* was the key thing that got he [her then thirteen-year-old son] and I really talking about reading and how you don't always have to read 'junk.'"[10] Finally, it seems *Catcher* is not only a "formative" book to be shared across generations but a text that is capable of actually transforming its reader, leading Julie Smith to conclude her *Catcher* scene in *New Orleans Beat* with this claim: "Anybody who reads this book . . . can talk any way they want . . . because you can't stop anybody after they've read it, can you? They come out a whole different person, don't they?"[11]

The question then becomes, What is this book, this story that catches the attention and often the affections of so many? Simply told, *The Catcher in the Rye* is the tale of a sixteen-year-old boy, Holden Caulfield, who is flunking out of his third prep school and suffers a breakdown of sorts when he leaves school early to spend three days on his own in New York City. Holden is the narrator of the story, which is told in retrospect from a sanitarium in California, and Salinger maximizes the impact of the narrative by adhering meticulously to the teenage vernacular of the late 1940s–early 1950s. The resulting text is peppered with mild obscenities as Holden expresses his disappointment and, often, disgust with much of the postwar adult world.

Holden's definitive sense of American life is that it is largely "phony" —a term he applies repeatedly throughout the tale to various contemporary definitions of success, ranging from the realms of corporate achievement, conventional marriage, social status, and "belonging" to physical attractiveness, Hollywood glamour, and athletics. The implied "craziness" of his perspective is enhanced by the fact that Holden is well on the way to such success himself if only he would accept it. The novel ends as it begins: with Holden in the sanitarium, expected to return to "normal life" in the near future yet with little indication as to how he will manage the return to normalcy, much less whether he desires to do so.

On the surface, then, *Catcher* appears to be a rather mundane novel with its greatest potential audience among teenagers: the audience most likely to identify with Holden, to find the novel's use of adolescent vernacular familiar, and to appreciate the critique of contemporary adulthood. It is not readily apparent why this particular novel has gained the lasting affection as well as engendered the vehement hostility of adult readers to the degree that they have been willing to debate over it for the past forty-odd years. While other contemporary novels may have found a similarly split audience (Vladimir Nabokov's *Lolita* comes to mind), they have neither spurred such lengthy controversy nor enjoyed the sustained popularity of *Catcher*. It is only by looking more closely at Salinger's carefully drawn characterization of Holden Caulfield and listening through the vernacular and the obscenities that one can isolate the eloquent critique that Salinger presents, catching his audience unaware. The argument is one in the long-standing "determining debate" of American thought and writing that has been given coherent definition in R. W. B. Lewis's *The American Adam*.

⁓

In 1955 R. W. B. Lewis put forward his analysis of and argument for a "native American mythology." Pointing out that the salient (and assumedly universal) characteristic of cultural maturation was the generation of a "determining debate over the ideas that preoccupy it: salvation, the order of nature, money, power, sex, the machine, and the like," Lewis believed that such debates were a crucial forum in which "a culture achieves identity not so much through the ascendancy of one particular set of convictions as through the emergence of its peculiar and distinctive dialogue."[12]

Lewis located the American debate in the voices of "articulate thinkers and conscious artists" of nineteenth-century America, and the resulting mythos he isolated was what he called the "American Adam": "the authentic American as a figure of heroic innocence and vast potentialities, poised at the start of a new history."[13] While much of *The American Adam* was devoted to definition and description of this mythological hero as he appeared in American fiction, the heart of Lewis's argument lay in his insistence that this cultural mythology was a motivational source toward human good and, as well, in his mourning of the absence of such a mythology in mid-twentieth-century America: "A century ago, the challenge to debate was an expressed belief in achieved human per-fection, a return to the primal perfection. Today the challenge comes rather from the expressed belief in achieved hopelessness.... We can hardly expect to be persuaded any longer by the historic dream of the new Adam."[14]

Looking at contemporary American literature from his 1955 van-tage, Lewis identified three novels in the post–World War II period as examples of "the truest and most fully engaged American fiction after the second war": *Invisible Man* by Ralph Ellison, *The Adventures of Augie March* by Saul Bellow, and *The Catcher in the Rye* by J. D. Salinger. Lewis saw each of these novels as among the very few to continue the Adamic fictional tradition of solitary experience and moral priority over the waiting world. He applauded the efforts of these mid-twentieth-century writers as they "engender[ed] from within their work the hopeful and vulnerable sense of life that makes experience and so makes narrative action possible," yet who did so by "creat[ing] it from within, since they can scarcely find it any longer in the historic world about them."[15]

Here, Lewis's recognition of the intersection between his own for-mulation of the "American Adam" as a once dominant yet recently shrinking force in American culture and the story of Holden Caulfield is the first clue as to the source of cultural tension created by *The Catcher in the Rye*. A story of traditional appeal and yet a contemporary oddness, both fit and lack of fit with the historic dialogue are evident when *Catcher* is examined in light of Lewis's argument.

The classic characterization of the American Adam was the nineteenth-century image of a "radically new personality, the hero of the new ad-venture," "happily bereft of ancestry," and free of the taint of inherited status to stand alone, "self-reliant and self-propelling, ready to confront whatever awaited him with the aid of his own unique and inherent resources." As the nineteenth century drew to a close, this characterization was modified as American literature reflected concurrent perceptions of social and environmental changes in American life: the movement of the "frontier" from forest to barren plain, and ultimately to closure. The American Adam, no longer situated in an Edenic world, found himself instead "alone in a hostile, or at best a neutral universe." Nevertheless, Lewis claimed that the Adamic character remained intact throughout the first half of the twentieth century, "for much of that fable remained ... the individual going forth toward experience, the inventor of his own character and creator of his personal history."[16]

Bearing these characterizations in mind, at this point I introduce to you Holden Caulfield, as J. D. Salinger did in the first page of *The Catcher in the Rye:*

> If you really want to hear about it, the first thing you'll probably want to know is where I was born, and what my lousy childhood was like, and how my parents were occupied and all before they had me, and all that David Copperfield kind of crap, but I don't feel like going into it, if you want to know the truth. In the first place, that stuff bores me, and in the second place, my parents would have about two hemorrhages apiece if I told anything personal about them .... Besides, I'm not going to tell you my whole goddam autobiography or anything. I'll just tell you about this madman stuff that happened to me around last Christmas.[17]

In Holden's statement of introduction, his position as a solitary individual in the Adamic tradition is not only evident but reinforced by the contrast to English literary tradition ("that David Copperfield kind of crap"). The initial assumption is that the mid-twentieth-century reader *wants* to know the family and position of a central character—an assumption that is immediately challenged as irrelevant to the telling of the story itself and as contrary to middle-class expectations of personal and family privacy. Hence, Salinger's introduction of his central character provided an opening defense for the Adamic narrative as well as an implicit jab at the movement of contemporary readers away from that very tradition.

Defense of the Adamic tradition is not surprising in light of Holden's apparent literary lineage. Searching for a fictional representative for his American mythos, "unambiguously treated" and "celebrated in his very Adamism,"[18] Lewis chose James Fenimore Cooper's Natty Bumppo: hero of *The Deerslayer* and, it seems, a direct if unacknowledged ancestor of Salinger's Holden Caulfield. In a central scene in *The Deerslayer*, Natty Bumppo's name is changed as the consequence of his fight with a Huron warrior. In their struggle, Natty kills the warrior, but Cooper characterizes it as a chivalrous battle, ending with the dying man telling Natty that he should now be known as "Hawkeye" instead of the boyish "Deerslayer."[19] In this pivotal moment, Natty takes on the heroic status of the American Adam: "born with all due ceremony during an incident that has every self-conscious quality of a ritual trial ... [,] Deerslayer earns his symbolic reward of a new name."[20]

If the notion of rebirth is characteristic of the American Adam, it is crucial to the overlapping American narrative of "regeneration through violence" in which acts of violence and destruction are seen as fair practice when they purportedly allow a morally strengthened consciousness to emerge.[21] And it is in keeping with both traditions, then, that early on in *Catcher*, Holden Caulfield purchases a red hunting cap that his prep school roommate calls a "deer-shooting cap." "Like hell it is," Holden retorts, and then clarifies to the reader of his narrative, "I took it off and looked at it. I sort of closed one eye, like I was taking aim at it. 'This is a people shooting hat,' I said. 'I shoot people in this hat'" (22).[22]

Further along, Holden battles an older and stronger classmate to protect the reputation of a female friend and finds himself on the losing end of the fight. Searching for his cap in defeat, Holden comes face-to-face with himself, and it is this critical moment of self-recognition that will lead to his leave-taking of Pencey Prep:

> I couldn't find my goddam hunting hat anywhere. Finally, I found it. It was under the bed. I put it on, and turned the peak around to the back, the way I liked it, and then I went over and took a look at my stupid face in the mirror. You never saw such gore in your life. I had blood all over my mouth and chin and even on my pajamas and bathrobe. It partly scared me and it partly fascinated me. All that blood and all sort of made me look tough. I'd only been in about two fights in my life, and I lost both of them. I'm not too tough. I'm a pacifist, if you want to know the truth. (45)

If the first passage recalls the heroic tradition of Cooper's *Deerslayer* (Holden donning the symbolic garb of the deer hunter and further identifying himself by his hawkeyed aim), then the second passage can be seen as a suggestion for a new errand for the Adamic hero: that of pacifism except when called to the protection of innocents. His ritual battle endured, Holden's reversal of the hunting cap brings to mind the cap of a baseball *catcher*. Holden is thus implicitly renamed and it is a name he will later explicitly claim.

Just as the moment of trial and rebirth was the creation of Lewis's Adamic character, it was his survival through a later "fall" from grace that brought the character to heroic status. Although the consequences of such a fall would entail some suffering, the fall itself offered an opportunity for learning necessary to the character's growth in moral understanding and conscience to fully heroic stature. In the writing of the elder Henry James, for example, the hero "had to fall, to pass beyond childhood in an encounter with 'Evil,'" and "had to mature by virtue of the destruction of his own egotism." The very act of "falling" opened the path to moral perfection, a state viewed by James as achievable "not by learning, only by *unlearning*."[23]

Considered within this framework of the "fortunate fall," Holden's experiences after he leaves Pencey Prep can be seen as necessary to his developing moral stature: from his introduction to the seamy side of New York City life via bar flies, stale cabs, hotel pimps and prostitutes to his confrontation with Mr. Antolini. Antolini is a teacher from one of Holden's past prep schools, "the best teacher I ever had" (174), and Holden turns to him for both moral support and physical shelter. Holden's visit to his home, however, is abruptly terminated when Holden interprets Antolini's consoling caresses as a homosexual advance.

Holden flees Antolini's apartment, disillusioned and less innocent than when he arrived; but before he can depart, Antolini makes a prediction as to Holden's future: "I have a feeling that you're riding for some kind of a terrible, terrible fall. But I don't honestly know what kind," Antolini warns Holden. "It may be the kind where, at the age of thirty, you sit in some bar hating everybody who comes in looking as if he might have played football in college." Fearing Holden will compromise himself in conforming to normative social roles and expectations, Antolini describes a future of miserable scenarios in which Holden might "pick up just enough education to hate people who say, 'It's a secret between he and I,'" or become a businessman "throwing paper clips at the nearest stenographer" (186).

Holden grasps Antolini's depiction but rejects and amends some of his predictions. Telling him, "you're wrong about hating football players and all. You really are. I don't hate too many guys," Holden asserts his own compassionate perspective: "What I may do, I may hate them for a little while . . . but it doesn't last too long, is what I mean. After a while, if I didn't see them . . . I sort of missed them" (187). Thinking Holden still doesn't understand him, Antolini tries to clarify the future of quiet desperation he fears for Holden:

> This fall I think you're riding for—it's a special kind of fall, a horrible kind. The man falling isn't permitted to feel or hear himself hit bottom. He just keeps falling and falling. The whole arrangement's designed for men who, at some time or other in their lives, were looking for something their own environment couldn't supply them with. Or they thought their environment couldn't supply them with. So they gave up looking. They gave it up before they ever really even got started. You follow me? (187)

In truth, Holden is already struggling against the fall from the idealism that Antolini assumes to accompany the loss of childhood innocence, but Holden is trying as well to maintain *the perception of hope* that is crucial to the struggle itself. It is in this sense that Salinger, in his development of Holden as a hero, perhaps unwittingly draws attention to a paradox within the tradition of the American Adam: heroic status is attained by gaining moral strength through "falling," yet the future role of the hero is to *prevent* (in actuality or figuratively) others from taking the same fall. Hence, in the passage that gives title to the novel, Holden's new-found purpose in life is to be "the catcher in the rye":

> Anyway, I keep picturing all these little kids playing some game in this big field of rye and all. Thousands of little kids, and nobody's around—nobody big, I mean—except me. And I'm standing on the edge of some crazy cliff. What I have to do, I have to catch everybody if they start to go over the cliff—I mean if they're running and they don't look where they're going I have to come out from somewhere and *catch* them. That's all I'd do all day. I'd just be the catcher in the rye and all. (173)

Although he wishes to prevent the fall of others, Holden cannot "catch" himself from his own fall—indeed, the "catcher in the rye" itself is a fantasy. The world of childhood innocence may exist outside of adult society but the inescapable process of maturity will eventually find all children becoming adult "insiders," participants in the larger social context, willing or not. In this sense, Holden's wish to remain "outside" the corrupting influences of adult society is again consistent with the mythos of the American Adam. The very heroism of the Adamic character rests on his ability to participate in and improve upon "society" even as he manages to sustain the moral certitude of his a priori innocence, a paradoxical stance that requires no small amount of skill on the part of the writer to maintain reader credibility.

Salinger manages this paradox through Holden's fearful sensation of "disappearing." In the duality of inside/outside relations, the outside "self" still depends upon the recognition of *other insiders* to validate one's very sense of existence. When Holden decides to leave Pencey Prep School—an action consistent with his outsider status—he painfully acknowledges his need for recognition of his leave-taking by those who remain "inside" Pencey:

> What I was really hanging around for, I was trying to feel some kind of good-by. I mean I've left schools and places I didn't even know I was

leaving them. I hate that. I don't care if it's a sad good-by or a bad good-by, but when I leave a place I like to *know* I'm leaving it. If you don't, you feel even worse. (4)

When the necessary "good-byes" are not forthcoming, Holden leaves in a state of limbo, neither insider nor outsider, and the perception of loss of self is palpable as Holden reports that he feels as if he is "disappearing" every time he crosses a road. This sensation is repeated toward the novel's end when Holden again takes flight in a state of near-total anomie in which he fears that he might "never get to the other side of the street" and would instead "just go down, down, down, and nobody'd ever see me again." In his desperation, Holden makes believe that he is talking to his dead brother, Allie, and manages to barely maintain his sense of identity through a series of incantations to Allie, pleading "don't let me disappear" (197–98).

Readers of the novel could construe Holden's sensation of "disappearing" as well as his reliance on his dead brother's support as evidence of incipient insanity rather than an imaginative preservation of self. Holden himself refers to his behavior as "crazy" and "madman stuff" throughout the novel. Yet this craziness is not only the consequence of Holden's alienation from society but also the very expression of that alienation. The only recourse Holden foresees is to "reappear" inside society, in a wholly different circumstance. In an extended fantasy sequence, he envisions himself structurally and functionally inside society while remaining outside in any meaningful sense:

> I'd start hitchhiking my way out West. . . . I'd be somewhere out West where it was very pretty and sunny and where nobody'd know me and I'd get a job. I figured I could get a job at a filling station somewhere, putting gas and oil in people's cars. I didn't care what kind of job it was, though. Just so people didn't know me and I didn't know anybody. I thought what I'd do was, I'd pretend I was one of those deaf-mutes. That way I wouldn't have to have any goddam stupid useless conversations with anybody. (198)

In his fantasy of moving West, Holden is attempting a further "new beginning," in which he will protect his innocence and idealism by physically moving out and away from the inauthenticity of adult society. A course of action that is familiar in American frontier experience, the idea of escaping into the wilderness of the "untracked American forest" is endemic to the American Adam and requires the creation of a fictional environment in which "the world always lies before the hero, and normally, like Huck Finn, he is able to light out again for the 'territories.'"[24]

Holden, however, is not in the midst of the "untracked American forest" but rather in the urban "jungle" of the mid-twentieth century. Salinger's use of this environment emphasizes the coldness of modern institutions and the lack of meaning in contemporary language, as evidenced through his continuing imagery of graffiti and obscenities scrawled over hard exterior surfaces. Time and again, Holden attempts to erase or rub out the obscenities from the walls of a railway station, a museum, and a school. Holden reads these obscenities as expressions of hostility that represent not only the loss of innocence but the perversion of that innocence. When Holden finds "Fuck You" scrawled on the wall of the school attended by his sister, Phoebe, it drives him "damn near crazy" to think that first the "little kids would see it" and "then finally some dirty kid would tell them—all cockeyed, naturally—what it meant," causing them to "*think* about it and maybe even *worry* about it for a couple of days" (201).

Consequently, when Holden confronts his own mortality, the perception of hope so crucial to the continuation of the American Adam is dashed by his recognition of the postwar cultural conditions of anonymity and alienation:

> That's the whole trouble. You can't ever find a place that's nice and peaceful, because there isn't any. You may *think* there is, but once you get there, when you're not looking, somebody'll sneak up and write "Fuck you" right under your nose. Try it sometime. I think, even, if I ever die, and they stick me in a cemetery, and I have a tombstone and all, it'll say "Holden Caulfield" on it, and then what year I was born and what year I died, and then right under that it'll say "Fuck you." I'm positive, in fact. (204)

Here, Holden's realization of the apparent futility of attempting to make his individual life fully distinctive, and the absurdity of trying to prevent the loss or perversion of innocence, does not stop him from continuing to try to erase the obscenities he personally confronts. In a revision of the Adamic plot that reflects the paradoxical sentiments of disillusionment and optimism prevalent in postwar America, Salinger requires his readers to entertain notions of Holden's defeat and demise only to salvage Holden's heroic status by emphasizing the relentless hopefulness of his actions.[25] Signifying the survival of Holden's optimism, Holden's repeated erasures of the obscene scrawlings take the form of what critic Ihab Hassan has termed the "rare quixotic gesture"—an eloquent act of hopefulness by the absurd yet heroic American character. Arguing that the "unmistakably American flourish" of the quixotic gesture is rooted in the "quest of American adolescents . . . for an idea of truth," Hassan believed that such actions were gestures "at once of pure expression and of expectation, of protest and of prayer, of aesthetic form and spiritual content," and finally, "behavior that sings."[26]

While the rubbing out of obscenities is the most self-conscious (and self-defeating) effort in *Catcher,* the very fantasy of being the "catcher in the rye" is itself a notion of quixotic hopefulness. Holden's account of his "madman" days ends with an expression of joy and momentary return to innocence as he watches his young sister, Phoebe, riding a carousel in the rain at his encouragement. Phoebe has just returned Holden's red hunting cap, placing it on his head and effectively acknowledging the temporal nature of his identity as "the catcher" when she tells him "you can wear it for a while."

Noting upon reflection that his hunting cap "really gave me quite a lot of protection, in a way," Holden sits in the rain and gets soaked watching Phoebe. It is a moment worth the drenching for Holden, who finds himself feeling "so damn happy, if you want to know the truth. I don't know why. It was just that she looked so damn *nice,* the way she kept going around and around, in her blue coat and all." Concluding by telling the reader, "God, I wish you could've been there," Holden's narrative here implies that while the *preservation* of innocence might indeed be impossible, the appreciation of that innocence is enough to restore the sense of hope (212–13).

Catcher closes with Holden's summary of his final state of convalescence—although whether he is recovering from a mental breakdown or physical exhaustion is unclear. Not surprisingly, the tale ends on a hopeful if enigmatic note as Holden first tells the reader that "if you want to know the truth, I don't know what I think about it. I'm sorry I told so many people about it." In the very next sentence, however, Holden goes on to acknowledge, "All I know is, I sort of miss everybody I told about. Even old Stradlater and Ackley, for instance. I think I even miss that goddam Maurice," leading Holden to warn the reader, "Don't ever tell anybody anything. If you do, you start missing everybody" (213–14). Hence, if Holden at last remains outside society, it is with an enriched sense of his kinship with those *inside*—an affinity ironically recognized through his struggle to distinguish himself from them.

In *The Myth of Sisyphus,* Albert Camus writes of the absurd hero:

"The struggle itself toward the heights is enough to fill a man's heart. One must imagine Sisyphus happy."[27] And so do I see Holden Caulfield, as both absurd hero and one ultimately happy at his task, balancing between actions of individual responsibility and engagement in a social community, a hero in the tradition of one of America's central fables. That the postwar context in which *Catcher* was conceived and read is itself a quixotic construction is the subject of the next chapter: a consideration of the perceptions of post–World War II intellectuals that the American errand had gone awry if not failed, and their wish to somehow sustain that selfsame sense of innocence.

2

The Question of Innocence

A book is not a thing like other things. When we hold it in our
hands all we hold is the paper: The book is elsewhere.
— Robert Escarpit, *The Book Revolution*

Most of what I have written thus far concerning Holden Caulfield and
The Catcher in the Rye echoes the beliefs of a series of American scholars
and critics of the period during and immediately after Salinger's novel
was released, and read, and had passed through its first major period of
controversy. Despite wide variances in their disciplines, training institutions, and areas of influence, all of these critics and scholars shared a
field of interpretation concerning American culture. If they undoubtedly
formed an elite cultural group, they also informed and expressed the
concerns of less articulate or privileged members of the broader culture.
Moreover, the expressed fears, the grumblings, the criticisms, and the
wistful hopes of these writers as they looked about their post–World War
II environment offer an open window for a retrospective consideration of
the cultural landscape of postwar America that is helpful to our understanding of the meaning and dynamics of the *Catcher* controversies.

Even as R. W. B. Lewis was busy conceptualizing the "American Adam"
as the central thematic structure and definition of heroic character in
nineteenth- and early-twentieth-century American fiction, he saw little
hopefulness or true Adamism in the creative discourse of the mid-
twentieth century. Pointing out in his introduction that "the old conviction of the new historical beginning seemed to vanish altogether" in
postwar literature, along with the previously "enlivening sense of possibility, of intellectual and artistic elbow-room, of new creations and fresh
initiatives,"[1] Lewis limited his acknowledgment of the Adamic presence
in the works of mid-twentieth-century writers to a single paragraph.

Writing in 1955, Lewis no longer saw the American Adam as a credible American character for post–World War II literature, because he believed that the postwar period was a bleak and chastened "age of containment" in which "we huddle together and shore up defenses; both our literature and our public conduct suggest that exposure to experience is certain to be fatal."[2]

Lewis's use of the inclusive "we" emphasizes that his statements were at least as much a part of his personal beliefs and experiences as they were of his scholarly analysis. Writing about American authors but speaking in the vocabulary of his own emotions and psyche, Lewis expressed beliefs that not only shaped his analysis of American literature but that reveal the broader intellectual climate in which *The Catcher in the Rye* was written and received. In the published scholarship of 1949–59, including Lewis's own work, there exists a perceptible intellectual worldview shaped by the impact of the Great Depression, totalitarianism, and the accompanying two World Wars as well as by the explicit evidence of man's capacity for inhumanity, revealed not only by the Holocaust but in America's first use of the atomic bomb in 1945.[3]

Long before the rise of the mythos of the American Adam in American literature, the rhetoric of public life (from sermons to political "speechifying") included familiar use of a narrative of America's fledgling history as a "city upon a hill," a beacon of Christian community in the midst of a world otherwise peopled by corrupt Europeans and ignorant primitives. Believing that their displacement to the rocky coast of what would become New England was not only God's will but a divine "errand into the wilderness," the Puritans eventually died out as a religious community, but their cultural legacy was a growing belief in the moral superiority of Americans. Amended over the centuries to include the element of innocence (born of the escape from and contrast to European corruption), the mythology of the city upon the hill was translated into that of "manifest destiny" as Americans sought to justify both expansion and intervention into other areas of the world.

In the summer light of August 1945 this shimmering cultural oasis became forever shrouded in the reflective debris of radioactive fallout. The American dropping of atomic bombs, first on Hiroshima and then three days later on Nagasaki, constituted acts of such deliberate and previously unknown destruction that the "innocence" of America's errand could scarcely be maintained any longer, creating a rupture in the most deeply held narrative of American privilege *and possibility.* If the Great Depression could be incorporated into the mythology as a lesson in humility and the brutality preceding and during World Wars I and II could be understood as evidence of the amoral forces against which the United States was destined to struggle, our actual use of "the Bomb" called America's moral stature into question. Consequently, the years since 1945 have not only shown a change in the worldview among scholars and academics but also frame a period of open controversy among scientists, civil and religious leaders, and the general public about America's development of and rationale for use of atomic weaponry.[4]

Typical of the earliest responses to the use of the atomic bomb was that of Edward R. Murrow of CBS radio. "Seldom, if ever, has a war ended leaving the victors with such a sense of uncertainty and fear," Murrow told his listeners, "with such a realization that the future is obscure and that survival is not assured."[5] Pensive from the first, the stream of dire observations ranged from the secular press—"[One] forgets the effect on Japan ... as one senses the foundations of one's own universe trembling" (*New York Herald Tribune*)[6]—to the religious—"[The bomb] cast a spell of dark foreboding over the spirit of humanity" (*Christian Century*).[7] In his radio address to the nation after the atomic bombing of Nagasaki, President Truman nevertheless attempted to invoke the sense of Adamic wisdom, gained postfall, to sustain credibility for America's global errand: "It is an awful responsibility which has come to us. We thank God that it has come to us instead of to our enemies; and we pray that He may guide us to use it in His ways and for His purposes."[8]

NBC radio news commentator H. V. Kaltenborn was more fearful of American actions than respectful as he challenged his audience: "As we listen to the newscast tonight, as we read our newspapers tomorrow, let us think of the mass murder which will come with World War III."[9] A few weeks later, Kaltenborn sharpened his imagery of American "innocence," observing, "We are like children playing with a concentrated instrument of death whose destructive potential our little minds cannot grasp."[10] Kaltenborn's imagery of dangerous adult naïveté here recalls the central metaphor of *The Catcher in the Rye*, in which Holden fears for the safety of children playing unaware of their risk as they near the edge of "some crazy cliff," which they might "start to go over ... if they're running and they don't look where they're going" (173).

In fact, J. D. Salinger—born in 1919 and writing *The Catcher in the Rye* in 1951—was a participant in a cultural cohort (those born between 1915 and 1925 and publishing after the end of World War II and into the early 1960s) that produced the diverse scholarship of intellectual historians such as Louis Hartz, Henry May, and David Noble as well as the literary and cultural criticism of Leslie Fiedler and R. W. B. Lewis, among others. The common theme of the most influential works of this cohort was best expressed by the point-blank title of May's 1959 examination of a "cultural revolution" in the sentiments of American intellectuals: *The End of American Innocence.*[11] In the conceptual infrastructure shared among this cohort, American experience was repeatedly divided into categories of pre-twentieth-century "innocence" and post–World War II "beyond innocence," making it clear that the end of World War II brought about a profound change in sensibility—that "something happened" that made America specifically, and the Western world in general, distinctly different from its historical past. What exactly that "something" was remained vague, as we shall see, as these writers made the drawing of distinctions between the "innocent" and "beyond" the central focus of their work, evading the illumination of how or why that innocence was lost.

To begin at the beginning, in his 1955 postscript to *On Native Grounds* social critic Alfred Kazin wrote simply that it "is not hopelessness one sees today, as the Marxists would say; it is a manifest feeling of strangeness before a kind of life that has actually outrun all the names we can give to it."[12] Similarly, critic Ihab Hassan stated in the first page of *Radical Innocence* (1961), "We are indeed here, past the meridian of the twentieth century, a devastating war behind us, and a war we dare not call by any name lowering ahead." And yet there were names by which the times could be addressed, and Hassan immediately did so in his discussion of "regimentation" in contemporary American life. Hassan theorized that regimentation was the consequence of an increased experience of duality in American life; citizens pursued stability and security through homogeneity but recoiled from the stagnation that was its cost. Hassan viewed this recoil as a contemporary version of "the old search for human innocence in the midst of a rat race," evinced in the paradoxical postwar "search for privatism in the midst of conformity and for contentment in the midst of frenetic bustle."[13]

Writing at very nearly the same moment, social scientists William Whyte and Betty Friedan unintentionally provided the documentation for Hassan's thesis in their complementary studies of middle-class suburbia in the 1950s. Whyte, in *The Organization Man* (1956), found Americans to be following what he termed the "social ethic" in pursuit of security and stability. The social ethic, according to Whyte, was grounded in the belief that the existence of the individual was secondary to the needs of society; "meaningless" as an individual, man found his worth in social collaboration, where "by sublimating himself in the group, he helps produce a whole that is greater than the sum of its parts." Practice of the social ethic, then, was aimed at "creat[ing] an equilibrium in which society's needs and the needs of the individual are one and the same"— an ethos that could best be accomplished by "applying the methods of science to human relations" so that conflicts ("breakdowns in communication" and "obstacles to consensus") would be eliminated.[14]

Based on his rigorous ethnographic study of a suburban community in Illinois, Whyte's book chronicled the loss of individual potency that occurs when one embraces the social ethic, and lamented the corresponding absence of social responsibility. He saw the loss as voluntary and one that would ultimately weaken the vitality of a democracy rooted in individual responsibility. Arguing that the fault lay not in the mode of organization itself but "in our worship of it," Whyte drew a similar line between the inherently benign nature of conformity by choice and the horrific consequences of "blind" or mindless conformity in Nazi Germany. Fearing that post–World War II America, in its "vain quest for a utopian equilibrium" through the suburban and bureaucratic organization of life, was pursuing an ethos that would foster such blind conformity, Whyte warned that while the social ethic might offer a "spurious peace of mind," its cost would be a forfeiture of individualism, and Americans would find they had "tyrannized" themselves.[15]

If the political consequences of social tyranny were the underlying concern for Whyte, the psychological consequences were predominant in Betty Friedan's *The Feminine Mystique* (1963). In many ways a parallel examination of suburban homogeneity, Friedan's study differed from Whyte's in two important ways. First, Friedan was concerned with individual consequences of social tyranny, and second, Friedan's focus was gender specific. After having confronted her own incipient loss of identity as a suburban housewife, both factors led to her conceptualization of "the problem that has no name":

> The problem lay buried, unspoken, for many years in the minds of
> American women. It was a strange stirring, a sense of dissatisfaction, a
> yearning that women suffered in the middle of the twentieth century
> in the United States. Each suburban wife struggled with it alone. As
> she made the beds, shopped for groceries, matched slipcover material,
> ate peanut butter sandwiches with her children, chauffeured Cub
> Scouts and Brownies, lay beside her husband at night—she was afraid
> to ask even of herself the silent question—"Is this all?"[16]

Indeed, it is difficult to conceive of women having the individual courage to ask at all given the glut of indoctrination Friedan documented as she captured the alienation of leisure-class postwar "homemakers" and analyzed the forms and origins of their anomie. In her summary delineation of the housewife's plight, Friedan inadvertently illustrated Hassan's schema of regimentation: the reliance of the mystique women on "experts" for instructions and decisions on everything from "how to catch a man and keep him" to the breast-feeding and toilet training of their own children, the purchasing of household goods and appliances, and "how to keep their husbands from dying young and their sons from growing into delinquents." Editorial columns and articles in women's magazines advised their readers that "truly feminine women do not want careers, higher education, political rights—the independence and the opportunities that the old-fashioned feminists fought for."[17]

While much of *The Feminine Mystique* implied that a male conspiracy was depriving women of self-realization, Friedan did acknowledge that the roots of enforced homogeneity lay in a collusive constriction of social participation. Pointing out that "the American spirit fell into a strange sleep" following World War II that went beyond sex roles, Friedan argued that women returned to the home "just as men shrugged off the bomb, forgot the concentration camps, condoned corruption, and fell into helpless conformity." That the "helpless conformity" of Friedan's subjects was the same as the willing passivity of Whyte's "blind" conformists was clear in Friedan's conclusion that for all postwar Americans "it was easier, safer, to think about love and sex than about communism, McCarthy, and the uncontrolled bomb."[18]

Locating the strained pursuit of identity and belonging within suburban and organizational life, both Friedan and Whyte effectively substantiated Hassan's notion of recoil in the strange slumber of middle-class conformity. It was, however, not the only manner of evading postwar insecurity. Hassan had described an alternative "other manifestation of recoil," conveyed in the "disaffiliation, apathy, silence, [and] coolness" that was "supposedly common among youth of college age."[19] There is perhaps no better spokesperson for this type of recoil from the contemporary "American Dream" than Holden Caulfield.

Throughout the course of his narrative in *The Catcher in the Rye*, Holden provides a continuing critique of "successful" marriage, careers, entertainment, and social interaction. Sometimes the critique is phrased in brief identifications of one sort of behavior or another as "phony," yet on occasion his commentary becomes more articulate. At one point Holden is sitting in the lobby of the New York Biltmore Hotel, reflecting upon the possible futures of the young women who pass by. Noting that it was "really nice sightseeing, if you know what I mean," he adds that it was also "sort of depressing" as he thought about what he imagined would happen to them: "You figured most of them would probably marry dopey guys." By Holden's definition, "dopey guys" were Whyte's copacetic "blind" conformists, always talking about "how many miles they get to a gallon in their goddam cars. . . . Guys that never read books. Guys that are very boring" (123).

Yet even as Holden criticizes the conformist "bores," his own familiarity with the repressive nature of the social ethos allows him to reconsider them with an empathy that attempts to recognize their hidden individualism. Telling his reader, "Maybe you shouldn't feel too sorry if you see some swell girl getting married to them," he goes on to point out that "they don't hurt anybody, most of them, and maybe they're secretly all terrific whistlers or something" (124). Empathy aside, Holden's view of contemporary "success" remains a bleak one in which the private rewards of personal actions and abilities are overwhelmed by the broader structure of social interaction. Social courtesy is identified as hypocrisy, and community—in both status and membership—is based on self-defense:

> You ought to go to a boys' school sometime. Try it sometime. . . . It's full of phonies, and all you do is study so that you can learn enough to be smart enough to be able to buy a goddam Cadillac some day, and you have to keep making believe you give a damn if the football team loses, and all you do is talk about girls and liquor and sex all day, and everybody sticks together in these dirty little goddam cliques. . . . Even the guys that belong to the Book of the Month Club stick together. (130–31)

Such is the "phony" success Holden rejects. Were he to embrace an alternative definition of success, even a cynical one, we might see him as moving "beyond innocence" and on to the development of a new perspective. Equally, were he to give in and emulate the "phonies," as he so readily could, he could also be viewed as "beyond innocence" through the trade of idealism for comfort and security. Yet Holden does neither, maintaining a stance of radical innocence in which hope lies in the questioning of social norms and authorities and is followed by the pursuit of genuine if painful answers.

Salinger's creation of a character of such "radical innocence" as Holden Caulfield was in fact sufficient to sustain Hassan's faith in the American future, as it held the possibility of "starting anew," but this belief was at the very least questionable for most of the next generation of postwar intellectuals. Social critic Marcus Klein was not nearly so optimistic about nor charitable toward the American conscience as Hassan, yet neither was he as gloomy as Lewis had been earlier. *After Alienation*, Klein's 1965 discussion of American culture and American literature in midcentury, begins evenly:

> But then came the Second World War and it left us, obviously, with a social situation different from that of the 1920's and 1930's, different in small and in great matters. On the one hand, the boobs were not now so dumb. The likely truth about the village was that it was an industrial suburb.... Then came the overwhelming tie, which is with us, of the prospect of absolute catastrophe.... One might have been partisan against the Bomb, but so was everyone against the Bomb, and that affected matters not at all.[20]

Like the earlier cohort of intellectuals, Klein observed the paralysis of engagement in postwar culture, arguing that American writers in the 1950s shared the "knowledge that we are all on the edge of dissolution and that at this point in history things must be salvaged." Their fiction, in consequence, "tend[ed] away from explicitly social subjects" even as it was "shaped by the social and political pressures of an age that is the most desperate in all history." Where according to Klein the first half of the twentieth century had been characterized by increasing alienation, midcentury was a period best described by the term "accommodation." Accommodation was a cultural "mood" that came into being "when rebellion had exhausted itself ... when there were no politics to speak of and when there were no orthodoxies to speak of to restrict one's freedom, and when all theories of society had been shattered." Where the point of accommodation was "the elimination of the distance between self and society" to achieve "the perfect union of self and society," Klein found midcentury literature to be "at best a lesson in the perpetual necessity of killing adjustments" that were required of the individual in the process.[21]

These selfsame "killing adjustments" were equally the concern of critic and historian Stephen Whitfield in his essay "The 1950's: The Era of No Hard Feelings," a masterful survey of the actions and perspectives of American leadership in the Cold War (both major and minor players). Whitfield's choice for the emblematic character of the decade was the junior senator from Wisconsin, Joseph R. McCarthy, who "displayed the arrogance of the roughneck who violates the rules, or rather makes up his own as he goes along." Disclosed in the title of the essay, the symbolic act of the decade was McCarthy's polite query of Edward R. Murrow following his accusation of Murrow as a conspirator with the Kremlin: "McCarthy sought [Murrow] out at a party, wrapped his arm around the liberal commentator's shoulder, and inquired, 'No hard feelings, Ed?'"[22]

For Whitfield, the absurdity reflected in McCarthy's question reflected an attitude that was commonplace in the cultural context of the 1950s. Humor and entertainment that concentrated on the absurdities of daily life in a "commercialized culture" prevailed as "satire and parody, the thinking man's comedies," declined. Like Friedan and Whyte, he found the atmosphere of the 1950s to be "fraught with moral ambiguity" and increasing alienation, creating a social and political environment in which "a terrible simplifier like McCarthy could flourish." McCarthy, Whitfield pointed out, embodied not only the absurdity but the considerable strain in cultural proscriptions of the time as he exhibited "not only the will to impose conformity and extinguish deviation" but, simultaneously, "the casual vulgarity, the smirking rebelliousness, the hint of violence which the web of civil society could barely restrain."[23]

The intolerability of living within the narrow boundaries of sheer good form was an issue highlighted by Salinger in *The Catcher in the Rye*. Early on in the novel, Holden critiques a simple standard of farewell that he receives from a teacher who had given him a failing grade: "I'm pretty sure he yelled 'Good luck!' at me. I hope not. I hope to hell not. I'd never yell 'Good luck!' at anybody. It sounds terrible, when you think about it" (15–16). Farther along, Holden recalls a speech class he found particularly frustrating in its emphasis on form over content. As Holden tells it, his teacher, Mr. Vinson, is a McCarthyesque "terrible simplifier":

> It's this course where each boy in class has to get up in class and make a speech. You know. Spontaneous and all. And if the boy digresses at all, you're supposed to yell "Digression!" at him as fast as you can. It just about drove me crazy. I got an F in it . . . . The trouble with me is, I *like* it when somebody digresses. It's more interesting and all . . . what I mean is, lots of times you don't *know* what interests you most till you start talking about something that *doesn't* interest you most. . . . I mean he'd keep telling you to *uni*fy and *sim*plify all the time. Some things you just can't do that to. (183–85)

Writing in Holden's adolescent voice, in this passage Salinger expresses frustration with the avoidance of meaning, of "interest," that was disguised in the postwar emphasis on style. Musing upon similar rites of ingenuous if correct courtesy permeating American life, Whitfield speculated that it was the "ominous presence (of) the Bomb" that rendered 1950s society "polite" in its impotence as Americans "who had once hoped to make life perfect decided to settle, with no hard feelings, for making life better."[24] Salinger also linked the threat of the Bomb to the self-annihilating pursuit of conventionality, but focused instead on the do-or-die perspective of the individual who *couldn't* "settle." Here, even as Holden appreciates the fatal courtesy of Fitzgerald's Gatsby, it is a course that Holden seeks to avoid at all costs—and in doing so he literally jumps to atomic annihilation:

> I was crazy about *The Great Gatsby.* Old Gatsby. Old sport. That kill'd
> me. Anyway, I'm sort of glad they've got the atomic bomb invented.
> If there's ever another war, I'm going to sit right the hell on top of it.
> I'll volunteer for it, I swear to God I will. (141)

If Holden's vision of individualistic escape from the deadly disingenuity of social courtesy is one that leads inescapably to self-destruction, it is a position at once appropriate to the "era of no hard feelings" and reminiscent of philosopher Albert Camus's definition of the universal absurd as the infinite pursuit of hope at any and all costs. Critic David Galloway correctly grounded his postwar analysis of *The Absurd Hero in American Fiction* in Camus's explication of absurdity in *The Myth of Sisyphus.* Paraphrasing Camus's characterization of Sisyphus as an individual "persist[ing] in his demands for truth in a universe that says truths are impossible," Galloway saw Camus's hero as perfectly suited to his understanding of American literature, in which "absurdity becomes a defiance of the universe, an extreme tension which will never permit the hero to rest, just as the tormented Sisyphus can never pause in his task."[25]

The "extreme tension" of the absurd in postwar American fiction, then, is one that is created through the protagonist's fictional recognition of the disjunctive gap between "the chain of mechanical daily gestures" and the void of purpose or meaning at bottom. The significance of the absurd, however, lies in the *consequences* of that recognition. It is this distinction that is missed in the focus on "accommodation" and its requirement of "an impossible reconciliation"[26] between the apparent security of postwar American life and the awareness of the inescapable jeopardy of that security in the Cold War context. To view the absurd as merely a series of "killing adjustments" is to *describe* the alienation and/or accommodation of the current age and yet to miss the potential for restoration stipulated in the notion of radical innocence. In the description of the absurd lie defeatism and nihilism whereas in the *consideration of potential actions,* inherently of and for the individual, lie hope and optimism.

The various "names" (which, in contradiction to Kazin, we had *not* run out of) for the worldview expressed in postwar American life and literature include, then, "accommodation" and "radical innocence," among many others: "the new nihilism, poetic naturalism, . . . a new concern for final matters, the rule of personality, the disappearance of manners, the death of dissidence, the end of social engagement,"[27] as well as "the literature of exhaustion" and "disruptive or surfiction."[28] Noting that these terms were most often imparted as "epithets" hurled by antagonistic critics with "programmatic expectations" toward the "the probationary, current discoveries of novelists," Klein himself found postwar literature to move outside the boundaries of accommodation, "signify[ing] that novelists in the last few years have been working within a sentiment that is generally felt to be different."[29]

The "different sentiment" of post–World War II writers is the set of varying responses to the prospect that dominated the cultural as well as the literary imagination—the prospect of nuclear annihilation. However, even without the atom bomb, the impact of World War II upon literature should have been expected, given the literary response to earlier wars. Alfred Kazin had argued as early as 1942 that the rise of modern American literature "did not begin with the discovery of sex alone, with the freedom to attack ugliness and provincialism, or with the need to bring our culture into the international modern stream" but was instead "rooted in nothing less than the transformation of our society in the great seminal years after the Civil War."[30]

A similar connection between war and creative cultural expression was the basis for Paul Fussell's acclaimed study *The Great War and Modern Memory* (1975). In his analysis of British fiction, poetry, journals, and memoirs, Fussell observed that one legacy of World War I was the shocking notion "of endless war as an inevitable condition of modern life."[31] For Britons, Fussell declared, World War I was a cultural watershed, "all encompassing, all pervading, both internal and external at once, the essential condition of consciousness in the twentieth century." The unique impact of World War I lay in the confrontation of man with the first technological war: man against machine, in the form of tanks, planes, and machine guns. Sounding much like the critics of post–World War II American culture, Fussell argued that World War I was "more ironic than any before or since," as it "reversed the Idea of Progress," and he described the post–World War I consciousness as a state in which "anxiety without end, without purpose, without reward, and without meaning is woven into the fabric of contemporary life."[32]

If Fussell's claim for the centrality of World War I for Great Britain is granted, World War II was the more ironic and apparent watershed for America. Succinctly capturing a sentiment shared among postwar American intellectuals, Ihab Hassan drew a distinction between the loss of individual "innocence" among American participants in World War I and the more extensive (and anxiety-producing) loss of national certitude that followed World War II: "When World War II came to an end soon after the holocausts at Hiroshima and Nagasaki, and millions of young men climbed out of uniform, a new age was ushered in. The men who went to war went, at best, with mixed idealism; they were not, it is often said, as innocent as their fathers who were sent from a Midwestern farm to a trench of the Marne."[33]

From its inception, America has both pursued and symbolized the ideals of hope and freedom, partly based on its stated belief in justice and equality (however historically inaccurate and ethnocentric) but more powerfully, if less tangibly, in representations of America as essentially innocent—a second Eden free from the taint of history and tradition. What greater irony could there be than that American potentiality would create and serve ultimate destruction. In this regard, Marcus Klein's reading of postwar American culture is both poignant and incisive:

> Something is missing: the old grievances don't begin to comprehend the evil with which in these years we have lived.... An imposing Puritanism has been sublimed into IBM machinery. A cruel industrialism has been replaced by a rampant scientism.... But such is the nature of the terror, that what in the culture is wrong, stupid and evil becomes trivial. Evil is not so important as once it was.... The terror beyond evil is the murder that occurred in the Second World War together with the prospect become familiar of entire and utter annihilation. We are all half-dead of it already, and there is to be opposed to it only a more strenuous and a more vivid sensing of human community ... the assertion that ... despite everything, the human community is possible.[34]

Yet we are only "half-dead of it already." The other half lies exactly in the remainder of American innocence—an innocence strengthened rather than weakened by the recognition of evil within us and forging the heroic characterization of radical innocence recognized by Hassan in the work of major postwar novelists such as Carson McCullers, Truman Capote, J. D. Salinger, and Saul Bellow. Similarly, Marcus Klein found protagonists who managed to effect heroism in the age of accommodation in the fiction of Bellow, Ralph Ellison, James Baldwin, Wright Morris, and Bernard Malamud. Finally, David Galloway located the absurd American hero in the writings of, again, Bellow and Salinger as well as John Updike and William Styron.

While Bellow is the author of common agreement, his characters are imperfectly suited as the exemplars of the new American hero in one aspect: that of age. Bellow's central characters are middle-aged, and given America's self-definition and external reputation as an adolescent culture, the new hero of the absurd age, the "radical innocent" in the fullest sense, must be youthful. In the post–World War II period two such young heroes stand out. The first is actor James Dean, whose work and life were representative of the Beat Generation. As critic John Clellon Holmes explained to the readers of *Esquire* in his 1958 essay "The Philosophy of the Beat Generation," "Everyone who has lived through a war, any sort of war, knows that beat means, not so much weariness, as rawness of nerves; not so much being 'filled up to *here*,' as being emptied out. It describes a state of mind from which all unessentials have been stripped, leaving it receptive to everything around it, but impatient with trivial obstructions. To be beat is to be at the bottom of your personality, looking up."[35]

But, Holmes argued, members of the Beat Generation of the 1950s were in fact different from the "beat" of past wars, as World War II came to an end in a context and a fashion that left young American men and women more dazed than "any [other] sort of war":

> It is the first generation in American history that has grown up with peacetime military training as a fully accepted fact of life. It is the first generation for whom the catch phrases of psychiatry have become such intellectual pablum that it can dare to think they may not be the final yardstick of the human soul. It is the first generation for whom genocide, brain-washing, cybernetics, motivational research—and the resultant limitation of the concept of human volition which is inherent in them—have been as familiar as its own face. It is also the first generation that has grown up since the possibility of the nuclear destruction of the world has become the final answer to all questions.... Everywhere the Beat Generation seems occupied with

the feverish production of answers—some of them frightening, some of them foolish—to a single question: how are we to live?[36]

Fascinating an audience that went beyond those who identified themselves as Beat, James Dean so personified the furious search for a life worth living that there was famously little separation between his film roles and his private life. "He lived hard and without complaint; and he died as he lived, going fast," wrote Holmes, ". . . a wistful, reticent youth, looking over the abyss separating him from older people with a level, saddened eye; living intensely in alternate explosions of tenderness and violence; eager for love and a sense of purpose."[37]

In contrast to the struggles of reconciliation among Bellow's middle-aged protagonists, the career of James Dean qualified for the depiction of the new American heroism by his very stance upon the ground of youth and his distance from his elders. The other possible "new hero" is one with whom we are now fully familiar—who also saw himself and others as living on the adolescent edge of "some crazy cliff" yet managed to literally embody the mature post–World War II generation as well. As Holden Caulfield describes himself,

> I was sixteen then, and I'm seventeen now, and sometimes I act like I'm about thirteen. It's really ironical, because I'm six foot two and a half and I have gray hair. I really do. The one side of my head—the right side—is full of millions of gray hairs. I've had them ever since I was a kid. . . . I get bored sometimes when people tell me to act my age. Sometimes I act a lot older than I am—I really do—but people never notice it. (9)

Holden Caulfield can thus be seen as a dual hero for mid-twentieth-century America: representing the perspective "beyond innocence" of his adult creator J. D. Salinger at the same time that he embraces the "radical innocence" of his fictional adolescent peer group. And it is among Holden's "real-life" peer group of multiple generations of postwar American adolescents that Salinger's achievement as author of the new American hero is most fully recognized. In the opening of their literary analysis of Salinger's work, critics Frederick Gwynn and Joseph Blotner observed that "whereas young readers of the Inter-War Period knew intimately the work of a goodly number of coeval writers (Hemingway, Fitzgerald, Dos Passos, Wolfe, Sinclair Lewis, for example)," by contrast "the only Post-War fiction unanimously approved by contemporary literate American youth consists of about five hundred pages by Jerome David Salinger."[38]

In sum, *The Catcher in the Rye* is written in the tradition of the American Adam yet conceived in a context of disillusionment and alienation from that very tradition. The heated controversy over the place of *The Catcher in the Rye*—whether it is an American classic, whether it is a "good" book or an "un-American" one—thus becomes less surprising yet still begs examination. The advance men for the debate are the literary critics, and the academicians who follow them are *The Catcher in the Rye*'s greatest proponents. It is to their voices we now listen as we enter the debate itself.

3

The Critical Perspective

Do you know why books such as this are so important? Because
they have quality. And what does the word quality mean? To me it
means texture. This book has pores. It has features. This book can
go under the microscope. You'd find life under the glass, stream-
ing past in infinite profusion. The more pores, the more truthfully
recorded details of life per square inch you can get on a sheet of
paper, the more "literary" you are. That's my definition, anyway.
Telling detail. Fresh detail. The good writers touch life often.
—Ray Bradbury, *Fahrenheit 451*

When *The Catcher in the Rye* was first published in July 1951, it was
simultaneously presented as the midsummer selection of the Book-of-
the-Month Club. In the board's report to the Book-of-the-Month Club
membership, literary critic Clifton Fadiman introduced *The Catcher in
the Rye,* writing that "that rare miracle of fiction has again come to pass:
a human being has been created out of ink, paper and the imagination."[1]
The fictional human being was, of course, Holden Caulfield, and his creation seemed all the more miraculous as this was J. D. Salinger's first (and,
to date, only) novel. Salinger had previously published twenty-eight
short stories and was known as a "*New Yorker* school" writer: although
several of his earlier stories had appeared in *Collier's* and *The Saturday
Evening Post,* among other magazines, seven of twelve short stories published between 1946 and 1951 were published in the *New Yorker.*[2] More to
the point, Salinger had described himself in 1945 as "a dash man and not
a miler, and it is probable that I will never write a novel."[3]

Reminiscent of the ambiguous mood of *The Catcher in the Rye* itself,
the unusual extent of literary attention to Salinger's single novel is both
curious and appropriate. As Marvin Laser and Norman Fruman note
in the introduction to their literary casebook, *Studies in J. D. Salinger*
(1963), "Salinger has been subjected to a range and intensity of critical

analysis which, before our century, was reserved only for the acknowledged masters of literature."[4] Indeed, Fruman and Laser's "casebook" was only one of four such books of criticism on Salinger and *The Catcher in the Rye* to be published in 1963 alone; three texts had already been published in 1958 and 1962, with four more to follow between 1965 and 1979. Literary criticism influences not only if but how a book will be read and thus bears analysis in the attempt to understand any novel as a cultural document. In this case, analysis of literary criticism is particularly important, as it was *Catcher*'s continued popularity among the broader public readership that reclaimed the attention of the literary critics in the late 1950s to mid-1960s and beyond. This reversal of the usual order of the dynamic of reader-critic relations in itself suggests *Catcher*'s importance as a cultural document.[5]

Nearly two hundred newspapers and magazines reviewed *The Catcher in the Rye* in the immediate period of its publication. As critic Robert Gutwillig wrote in his reflective 1961 review, "Looking back over the contemporary reviews of *The Catcher in the Rye* one is immediately struck by two things: how many of them there were and how poor they were, too."[6] While the clear majority of the early reviews were favorable, they were also characterized by inaccuracy (misspelling Holden, confusing both his age and the number of days that his narrative covers) and superficial, if clever, summaries and evaluations.

The inadequacy of these early reviews can be attributed at least in part to the time pressures confronting critics for daily or weekly publications, leading to judgments based on cursory readings and necessarily quick analyses. In fact, most of the 200-odd reviews were simply brief notices in local newspapers hailing *Catcher*'s publication, intended to introduce readers to a new book and author rather than critique the novel itself. These reviews are of import primarily as evidence of the widespread attention *Catcher* received. Several of the early reviews did reflect a closer reading and more probing evaluation of the novel. Though still favorable overall, they foreshadowed the future controversy as well as the continued significance of *The Catcher in the Rye*—for critics and popular readership alike.

Among the earliest reviews were two that appeared in journals devoted to the professional concerns of librarians and publishers as well as booksellers. The *Library Journal* gave *The Catcher in the Rye* high recommendations but cautioned that although it was about an adolescent it was "an *adult* book (very frank)" and "may be a shock to many parents who wonder about a young man's thoughts and actions, but its effect can be a salutary one."[7] A review in *Booklist* was equally cautious, suggesting that *Catcher* was an important book yet potentially controversial. Making note of the "imaginative, repetitious and often coarse language," the review termed *Catcher* "an unusual book on a pertinent theme" that "might not appeal to everyone but is certainly worth attention for its sensitive insight into a currently important topic, as well as for the quality of the writing."[8] However "pertinent," neither the theme nor the "currently important topic" was given any further explication in this scant single-paragraph review.

The first review to give expanded consideration to *Catcher* was written by Harrison Smith for the *Saturday Review* and shed some light on the "important topic" noted by *Booklist*. Titled "Manhattan Ulysses, Junior," Smith's review opened with a summary statement about contemporary literature, bemoaning the trend of "despair and frustration" in novels by recent authors in which "the sour note of bitterness and the recurring theme of sadism have become almost a convention." The portrayal of the "restlessness and bewilderment of our young men and boys" that contemporary authors put forward had been accepted, Smith explained, "because no one had anything better to offer." Finally, it seemed something better had been offered by J. D. Salinger. Smith termed *The Catcher in the Rye* "a remarkable and absorbing novel" that was both "profoundly moving and a disturbing book," and although "pathetic rather than tragic," it was above all "not hopeless."[9]

While Smith felt the convincing aspect of Holden's narrative was the authenticity of language, emotion, and memory it encompassed, he read the hope of the novel to be embodied in Holden's stance of "moral revulsion against anything that was ugly, evil, cruel, or what he called 'phoney' and his acute responsiveness to beauty and innocence, especially the innocence of the very young." Smith cautioned his audience, as did the *Library Journal* and *Booklist* reviewers, that "what happens to him is heart-rending," and that "some of his words and the accidents that befall him may seem to be too raw to be expressed in the words of a childish youth." The very honesty of Holden's narrative caused Smith to warn, "If readers can be shocked in this manner they should be advised to let the book alone" even as he advised his audience that *Catcher* was "a book to be read thoughtfully and more than once." Anticipating that for some readers *Catcher* might induce anxiety more than offer a recognition of hope, Smith addressed the question of what it was that these readers were shocked by. If all boys were "unusual and worthy of understanding" and, like Holden, "bewildered at the complexity of modern life, unsure of themselves, shocked by the spectacle of perversity and evil around them," Smith asked whether adult readers were not "equally shocked by the knowledge that even children cannot escape this contact and awareness?"[10]

Even in this earliest of reviews, the fault lines of the coming controversy over *Catcher* were apparent: the recognition of contemporary America as a society "beyond innocence," which is forced by the painful honesty of Holden's narrative; the "radical innocence" within which hope lies; the use of language that purposefully disassociates the pursuit of innocence and hopefulness from polite expression and social convention.

On 15 July 1951, the *Chicago Sunday Tribune,* the *New York Herald Tribune Book Review,* and the *New York Times Book Review* published reviews of *The Catcher in the Rye.* The review in the *Chicago Sunday Tribune* exemplifies the numerous mediocre reviews of moderate length that appeared across the country in this early period. Barely a page in length (six brief paragraphs), the review deemed *Catcher* successful as an "accurate and yet imaginative as possible" account of adolescent angst. This success was attributed to the authenticity of Holden's first-person narrative, leading to the review's title, "Honest Tale of Distraught Adolescent." The review itself, however, reflected a hasty reading. The final judgment of *Catcher* was that it was a worthy book, but for reasons that seriously call into question the reviewer's understanding of Holden's essential struggle toward maturity with integrity—hailing *Catcher* instead as a story with "a wonderful sort of grasp of how a boy can create his own world of fantasy and live form."[11]

Bearing in mind that the *Chicago Tribune* review was a lengthier consideration of *Catcher* than many of the early reviews, a concurrent review in the *New York Times Book Review*—"Aw, the World's a Crumby Place," written by James Stern—also demonstrates the inadequacy of the early critical treatment of *Catcher.* In Stern's review, the problem was an almost too-familiar grasp of *The Catcher in the Rye.* Writing entirely in what came to be termed "Holdenese," Stern presented an accurate and entertaining summary of *Catcher*—assuming the reader has already read it. If at least a partial intent of a book review is to introduce books to new readers, imagine the incomprehensibility of the following excerpts from Stern's review for the uninitiated:

> This girl Helga, she kills me. She reads just about everything I bring into the house, and a lot of crumby stuff besides. She's crazy about kids. I mean stories about kids. But Hel, she says there's hardly a writer

alive can write about children. . . . You should've see old Hel hit the
ceiling when I told her this Salinger, he has not only written a novel,
it's a Book-of-the-Month Club selection, too. For crying out loud, she
said, what's it about? About this Holden Caulfield, I told her, about the
time he ran away to New York from this Pencey Prep School in Agers-
town, Pa. . . . You see, this Holden, I said he just can't find anybody
decent in the lousy world.[12]

Following his summary, Stern offered a dualistic evaluation of
Catcher, continuing in "Holdenese" and using the imaginary Helga's
adolescent perspective with which to buttress his own adult viewpoint:
"You needn't swear, Hel, I said. Know what? This Holden, he's just like
you. He finds the whole world's full of people who say one thing and
mean another and he doesn't like it; and he hates movies and phony
slobs and snobs and crumby books and war. Boy, how he hates war. Just
like you, Hel, I said. But old Hel, she was already reading this crazy
'Catcher' book all over again. That's always a good sign with Hel."[13]

The likely confusion of the naive reader aside, Stern's review did
highlight several points that were to become commonplace in the criticism and controversy over *The Catcher in the Rye.* Stern's recognition of
Salinger's skill as a writer about children as well as criticism of Salinger's
overextended immersion of the reader into the world and language of
adolescence were repeated in later reviews of *Catcher.* Importantly, Stern
emphasized Salinger's presentation of contemporary social hypocrisy as
valid—and consonant with the beliefs and experiences of contemporary adolescent readers. Yet this left the reader of Stern's review further
confused: was *The Catcher in the Rye* a book, then, for adolescents, or
adults—or both?

Virgilia Peterson's review, "Three Days in the Bewildering World of
an Adolescent," appeared in the *New York Herald Tribune,* also on 15 July
1951. Peterson's review resembled Stern's, albeit without the too-clever
Holdenese. Like Stern, Peterson responded to *Catcher* as a book written
for an adult audience, assuming audience familiarity with Salinger's *New
Yorker* fiction, yet she reserved final judgment of *Catcher* for Holden's
real adolescent contemporaries. The tension between these dual perspectives was evident in Peterson's location of *Catcher*'s significance in
its rendering of a "portrait of a so-called privileged American youth"
for adult consideration. The "integrity" of Salinger's portrait, however,
could not be judged by adults such as herself but required evaluation by
Holden's peers. "It would be interesting and highly enlightening to know

what Holden Caulfield's contemporaries, male and female, think of him," Peterson proposed. "Their opinion would constitute the real test of Mr. Salinger's validity. The question of authenticity is one to which no parent can really guess the reply."[14]

Parents or not, if adult readers could not gauge the authenticity of *The Catcher in the Rye,* it was perhaps due to their closely held beliefs about adolescence rather than a lack of familiarity with adolescent experience. Peterson noted that *Catcher* "should provoke a tempest of reactions," and her own reaction was decidedly against the language used in the book. Acknowledging that "recent war novels have accustomed us all to ugly words and images" and that "there is probably not one phrase in the whole book that Holden Caulfield would not have used upon occasion," she found the language "peculiarly offensive" when coming "from the mouths of the very young and protected"—leading to her flat statement that "when they are piled upon each other in cumulative monotony, the ear refuses to believe."[15] Peterson's reading of sixteen-year-old Holden Caulfield's narrative as one told from "the mouths of the very young and protected" in fact demonstrates Peterson's own refusal—the "bewildered" adult mind behind the ear—to accept the tale as an explicit articulation of adolescent experience. As we will see, as the debate over *Catcher* unfolds, the procensorship position is often rooted in similar feelings of bewilderment and denial.

On 16 July 1951, *Time* and *Newsweek* magazines published their reviews of *Catcher.*[16] In both cases, most of the space in these meager half-page reviews was devoted to a thumbnail summary of the novel. While the *Newsweek* reviewer apparently had little to say beyond the summary, the reviewer for *Time* did applaud Salinger on two counts. Complimenting Salinger for writing "some of the most acidly humorous deadpan satire since the late great Ring Lardner," the reviewer believed the greatest strength of *Catcher* was the accuracy of Salinger's portrayal of American adolescence. In contrast to Peterson's review, the *Time* review admires rather than questions the authenticity of Holden and his world, concluding with the pronouncement that "the prize catch in *The Catcher in the Rye* may well be Novelist Salinger himself. He can understand an adolescent mind without displaying one."[17]

Three days later, another review appeared that provided a singular interpretation and the first full rejection of *Catcher* as unfit for any audience. The untitled review, written by T. Morris Longstreth for the *Christian Science Monitor,* opened with the statement, "A sixteen-year-old schoolboy, Holden Caulfield, tells the story—with the paradoxical result that it is not fit for children to read." After quoting J. D. Salinger as saying, "All of my best friends are children. It's almost unbearable to me to realize that my book will be kept on a shelf out of their reach," Longstreth expressed his disbelief that "a true lover of children could father this tale," and cautioned his readers that "many adults as well" would not "wish to condition themselves to Holden's language."[18]

In introducing his argument, Longstreth paralleled *Catcher* with the definition of life given in Shakespeare's *Macbeth:* "a tale told by an idiot … signifying nothing," and the summary that followed contained more thoroughgoing damnation. Holden's conduct in the novel was reduced to "a nightmarish medley of loneliness, bravado, and supineness," his narrative "wholly repellent in its mingled vulgarity, naiveté, and sly perversion," and Holden himself was termed "psychopathic" and "as unbalanced as a rooster on a tightrope." Significantly, Longstreth's concluding paragraph provided a premonitory expression of the near-paranoia that would characterize the censorship debates in the years to come. "Fortunately, there cannot be many of him yet. But one fears that a book like this given wide circulation may multiply his kind," he worried, "as too easily happens when immorality and perversion are recounted by writers of talent whose work is countenanced in the name of art or good intention."[19]

In August 1951, two reviews appeared that did "countenance" *Catcher*—for sheer enjoyment as much as for art or good intention. Indeed, critic Harvey Breit in his review for the *Atlantic* seemed suspicious of his own pleasure in reading *Catcher*. Breit was the first critic to contrast resemblances between Holden and Huck in *The Adventures of Huckleberry Finn,* drawing positive parallels between the two characters first and then distinguishing the difference between the two books:

> T. S. Eliot once pointed out that we see the world through Huck's eyes. Well, we do not see it through Holden's. We see Holden as a smiling adult sees a boy, and we smile at his spectral, incredible world. I think that is the decisive failure: whatever is serious and implicit in the novel is overwhelmed by the more powerful comic element. What remains is a brilliant tour de force, one that has sufficient power and cleverness to make the reader chuckle and—rare indeed—even laugh aloud.[20]

Breit himself was not misled by the humor nearly as much as he suggested. In his opening paragraph, Breit argued for recognition of *Catcher* as significant "because the novel, for all its surface guilelessness, is a critique of the contemporary, grown-up world."[21] Here, Breit is over-looking his own role as reader: as Breit apparently shared Salinger's critique of contemporary America, he was thus able to indulge more fully (and perhaps seek relief) in the comic aspects of Holden's narrative. It is certainly difficult to imagine readers of Longstreth's perspective smiling at Holden's "spectral incredible world."

The other August review was S. N. Behrman's near-extravagant accolade of *The Catcher in the Rye* that was published, not surprisingly, in the *New Yorker*. The review was a lengthy five pages and had the tone of a tribute to a "local boy made good," including occasional lapses into "Holdenese." Of particular note in this review was Behrman's closing summary. He not only emphasized the interpretation of Holden as a willful innocent but could scarcely restrain himself from writing a happy ending in place of the circular and ambiguous conclusion that Salinger had written:

> Holden's difficulties affect his nervous system but never his vision. It is the vision of the innocent.... Holden will be all right. One day, he will probably find himself in the mood to call up Jane. He will even become more tolerant of phonies—it is part of the mechanics of living.... He may even, someday, write a novel. I would like to read it. I loved this one. I mean it—I really did.[22]

Behrman's extension of *Catcher* here recalls Marcus Klein's faith in accommodation—he believes Holden can mature and somehow maintain the idealism of his innocence.

With the exception of an unremarkable review by Ernest Jones for the *Nation* (1 September 1951), Behrman's review marked the temporary close of critical attention to *The Catcher in the Rye* itself. In reconsidering these early reviews, we find the majority were quite favorable, yet there was enough caution and complaint in the more probing pieces to foreshadow the coming controversy over *Catcher*'s place in American culture.

Indeed, *Catcher* began to be censored from bookstores and public libraries as well as schools not long after this initial review period closed—perhaps in part as a consequence of its 1951 publication date. In the 1950s, the censorship of books became a well-organized activity across America, a matter that will be addressed at length in the next chapter. Suffice it to say at this point that while 1954 is the first date for which there is formal record of a censorship attempt of *Catcher*, this attempt and others in the 1954–60 period were based on a circulated list of twenty "objectionable" books.

The inclusion of *Catcher* on this early listing suggests that earlier informal and/or unrecorded attempts to censor it may have led to its 1954 status as objectionable. *Catcher* was formally censored first in Los Angeles and Marin Counties, California (1954), and then in Boston, Port Huron, Buffalo, and Baltimore (1955). By 1956, *Catcher* was also banned in Fairmont, McMechen, and Wheeling, West Virginia, as well as St. Louis, and the censorship continued to expand throughout the 1950s.[23] However, in contrast to the experience of the majority of books on the censors' list, *Catcher* often received focal attention and stirred a local controversy in nearly every case.

While literary critics would largely refrain from engagement in the censorship controversies, their own internal debate over *Catcher* quietly flourished. The dividing question was whether or not to view Salinger as a major writer in the field of mid-twentieth-century literature—the answer to which largely depended upon whether *Catcher* was seen as the product of years of short-story-writing apprenticeship with further novels to follow or as a one-time fluke, an "accidental" novel. In fact, one explanation of the near-absolute public silence of literary critics regarding *Catcher* through 1956 is that they were waiting to see if Salinger would publish another novel. While some unsupported claims were made that Salinger was writing another novel, his only publications following *Catcher* were five new short stories (1953–59) and three book-length collections of his short fiction (*Nine Stories*, 1953; *Franny and Zooey*, 1961; *Raise High the Roof Beam, Carpenters* and *Seymour: An Introduction*, 1963).

The publication of *Nine Stories* and its sustained presence on the *New York Times* "best-seller" list did give rise to reviews that contained frequent references to *Catcher*, making criticisms and comparisons that were "presented in such a way as to reveal that *The Catcher* was still a much-discussed book."[24] Many of these criticisms were of a negative sort, explained perhaps by the critics' growing frustration with Salinger as a second novel failed to materialize. In a representative review of *Nine Stories*, critic Seymour Krill voiced the professional jealousy of critics who felt Salinger was wasting a talent that they, at least implicitly, would cherish: "When you come right down to it, the chivvying of a genuine writer is a form of complimenting him. In the majority of cases, the 'magic' simply isn't there, and one makes criticism a form of duty; in Salinger's instance, where the gem of his talent shines, there is real concern that the author make the very best use of it. Such freshness isn't given freely, and its ownership implies a responsibility which transcends self."[25]

It was the irresponsibility of the critics themselves, however, that irritated critic David L. Stevenson as he took the literary profession to task for their neglect of Salinger in the March 1957 issue of the *Nation*. In his essay "J. D. Salinger: The Mirror of Crisis," Stevenson opened with this statement:

> It is a curiosity of our age of criticism that J. D. Salinger, one of the most gifted of the young writers to emerge in America since World War II, is rarely acknowledged by the official guardians of our literary virtue in the quarterlies. He was extravagantly praised by the nation's book reviewers for his best-selling novel of 1951, *The Catcher in the Rye*.... His work has become standard reading in Freshman English. One hears his name occasionally above the noise of a cocktail party when a new story appears, in the last few years usually in *The New Yorker*. But he has remained outside the interest of our seriously dedicated critics.[26]

Stevenson went on to explain this lack of attention to Salinger with revealing insight into the real processes of contemporary literary criticism. The problem, it seemed, lay not in Salinger's work but in his "diffidence to things dedicatedly literary" and his social existence "wholly beyond the fixed orbit of their [critics] attention." Having thus acknowledged the elitism of the literary profession, Stevenson analyzed Salinger's work from several angles. Noting Salinger's place in the *New Yorker* school— how his work was both characteristic and uncharacteristic of *New Yorker* short fiction—Stevenson then contrasted Salinger's "Pretty Mouth and Green My Eyes" with Hemingway's "The Short Happy Life of Francis Macomber," and included brief analyses of several of Salinger's other short stories. For Stevenson, the distinctive element of Salinger's fiction and particularly of *The Catcher in the Rye* was that Salinger did not "take you out of yourself into a living, substantial world of fiction" but instead kept returning the reader "back into your own problems, or into an awareness of them in your contemporaries."[27]

It was within this modality of necessarily reflexive reading that the "mirror of crisis" came into play. Stevenson discussed *Catcher* at some length as "Salinger's most ambitious presentation of aspects of contemporary alienation, and his most successful capture of an American audience." *Catcher* was a "mirror" of full-length clarity, causing the reader to reflect on the experience of alienation that was particularly suited to the social environment of post–World War II America. In addressing the nature of the crisis reflected in Salinger's fiction and its audience appeal, Stevenson wrote that "in our time and place the individual estranged from his fellows seems peculiarly understandable and therefore touching to us." "It is not that we, as a generation, are defeated, or without will," he asserted, but that perhaps "our religion, our family ties, our cultural traditions now give us a lighter armor than our predecessors wore."[28] It was not, therefore, that the experience of alienation was new to Americans, nor that the struggle against anomie was a lost cause for postwar Americans anymore than it had been for earlier generations, but that a gradual disintegration in the fabric of social institutions had laid bare the isolation of the individual.

Stevenson's perspective closely resembled that of Arthur Heiserman and James E. Miller Jr. in their essay "J. D. Salinger: Some Crazy Cliff." Published in 1956 and apparently overlooked by Stevenson, it was in fact the Heiserman and Miller article that truly broke the silence of "serious" critics toward *Catcher*.[29] Heiserman and Miller argued that while *Catcher* was in the universal tradition of "the Quest"—"a seeking after what is tremendous, greater than the love of woman ... [, in which] protagonists place themselves outside the bounds of what is known and seek not stability but a Truth which is unwarped by stability"—it was more specifically American, and contemporary American, at that.[30]

In a manner reminiscent of Lewis's *American Adam*, Heiserman and Miller wrote that "American literature seems fascinated with the outcast, the person who defies traditions in order to arrive at some pristine knowledge, some personal integrity." Conjuring the fictional heroes created by novelists James Fenimore Cooper, Mark Twain, and John Knowles, Heiserman and Miller presented a character profile against which Salinger's characterization of Holden could be evaluated. Beginning with the observation that "the virtues of these American heroes are personal ones: they most often, as a matter of fact, are in conflict with home, family, church," Heiserman and Miller pointed out that "the typical American hero must flee these institutions, become a tramp in the earth, cut himself off," because "only by flight can he find knowledge of what is real. And if he does not flee, he at least defies."

Holden Caulfield was seen to be an American hero in this vein but with a twist: while the "phoniness of society forces Holden Caulfield to leave it," explained Heiserman and Miller, he is seeking "nothing better than a home, a life embosomed upon what is known and can be trusted." Interestingly, Heiserman and Miller applauded Holden's heroism in one

of the most openly self-deprecating expressions of the "beyond innocence" perspective. Writing early on in their essay that "for Holden, there
is no place to go," and that "unlike all of us, Holden refuses to compromise with adulthood and its necessary adulteries; and his heroism drives
him berserk," Heiserman and Miller concluded that it was "not Holden
who should be examined for a sickness of the mind, but the world in
which he has sojourned and found himself an alien."[31]

In the 1957 summer issue of the *American Quarterly,* the essays by
Stevenson and Heiserman and Miller were joined by another of similar
persuasion. Written by Edgar Branch and titled "Mark Twain and J. D.
Salinger: A Study in Literary Continuity," it marked the first lengthy
attempt to place *Catcher* in the tradition of American literature. While
stating that "*The Catcher in the Rye,* in fact, is a kind of *Huckleberry Finn*
in modern dress," Branch further cautioned that the purpose of his
paper was not "to reveal any direct, 'real' or conscious 'influences' . . . that
Huckleberry Finn had upon Salinger's novel" but was rather an attempt
"to bare one nerve of cultural continuity in America by dissecting some
literary relationships between the two novels."[32]

Branch began his comparison of the two novels by discussing the
parallels in narrative pattern and style, followed by a review of the similarities in the characterizations of Huck and Holden. In both cases the
novels were found to be much alike and, although he did not explicitly
address the Adamic tradition, Branch's contrast and comparison did
follow the outline of Lewis's argument. Branch's essay concluded with a
contrast of "ethical-social import," as he found *Huckleberry Finn* and
Catcher to be essentially alike yet different as they reflected their own
sociohistorical context. Both books, according to Branch, contained "a
devastating criticism of American society" and expressed "a morality of
love and humanity," yet *Catcher* "assume[d] a cultural determinism"
whereas *Huckleberry Finn* answered challenged determinism with its
portrayal of "freedom through self-guidance."

In his closing comments, Branch metaphorically linked the two novels in such a way as to highlight the change in social context and to suggest that he, like Stevenson, Heiserman, and Miller, was of the "beyond
innocence" perspective that found *The Catcher in the Rye* so appropriate
to the post–World War II period:

> So Huck on a raft, as profoundly symbolic today as Thoreau in his
> cabin, is ever more meaningful as our national experience hurtles us
> along routes more menacing than the Mississippi. *The Catcher in the*

Rye, always cautionary, often horrifying in moral tone, creates an over-
whelming sense of that hurtling. The point is not that Salinger's moral
vision is therefore defective. Rather, because his vision is lit by the sick
lamps of civilization, *The Catcher in the Rye* is as appropriate to our
age as *Huckleberry Finn* is to an earlier America. Salinger's novel, in
fact, suggests great truths about our times.[33]

If Stevenson, Branch, Heiserman, and Miller were isolated voices in
1956–57, they did not remain so for long. In 1958 came the publication of
the first book-length analysis of Salinger's fiction, Frederick Gwynn and
Joseph Blotner's *The Fiction of J. D. Salinger,*[34] followed in 1959 by five
review articles that returned the focus to *The Catcher in the Rye.* The last
of the articles was "The Salinger Industry," written by George Steiner for
the *Nation* in late 1959.[35] Steiner's essay is of particular interest here as it
was at once a response to David Stevenson's 1957 *Nation* article and a
review of the surge in Salinger criticism that appeared between the two
essays. Noting that Stevenson "can now rest assured . . . the heavy guns
are in action along the entire critical front," Steiner found the attention
to Salinger undeserved and disproportionate.[36]

Where Stevenson held the elite machinations of the literary profession responsible for the inattention to Salinger, Steiner placed the blame
for the increasingly abundant criticism of Salinger's fiction at the door
of the profession itself. Steiner agonized that, in consequence of both the
impact of the New Criticism and the economics in which the English
professor is promoted on the basis of what he publishes, "American literary criticism has become a vast machine in constant need of new raw
material," a field with "too many critical journals, too many seminars,
too many summer schools and fellowships for critics." "There has never
been, and cannot be," he argued, "enough good literature produced at
any given moment to supply a critical industry so massive and serious."[37]

The cost of this overproduction of criticism in Steiner's view was that
merely "competent" works such as *The Catcher in the Rye* become indis-
tinguishable in literary treatment from the "great" works of Cervantes,
Chekhov, or even Mark Twain. Steiner clearly distinguished between the
import of elite and popular literature and held it the "task" and "responsibility" of the literary profession to elucidate that distinction for the
review audience. Perhaps unintentionally, Steiner was arguing for the
preservation of an elite body of literature as defined by an equally elite
body of interpreters. Yet the actual practice of writing, criticism, and
reading calls such elitism into question, and nowhere so clearly as in

the criticism and reading of *The Catcher in the Rye*. As Steiner himself acknowledged, the very popularity of *Catcher* with the public caused a reversal of the usual direction of influence between critic and reader.

Steiner opened his essay by noting that Gwynn and Blotner, along with the other four 1959 reviewers of Salinger's fiction, had recognized Salinger's popular significance (e.g., Arthur Mizener's comment that "Salinger is probably the most avidly read author of any serious pretensions in his generation," and Granville Hicks's similar comment that "there are, I am convinced, millions of young Americans who feel closer to Salinger than to any other writer"),[38] then stating that "obviously, critics are interested to find out why this should be so."[39] While the idea that the critics might take instruction from the popular readership was apparent anathema to Steiner and the normative practice of literary critics, it is of vital interest in considering *The Catcher in the Rye* as a cultural document.

Indeed, Robert Gutwillig, in his 1961 review in the *New York Times Book Review,* had pointed out that *Catcher*'s popularity with students had surely stimulated critical attention to it because of the dual role of teacher and critic. "Salinger and Caulfield continue to move and amuse the current school and college generation," Gutwillig commented, "and the quarterly critics, most of whom are college teachers, know it."[40] While Steiner was characteristically suspicious of the "academic critic" who, having selected "a small though clearly interesting fish like Salinger" for classroom use, can then "do his piece with few footnotes" and mark off "another tally on the sheet of his career,"[41] Marvin Laser and Norman Fruman proposed that the spate of articles by academic critics was instead a response to the widely expressed popular interest in *The Catcher in the Rye* and a more genuine attempt to understand and explain its continued importance.[42] A look at the later reviews and essays regarding *The Catcher in the Rye* supports Laser and Fruman's viewpoint and provides further evidence of the significance of *Catcher* among the popular readership.

Titling his review "Everybody's Caught *The Catcher in the Rye*," Gutwillig opened his essay with a summary of the academic appeal and current consumption of *Catcher* among university and secondary students.

Of the 250,000 paperback copies sold this year, a goodly number went to students of Yale, Northern Baptist Theological Seminary and 275 other colleges and universities across the country who have adopted the book for required or supplementary reading in English, psychology and other courses. The appeal of *The Catcher in the Rye* extends also to the younger brothers and sisters of the college crowd. Thousands of secondary school students find themselves academically involved with Holden Caulfield and the week-end of his flight from Pencey Prep.

In fact, the reason for the appearance of Gutwillig's review in 1961 — ten years after the initial publication of *The Catcher in the Rye*—was that for the second year in a row "so many bookstores, especially those in college communities, reported it among their most-wanted paperbacks that it has won a place on this *Review*'s paperback best seller list."[43]

Evidence of student commitment to Salinger (and particularly *The Catcher in the Rye*) as well as of the "Salinger industry" is abundant in the belated wave of critical attention to *Catcher*. In the span of four years between 1959 and 1963, at least twenty scholarly essays were devoted to *The Catcher in the Rye*, while the publication of Salinger's *Franny and Zooey* in 1961 occasioned numerous discussions of *Catcher* in the course of the reviews. With six full-length books on him appearing between 1962 and 1963 alone, Salinger received additional consideration in two surveys of the contemporary American novel: Hassan's *Radical Innocence* (1961) and Klein's *After Alienation* (1962).[44] As we have seen in the examples given by Gwynn and Blotner, Stevenson, Hicks, Mizener, and Gutwillig, the popularity of *The Catcher in the Rye* among American youth and particularly college students was extravagant, leading Laser and Fruman to comment that "observers of the American scene know that Salinger is by far the most popular author, living or dead, among college students."[45]

Laser and Fruman, like so many of Salinger's critics, were professors of English, and many of these academic critics quoted classroom examples in an attempt to fully document the voluntary engagement of students in Salinger's fiction. Arthur Mizener, at the time a professor of English at Cornell University, opened his 1959 essay for *Harper's* with a classroom example. "A few months ago I gave a lecture in the Middle West, on F. Scott Fitzgerald, before about as intelligent an undergraduate audience as you are likely to find," Mizener wrote, and then recounted the "humbling non-sequitur" that he believed his colleagues would find "too familiar to be any surprise": "When I finished, the first question from the floor was about J. D. Salinger."[46]

Similarly, in introducing her review of *Franny and Zooey*, Joan Didion described a 1956 cocktail party in New York where "a stunningly predictable Sarah Lawrence girl" attempted to engage Didion in a discussion of Salinger, only to declare that Salinger was "the single person in the world capable of understanding her." Reflecting that in the five years since the party few areas in life had gone *un*changed, Didion noted that J. D. Salinger's appeal remained consistent. Acknowledging that "among the reasonably literate young and young at heart, he is surely the most read and reread writer in America today," she observed that Salinger "exert[ed] a power over his readers which [was] in some ways extra-literary." "Those readers expect him to teach them something," she claimed, "something that has nothing at all to do with fiction."[47]

While the balance of Didion's review was filled with cynical and scathing criticism of Salinger (*Franny and Zooey* is termed "spurious . . . self-help copy: it emerges finally as *Positive Thinking* for the upper middle classes"),[48] the preceding passage highlighted a significant difficulty for the critics who sought to understand the popularity of *The Catcher in the Rye*. One after another, critics first acknowledged popular-reader appreciation of *Catcher* and then tried to explain that popularity in structural analyses of the novel that not only conflicted with one another but often conflicted internally as well.

Consequently, the student qua future literary critic who reads the casebooks of Salinger criticism may finish them confused as to the real contents of *The Catcher in the Rye* but certainly educated as to the various modes and techniques of literary criticism. The bulk of the "Salinger industry" criticism presents an ironic and revealing look at the profession of literary criticism: with the return of critical attention to *Catcher*, an irritating necessity commanded by its sustained popularity, critics sought explanation in the modality of an "Ideal Reader." Seeking to determine the "objective" meaning and significance of the novel through the application of critical aesthetics and standards shared among members of the literary establishment, *Catcher*'s success could only be understood as a fluke. For the majority of literary critics, the incomprehensibility of *Catcher*'s immediate and continued appeal may at least partly be explained by their disinterest in, if not outright dismissal of, the popular readership.

There is one academic critic within this period who did attempt to comprehend *The Catcher in the Rye* as it was popularly read. Edward Corbett, then a professor of English at Creighton University, Nebraska, wrote an essay that was published in *America* in 1961. Titled "Raise High the Barriers, Censors: Some Thoughts on *The Catcher in the Rye*," Corbett's essay was remarkable on two counts. Not only did he attribute intelligence to the popular readership and respect reader explanations of *Catcher*'s value but he also sought to understand the censorship of *The Catcher in the Rye*, where other critics rarely acknowledged that censorship was even occurring.

Corbett opened his essay with two examples of campus censorship of *The Catcher in the Rye* (at a West Coast college and a Midwestern high school), to which he responded with a personal anecdote of student appreciation of *Catcher*. He recounted as "firsthand evidence" the previous year's annual Jesuit English contest in which students from ten Midwestern Jesuit colleges wrote essays on one of three novels. The three novels for 1959 were *The Catcher in the Rye*, Huxley's *Brave New World*, and Conrad's *Under Western Eyes*. Fully 90 percent of the students at Creighton chose to write on *Catcher*, and Corbett "[had] never witnessed on our campus as much eager discussion about a book as there was about *The Catcher in the Rye*."[49]

Having thus identified *Catcher* as a central text for the "young people of the postwar generation," Corbett discussed the possible grounds for censorship, balancing the perspective of the censor against one of more liberal consideration. He isolated three central areas of conflict: the language of the book, "scandalous" episodes in the book, and the perception that Holden, "constantly protesting against phoniness, is a phony himself." The first two were dismissed by Corbett, albeit thoughtfully, on the basis that adult guidance and open discussion of the novel would keep any profanities, obscenities, or scandalous behavior within the context of art and realism. The third aspect—Holden's own "phoniness"—was one that Corbett found more difficult to refute. The complaint was that, however apt Holden's criticism of academic and social conformity around him, it was difficult to find in Holden a model of some alternative behavior. While Corbett found in Holden's behavior both present hope and future wisdom, he empathized with the objecting reader on this point: "I suspect that adults who object to Holden on the grounds of his apparent phoniness are betraying their own uneasiness. Holden is not like the adolescents in the magazine ads—the smiling, crew-cut, loafer-shod teenagers wrapped up in the cocoon of suburban togetherness. He makes the adults of my generation uncomfortable because he exposes so much of what is meretricious in our way of life."[50]

Significantly, in his conclusion Corbett raised the question of exactly who the appropriate reader for *The Catcher in the Rye* might be. Foreseeing that "future controversy will probably center on just what age an adolescent must be before he is ready for this book," Corbett himself took the position that "*Catcher* is a subtle, sophisticated novel that requires an experienced, mature reader."[51] Recalling the earlier reviews for a moment, the question of appropriate audience had already been reflected in the mixed evaluations of *Catcher* as a book whose validity might best be judged by adolescents, even as most reviewers assumed that it was an adult book. For Salinger himself, the question of audience was all-inclusive, reflected in his early statement that *Catcher* was intended for children as much as for adults.[52]

While Corbett's essay demonstrated the successful reading of *The Catcher in the Rye* in the university setting, if assuredly by the "experienced" and "mature" readers of junior and senior literature classes, *Catcher* was the source of two serious censorship incidents on university campuses at the time of his essay. Corbett described one such incident, which led to the firing of an English professor at an unidentified West Coast college for requiring his freshman class to read *The Catcher in the Rye.*[53] The other case occurred in April of 1961, when the parents of a twenty-year-old University of Texas student protested the inclusion of *Catcher* in the required readings of her sophomore English class. The university in this incident supported the professor and the English Department and retained *The Catcher in the Rye.* Consequently, the student's father, a Houston attorney and port commissioner at the time, stated that he would withdraw his daughter from the university.[54]

Although Corbett's essay implied that censorship of *The Catcher in the Rye* was being attempted on college campuses beyond these two cases, there is an absence of formal record of such attempts in his essay or elsewhere. This is not to say that Corbett was incorrect but rather that university censorship may have been dealt with covertly. By contrast, high school censorship of *Catcher* was clearly in evidence.

Between 1961 and 1965, eighteen separate attempts to censor *Catcher* on high school campuses created sufficient dispute to merit attention in local and national newspapers.[55] Occurring in both small and large school districts in California, Nevada, Ohio, Delaware, Connecticut, Oregon, Pennsylvania, Georgia, New York, and Virginia, the frequency and vehemence of the attacks on *The Catcher in the Rye* caused the American Book Publishers Council to state in late 1963 that "J. D. Salinger's novel of youth in search of identity now has the dubious honor of being the most consistently damned book in this country's public school systems."[56] Interestingly, an adequate defense was able to be made in the majority of these incidents, and *Catcher* was ultimately retained in the high school system—if in a recommended or restricted capacity rather than as required reading.

As the literary critics did not often concern themselves with the general question of audience, their abstention from the censorship debates or even recognition of attempts to censor *The Catcher in the Rye* is not surprising. Except for one incident (in Connecticut, May 1964) in which four academic critics agreed to testify in defense of *Catcher* at a Board of Education hearing,[57] the literary establishment did not become involved in the growing public controversy, even as debate participants made secondhand use of their reviews. As the censorship debates over *The Catcher in the Rye* escalated, critical attention to the novel once again declined.

Having apparently reached its peak in 1963, the "Salinger industry" slowed down between 1964 and 1966. The few articles in this period were essentially repetitive structural analyses, a trend initiated in James E. Miller's 1965 pamphlet essay on J. D. Salinger. *The Catcher in the Rye* was discussed at length in the context of contemporary American fiction in the critical surveys of Jonathan Baumbach (*The Landscape of Nightmare*, 1965) and David P. Galloway (*The Absurd Hero in American Fiction*, 1966). Both authors explained the meaning and significance of *The Catcher in the Rye* in terms of its contributions to post–World War II discourse within the literary establishment, yet their analyses neglected the possible interpretations of the broader audience of American readers.[58]

The "Salinger industry" then gasped its last breath with the publication of Kenneth Hamilton's *J. D. Salinger* in 1967. Published as a part of the series "Contemporary Writers in Christian Perspective," Hamilton's brief book was concerned with the religious quality of Salinger's work and *The Catcher in the Rye* in particular. While applauding the book's spiritual significance, Hamilton's work is striking in its absence of recognition of censorship of *The Catcher in the Rye*—particularly as one of the grounds of censorship at this time was *Catcher*'s "atheistic" mood.[59]

One essay stood in contrast to this trend : Mary Ely's "A Cup of Consecrated Chicken Soup," published in *The Catholic World* in February of 1966. Ely, a teacher of English and religion at a Midwestern high school, was concerned, like Edward Corbett, over the censorship of *The Catcher in the Rye* and, like Kenneth Hamilton, with the relation of "religion to literature and life."[60] A teacher with eighteen years of experience, the occasion that inspired her essay was a set of informal notes passed between two students during her religion class and confiscated by Ms. Ely. Both students were outstanding twelfth-graders: Lennie, "a science-math sharpie," and Bill, "a merit finalist." Ely offered the notes unedited in her essay, and this clandestine dialogue is rare evidence of unsolicited reader response:

> **Lennie:** Bill, Do you think J. D. Salinger's *Catcher in the Rye* is a satire on the world today and is the author pessimistic on life?
>
> **Bill:** It is a satire, but whether or not he is pessimistic is an undecided question among critics. Salinger asks, "How can a person who is exceptional in his observation of life (such as Holden) live in a world which does not appreciate the skill of observation?" In Franny and Zooey he answers the question by saying that the person who is exceptional. . . . must consider all worldly, phony people as symbolizing Christ & thus be loved. You can hate the phoniness of people, but you must love the people.
>
> **Lennie:** When I read it, I thought how can a guy with the observing piercing mind of Caulfield be flunking out. His attitudes are very childish. There would seem to be a contradiction in Holden's character: his good observing mind, which, while looking at life, fails to see that others adapted themselves and he must.
>
> **Bill:** These people adapted themselves to a phony world. This Holden thought he could not do. His attitude is one of rejecting the phony world. According to Salinger, Holden's attitude is wrong because he hates people as individuals, but, at the very end of the story, Holden feels sorry for all the phonies he has met. This shows that although his early rejection of phonies was very obvious, his later pity, compassion, and love for them is just as obvious.

Regretting that her actions ended the interchange, Ely thought that the notes demonstrated *Catcher*'s potential for classroom usage, asking whether it wouldn't "be sensible teaching to share this perceptive view of life with the rest of the twelfth graders by a discussion of Holden's dilemma in English or religion class." "What English teacher has ever found any stimulating notes concerning the problems of Ivanhoe or Little Eppie," she asked, "yet we continue to teach *Ivanhoe* and *Silas Marner* to the 'hitchhiking' and 'gorilla' dancing generation."[61]

While I confess I cannot imagine discovering such a set of surreptitious notes on even *The Catcher in the Rye* in my university-level classes, Ely's point that *Catcher* may provide an appealing context for the classroom discussion of ethics and values is well-taken. As if anticipating the skepticism of less-blessed teachers, Ely offered a further example of *Catcher*'s ability to bridge the gap between education and extracurricular experience. Intended as evidence of "Holden's hold on the heartstrings" and noting that "many students candidly admit a fondness for Holden because he is more confused than they are," Ms. Ely described a "masquerade school dance when a seventeen-year-old wore an old red hunting cap backwards, rating applause and accolade from teacher and teenager alike."[62]

Identification with Holden apparently bridges the gap between teenager and critic as well—and the span of generations. In the midst of his 1961 review for the *New York Times*, Robert Gutwillig had paused for a reflexive consideration of his own relationship to *The Catcher in the Rye*:

> What was it about the novel that struck Americans so squarely ten years ago and continues to hit the mark still? Primarily it was, I think, the shock and thrill of recognition. Many of my friends and this writer himself identified completely with Holden. I went to a school much like Pencey Prep. One of my friends had a younger brother like Allie, who had died, another an older brother like D.B., still another a younger sister like Phoebe. After reading the novel, several of us went out and bought ourselves red caps with earflaps, and we all took to calling each other "Ace" and "Prince."[63]

If his explanation of the identification with Holden based on similarities of schooling and family relationships seems somewhat superficial in hindsight, Gutwillig stands virtually alone in including his personal sentiments in a professional review. Indeed, the literary critics' lack of attention to readership experience reflects the intentions of literary criticism at the time. In their attempt to maintain professional standards of objectivity, literary critics necessarily eschewed their own personal responses and largely ignored the reading public because of the difficulty of assessing and proving the varied readings of any text. Ely's closing statement stands as a case in point: "Until I found the notes quoted," she wrote, "I had decided to stop fighting for Holden. But somehow now the fight seems not altogether hopeless, victory not too Utopian."[64] It was her exposure to unsolicited and, arguably, objective evidence that allowed Ely to go beyond the accepted parameters of critical analysis.

While many present critics continue to analyze literary texts in the modality of the Ideal Reader and are skeptical at best of the possible value of broader reader interpretations, a shift away from this perspective is evident in recent literary criticism and cultural analysis. This shift can perhaps be attributed to two factors: post-1960s awareness of and emphasis on the experience of American diversity and the impact of the theoretical work of European scholars in semiotics and cultural criticism.

Stanley Fish's 1980 manifesto, *Is There a Text in This Class?* is the landmark argument in this shift. Writing as a radical literary critic, Fish did not explicitly recognize semiotic theory, although cultural historian Janice Radway has aptly pointed out that "the theory of the text he sets forth implicitly in those essays is essentially a semiotic one."[65] Fish emphasized the role of the reader in constituting the meaning of any text and, furthermore, asserted that the membership of the reader in reference groups (as he termed them, "interpretive communities") will direct the reader's reading of the text. Interpretive communities structure the very existence of the text because, as Fish explained it, "the act of recognizing literature is not constrained by something in the text, nor does it issue from an independent and arbitrary will." The very recognition of a text as literature "proceeds from a collective decision ... [,] a decision that will be in force only so long as a community of readers or believers continues to abide by it."[66]

Fish's argument was directed toward literary critics and the very notion of the objectivity of their analysis. Fish pointed out that such objectivity is a fallacy, paired with the equivalent fallacy that a text is necessarily subjective. Fish argued that both the production of a text (writing and publication) and the consumption of a text (reception, reading, and analysis) take place within shared frameworks of reality: each an interpretive community that could not be defined as objective because "its perspective is interested rather than neutral." Similarly, Fish continued, the production of meanings and of the texts themselves cannot be truly subjective "because they do not proceed from an isolated individual but from a public and conventional point of view."[67]

If Fish's argument undermined the very foundations of traditional literary criticism, it has been significant in its implications for cultural historians as well. In a sense, the literary text becomes a semiotic transaction in which any attempt to discover the "meaning" of the text must necessarily rely on discovery of the reader, his response, and the interpretive communities that direct the reader's recognition and understanding of the text as a signifier. Hence, in treating literature as a cultural document, scholars must address the question of audience as much, if not more so, than authorship. This approach limits the critic's conduction of structural and symbolic analyses as it privileges the interpretations of the actual reader and negates notions of an Ideal Reader.

Perhaps the most difficult of the implications of Fish's work is not the reformulation of one's approach to literary texts but the development of ways to investigate, as Janice Radway put it, "the ways real readers read."[68]

As Robert Gutwillig's personal account demonstrated, even literary critics are not comfortable with the self-consciousness required in explaining one's response to a text. Mary Ely's accidental discovery of reader response highlights the fact that unselfconscious reader response exists, but in ways and places that the cultural historian might not recognize as worthy of investigation.

In the case of a text such as *The Catcher in the Rye,* the continued and voluntary debate over its meaning and value offers reader interpretations of the text as well as assumptions about how other readers are reading and judgments as to what they should be reading. The participation of the literary critics in the debates, if it can be called participation, was consistent with the very practice of their profession. Writing analyses and evaluations of books for an audience of readers they cared not to understand, they had little interest in whether or not and by whom *Catcher* was read at all. Yet it seems the audience of readers has found enough meaning and value in the novel to come forward with their interpretations. In the censorship controversies, parents, librarians, school teachers and administrators, religious leaders, civic activists, and, on occasion, students all volunteer their readings and opinions of *The Catcher in the Rye.*

4

Interpretive Communities

For a society is not made up merely of the mass of individuals
who compose it, the ground which they occupy, the things which
they use and the movements which they perform, but above all is
the idea which it forms of itself. It is undoubtedly true that it hesi-
tates over the manner in which it ought to conceive itself; it feels
drawn in divergent directions. But these conflicts which break
forth are not between the ideal and reality, but between two different ideals, that of yesterday and that of today.
—Emile Durkheim, *The Elementary Forms of Religious Life*

The immediate difficulty in discovering the "ways real readers read" *The Catcher in the Rye* lies in determining who the reader is—which of several audiences one is addressing. Whether *Catcher* as a book about an adolescent was intended for an audience of former adolescents or future adults has been a point of contention for both censors and supporters of *The Catcher in the Rye*. In 1985, critic Richard Stayton argued that *Catcher* is a "classic" of "timeless power" based on his personal experience as a reader across three decades. Titled "Why Holden Caulfield Still Catches You," Stayton's review is an example of adolescent reader response via recollection *and* of present adult reading. As Stayton recalled: "For me and my friends growing up absurd in the early 1960's with pimples and masturbation and parents who kept getting weirder and weirder, 'The Catcher in the Rye' was a kind of Bible. We understood Holden ... official affirmation of all this came when my high school *advanced* English class wouldn't permit me to review or even *read 'The Catcher in the Rye.'* We loved the controversy. It validated our alienation, sort of."[1]

A college student in the 1960s, Stayton remembered that the counter-cultural slogan "Don't trust anyone over 30" "seemed to come right out of Holden Caulfield's mouth," although as post-sixties disillusionment turned to apathy in the 1970s, Stayton necessarily "kept (his) distance from Holden Caulfield's identity crisis." Even so, Stayton acknowledged that when he would come across a copy of *Catcher* in a bookstore, Salinger's tale "always triggered memories of adolescence, of first discovering that I wasn't quite alone with my impure thoughts, that being an outsider wasn't all bad."[2]

"Re-re-reading" *The Catcher in the Rye* in 1984 at the age of thirty-seven, Stayton found that he responded to the book on two new levels. Reading at first with a cynicism born of his maturity, Stayton found that although he still "liked a lot of characters in the book ... in my *mind* ... Holden Caulfield seemed phony as hell." Yet when in the course of the novel Holden declared that what he loved about museums was "that everything always stayed right where it was.... Nobody'd be different. The only thing that would be different would be you," his words nagged at Stayton and brought him to an epiphany of recovered idealism: "Salinger's spiritual odyssey had reached out beyond two decades to teach me a new perspective on myself. In midlife, I realized—thanks again to '*The Catcher in the Rye*'—who I was in relation to the world: another phony asking, 'When in hell are you going to grow up?'"[3]

If Stayton saw *The Catcher in the Rye* as a novel of continuous value, deepening in meaning as the reader matured, others have seen *Catcher* as equally timeless in its appeal to the particular age of adolescence. When critic Tracy Young interviewed English writer Ian Hamilton regarding his recent and controversial biography of J. D. Salinger,[4] she learned that Hamilton's interest in Salinger began with an adolescent appreciation of *Catcher* that was rekindled when his own sixteen-year-old son began "raving" about the book after reading it in school. "I'd never heard him say he'd read a wonderful book before," mused Hamilton.[5]

However beloved by adolescent readers, *Catcher* has been seen by still other readers as a book that is about adolescence but is strictly for adult readers. In a 1986 article for the *New York Times Book Review* titled "Should Holden Caulfield Read These Books?," critic Donald Barr challenged the inclusion of four "disposable classics" in the secondary school curriculum: *The Catcher in the Rye,* William Golding's *Lord of the Flies,* Harper Lee's *To Kill a Mocking Bird,* and John Knowles's *A Separate Peace.*[6] Barr found that the actual readership of these "ordinary trade books for adults" ranged from adults to preadolescents, explaining that the reading of these books began as "'in' books among college students," and then "moved down through the schools" where they "jostle(d) 'Romeo and Juliet' in middle school and high school reading lists."[7]

Recognizing that possibly "the college students chose these books themselves," what concerned Barr was that high school students and younger readers did not choose such reading but that, "in general, the American adolescent is given books to read, and less often by his parents than his teachers." This bothered Barr because in his *adult* reading of these novels he found the adult choices inappropriate for *adolescent* consideration. For Barr, novels such as *David Copperfield, Oliver Twist,* and *Great Expectations* were appropriate adolescent reading because they "are stories about growing up and the difficulties of growing up." By contrast, *Catcher in the Rye* and *Lord of the Flies* "are about not growing up" and in Barr's opinion "may even provide half-seductive images of alienation" to adolescent readers who are "not grown up enough to discern their moral structure." From Barr's adult perspective, even "Holden Caulfield, whose symbolic dream was to be the protector of children, would not have given children 'The Catcher in the Rye' to read."[8]

Barr did acknowledge that the act of reading itself is dependent upon the nature of the reader—and he somewhat confusingly took comfort in his view of the child as a reader. Positing children's reading as "a wonderful and powerful activity," he described this activity as essentially self-protecting, as "it can censor imperceptibly. . . . Children can be made to read all sorts of things; but in *reading* they mostly read what they want." "Mostly" is the operative word here, as Barr's question throughout the essay is ultimately whether children read by choice and with free interpretation or whether they are pushed to read adult books and probed for equally adult interpretations. Bringing his argument to a close, Barr asked, "What is one trying to teach when one assigns to preadolescents and adolescents a story about the ambiguity—perhaps even the impossibility—of friendship? *Should* we invite them to contemplate the dark forces brooding over the tortured world of adolescence?"[9]

In a similar albeit much more simplistic manner, the writers of the television series *Archie Bunker's Place* contrasted adult and adolescent reader response to *The Catcher in the Rye*. In a 1982 episode, central character Archie Bunker was asked to join a group of parents protesting sex education in the schools and pornography in the libraries. The leader of the group singularly described *Catcher* as a book in which "a teenager utters obscenities from cover to cover." Before Archie could respond, a student objected to this description, stating that *Catcher* was instead a book "about a teenager growing up."[10] This contrast between adult and adolescent interpretation of the book exemplifies Barr's argument by unwittingly emphasizing the process of signification in which the meaning of a text (as signifier) is understood on the basis of reader experience and expectations. Moreover, such recognition of the signification process is not limited to critical theorists, as the following conclusion to a student's essay on *Catcher* demonstrates: "Salinger writes about feelings and attitudes without explaining them. There is no need to, for you either understand the character or you don't. Empathy makes the fine line between *The Catcher in the Rye* being profound or just vulgar; between its being authentic or an exaggeration. I thought the book was magnificently written.... *The Catcher in the Rye* is a very personal book, and if you can find a part of yourself in it, then Holden Caulfield lives!!!"[11]

This essay, written in 1969 by a sixteen-year-old California public high school student, offers a rare glimpse of student reader response to *The Catcher in the Rye.* Sandra Christenson opened her essay with a summary description of *The Catcher in the Rye* in which explication of the concrete text is nearly inseparable from the interpretive perspective of the reader: "*The Catcher in the Rye* is a story concerned with self-identity; the search of a boy for himself, for his place, and for his reason. It is at a time when childhood and its innocence are at one end, and the patterned stamp of adulthood lurks at the other. Holden Caulfield represents the person caught in the vacuum, an offspring of its emptiness. He is someone who is trying to find out who he is and what he is looking for so that he will have some pattern to fit in and something permanent and real to identify with and to cling to when he is left alone to make his own way." Christenson then moves on to address the themes of bitterness and resentment that she found contained in Holden's "migration" from the world of childhood to that of adulthood: "Bitterness comes, too, when you look around in order to find something or someone real to see your reflection in, and everything and everyone that you touch is phoney. You witness people respecting the wrong thing for the wrong reason; teachers laughing at the 'right' jokes that aren't even funny; neighbors grinning at one another under a guise of interest and friendship instead of the indifference and dislike they really feel."[12]

And finally, *Catcher* is no longer the subject but becomes the frame for Christenson's own views: "There is resentment, too, when your childhood is dirtied by life, and your innocence is gone. The dirtiness is indelibly inscribed in your mind, and you are changed inside and on the surface, too, like a wall with a profanity scratched on it with a knife. You can turn profanity and ugliness around and use them for your own weapons, but it is a small defense against the hurt and confusion you feel."[13]

Importantly, in Christenson's response a certain amount of the "brooding over the tortured world of adolescence" that Donald Barr feared is evident, but it is an interpretation of *The Catcher in the Rye* established primarily through the frame of Christenson's own perspective and implicitly preexisting experience of struggle to define her own identity and sense of purpose. In another example of adolescent reader response, a male high school student in Madison, Wisconsin (1964), found *The Catcher in the Rye* to be reassuring rather than disturbing: "If I were a writer, I would like very much to have the qualities of Mr. J. D. Salinger.... I cannot remember reading a story of any type which brought out thoughts so perfectly as this book. They were common thoughts and ideas expressed so as to give you a feeling of security. They were so much like your very own, which you were afraid to admit for fear they were different."[14]

Thus, the reader not only censors and edits the concrete text but reads individual experience and belief into it as well—and this is true for the adult reader as much as the child.

One difference between the reader response of adolescents and that of adults in the *Catcher* debates is that very little adolescent response exists for consideration whereas adult response is voluminous. This discrepancy may be due in part to the consonance that adolescents seem to experience in reading *The Catcher in the Rye:* as Sandra Christenson stated, "I accept *The Catcher in the Rye* as a part of myself."[15] In one English composition assignment recounted in the education journal *Clearinghouse,* when students were asked to comment on episodes or elements in *Catcher* that they thought were "shocking," they responded that they were not shocked by anything in the novel.[16] One explanation for the relative lack of student response, then, is that the entire *Catcher* controversy may simply seem to be much ado about nothing to many adolescents.

This line of reasoning falters in light of the observations of teachers and critics concerning the popularity of *The Catcher in the Rye* with students, and the general absence of student participation in the debates remains striking. The better explanation is that the *Catcher* debates were perceived by the participants to be adult affairs. Adolescent views were not solicited, and in the few cases in which they were volunteered, they were paternalistically dismissed. Consequently, whether or not *The Catcher in the Rye* was intended for or read by adolescents, the debates themselves exist as an expression of the audience of adult readers.

While the *Catcher* debates provide an opportune setting for the study of reader response, the accessible response is primarily that of adults and is further limited to the adults who came to be involved in censorship action. Although participants in the *Catcher* debates were diverse in their communities of residence, fields of employment, religious beliefs, and political commitments, this primary limitation of the response has two consequences. First, the participants in the *Catcher* debates are largely white and middle class.[17] While this is perhaps fitting for debates over a novel that is in itself white and middle upper class, it also reflects the social context of censorship in America historically. Furthermore, the increasingly inescapable tendency of mid- to late-twentieth-century Americans to think in terms of the middle-class categories represented in the national media means that nonparticipants are at least familiar with—and likely to share in—the beliefs and concerns expressed by debate participants despite differences of class and ethnicity.[18] Second, while most participants were readers of *The Catcher in the Rye,* some became involved in the censorship actions because of their parental and professional positions and read *Catcher* only when the controversy made it necessary. For these latter readers the very question of censorship was the guiding framework in both their reading and response.

Hence, the censorship debates over *Catcher* are most intriguing as they open dialogue concerning what is "American" or "un-American" about the novel, and in doing so they make audible some of the deeply held assumptions and tensions of the middle class. Perhaps indicating the insufficiency of such amorphous social membership, individual readers who became involved in the *Catcher* debates voluntarily sought to distinguish or identify themselves to other participants by stressing their relationship to the professional communities of librarians and educators, the ideological community of the New Right, and the status community of parenthood. Literary critics formed an important if unintentional fifth community, although they did not directly involve themselves in the controversies.

Essentially, the reviews written by literary critics were used on occasion by the actively involved participants as a resource and did serve to add validity to claims that *The Catcher in the Rye* was "serious" fiction that ought to be included in the contemporary literature curriculum—particularly as a "young adult" or "coming of age" novel. Though their words were influential when called upon in their published voice of expertise, the literary critics as individuals refrained from any direct engagement with or acknowledgement of concern about the reception of the novel among the public readership, whether appreciative of or hostile to the text. However passive or disengaged from the public debate, literary critics were nonetheless crucial in their certification of *Catcher* as a significant work of contemporary literature.[19]

In the interpretation of the *Catcher in the Rye* controversies as a cultural debate, the preliminary task of the observer, required if one is to enter the worldview of the participants, is to bring forward *in their own terms* the background assumptions that shaped the response of each participant community to *Catcher* and to the larger debate. To this end, I have analyzed the magazines, texts, and professional journals that serve as forums for the four communities of active participants and have isolated their role conceptualizations and internal beliefs about American society, censorship, and the education of adolescents. In presenting their perspectives, I choose to examine them in the order of their appearance in the debate itself.[20]

Defenders of the Faith

The earliest attempt to censor *The Catcher in the Rye* for which there is formal record was in 1954, in Marin County, California, and shortly thereafter in Los Angeles County. In 1955–56, eight more attempts occurred across the nation.[21] These first ten attempts represent not only the opening of censorship of *The Catcher in the Rye* but also a well-organized nationwide effort to censor high school reading materials in general. The base of censorship operations in this period was the National Organization for Decent Literature (NODL). In each of these ten early attempts, a parent or "concerned citizen" approached the local school board with a list of books to be banned, including *The Catcher in the Rye*, because of these books' "immoral," "atheistic," or "communist" content. The lists and brief appended comments on each "suspect" book were generated through the NODL and set the tone for the arguments of procensorship religious leaders and affiliated citizenry for years to come. While this group eventually blended into the New Right as it matured in the late 1970s, to understand the development of the community of debate participants aligned with the New Right first requires a look at the history and ideology of the NODL.

The NODL was established in 1938 by the Catholic Bishops of the United States. The stated purpose of the organization was "to organize and set in motion the moral forces of the entire country ... against the lascivious type of literature which threatens moral, social and national life."[22] The explicit concern of the NODL in the early years was the content of magazines and comic books aimed at the expanding adolescent market. Bookstores were targeted for censorship action (requesting removal of materials, publishing lists of offending titles, and spurring boycotts of the bookstores that carried them), and NODL task forces were made up of Catholic women active in their local communities.

By the early 1950s, the targets, tactics, and the task forces themselves had changed. The previous focus on magazines and comic books shifted to paperbacks, particularly those paperbacks placed in high school libraries and encouraged as student reading materials. Concurrently, textbook content came under increased review with the formation of textbook commissions within local school districts. NODL members as well as local citizens responding to their efforts increasingly sought seats on these commissions. Objectionable material was defined not only on moral or religious grounds but out of "patriotic" concerns that reflected the influence of McCarthyism.

In 1953, for example, a community member of the Indianapolis textbook commission, Mrs. Thomas J. White, argued for the removal of *Robin Hood* and all mention of Quakers from textbooks. "There is a Communist directive in education now to stress the story of Robin Hood," she claimed. "They want to stress it because he robbed the rich and gave to the poor. That's the Communist line." As to the problem with the inclusion of Quakers in American history texts, "Quakers don't believe in fighting wars." Fearing that "all the men they can get to believe that they don't need to go to war, the better off the Communists are," White conflated Quaker pacifism and Communist aims as she insisted, "Its [*sic*] the same as their crusade for peace—everybody lay down their arms and they'll take over."[23]

In a similar instance, *The Wonderful Wizard of Oz* was excluded from classroom use in Pacific Palisades, California, in 1961 along with *The Young Russia*, which was described as "a recent volume of pictures from a national photo magazine showing smiling Soviet youngsters." Assuming that the menace in these books was obvious to adult Americans (if not to the audience of young American readers), then Associate Superintendent for Instructional Services (Los Angeles District) Everett Chafee explained the exclusions by simply stating, "Communist tone and Communist authors are among the things we look for."[24]

If the fear of a communist takeover through the reading of *Robin Hood* and *The Wizard of Oz* and study of the Quakers seems extravagant, consider the 1954 resolution of the more sedate National Council of Juvenile Court Judges, who feared increasing juvenile crime if not communism as an effect of the presence of paperbacks in the schools: "There is a growing realization that such foul publications, through their distribution to children and youth and their extensive encouragement to read them, contribute to the breakdown of the moral sense in children which today is causing an increase in juvenile delinquency."[25]

Although specific paperbacks were not isolated in the judges' resolution, one can assume they were of the same generic sort investigated by a Rhode Island commission on pocket-size books in 1956. The findings of this commission were based on a survey of thirty-three paperbacks conducted by Mary Kiely, librarian of a large Rhode Island high school. In her analysis of story plots and themes in these books, Kiely found that "11 out of 33 dealt with seductions; five had perversion, incest or sex abnormalities as their theme; five dealt with teen-age violence," and three of the paperbacks were described by Kiely as "illustrated manuals of sex instruction."[26]

The perceived threat of such indecent literature in the hands of American youths fostered the development of other small and localized organizations across the country such as the Crusaders for Decency in Literature in Albuquerque, New Mexico. As early as 1954, Rabbi Moshay P. Mann of the Albuquerque Ministerial Alliance led a fund-raising drive for the expansion of the Crusaders, alleging that "religion is the first line of attack by indecent literature," and that the reading of indecent literature posed a nondenominational threat, "as all the ethical and moral teachings of religion are nullified by the ill effects of unwholesome reading material."[27]

Recognizing that interest and support for its efforts were not limited to the Catholic community, NODL opened its first actual office in 1955. Set up in Chicago, the office was intended to "coordinate the work nationally" as "civic, fraternal, and Protestant" groups joined the concern.[28] In 1956 Monsignor Thomas Fitzgerald chronicled the history of NODL in his essay titled "The Menace of Indecent Literature." Stressing that NODL was no longer "concerned primarily with recruiting just the Catholic forces of the country in a campaign against objectionable literature," he implored "all right-thinking and decent people to join in this movement to preserve the ideals of our young people."[29]

What was crucial to each of these arguments was the belief that the "indecencies," which ranged from "obscene" language and explicit sexuality to perceived proposals for atheism and communism, were threats to the moral fiber of the American youth. Equally important, these individuals and organizations believed that such threats could not be combated in any way other than through censorship. In dismissing, when considered at all, the possibility that the American youth might read these materials critically or at least in conjunction with contrasting instruction from home, school, and church, the procensorship arguments reveal considerable insecurity about the stability of their own beliefs.

A 1956 NODL "bulletin" that started off by admitting, "We have to hand it to the Communists who, within the enslaving Bamboo Curtain of Red China, have launched a nationwide campaign against pornographic trash," continued on to confess, "Here is zeal—even though misguided zeal—for the cause of a materialistic, atheistic state. Its action shames us, the complacent, compromising West." The author's recognition that "pulp novels and horror books and obscenities in print must go from their land" then led to the suggestion that NODL might model itself upon—incredibly—the very communists they feared: "Should not this example provoke a similar literary clean-up in our own land where the morality of our actions is gauged by service to God and not to an atheistic state?"[30]

As if heeding NODL's call, enter Charles H. Keating Jr. of Cincinnati, Ohio. Keating became concerned about indecent literature in 1956 when he came upon a group of youths at a newsstand, snickering over "girlie" magazines placed on an isolated display shelf.[31] By 1958, he had founded a fast-growing organization called Citizens for Decent Literature (CDL).[32] By 1962 CDL had nationalized, keeping the headquarters in Cincinnati (housed in Keating's law office) and publishing a biweekly bulletin, *The National Decency Reporter.*[33] Two years later, Keating captured the attention of *Reader's Digest,* which portrayed him as the paradigmatic gladiator of American decency. "Fearing a phony cry of censorship, we have been jeered into a national sheepishness about taking action against this evil," Keating scolded his national audience, "Lick that timidity and you've gone a long way toward licking the problem."[34]

"Keating should know," *Reader's Digest* declared in response, reminding their audience that as "a former All-America swimming champion and U. S. Navy fighter pilot, the six-foot-four young lawyer" had the necessary stature to lead his army of citizens and had "effectively proved that the tide *can* be swept back by concerted community action." Continuing with a description of Keating's heroic battle with indecent literature in cases across the United States and the strengthening of the CDL, *Reader's Digest* highlighted its youth organization, "a growingly potent arm of CDL" with a membership "carefully chosen from school leaders and top athletes" and divided into more than two hundred chapters. CDL youth were "given training in the art of letter-writing to law-enforcement officials" and encouraged to "attend court trials in force, serve as volunteers in getting out CDL mailings, [and] publish their own nationally distributed newsletter," all of which was "great training for citizen action in later life," according to Keating.[35]

Some fifteen years later, the challenge of "citizen action" against indecency was again championed, but this time by a religiously inspired leader. "The church should be a disciplined, charging army. Christians, like slaves and soldiers, ask no questions," Jerry Falwell lectured to his "Moral Majority." "For our nation this is a life and death struggle and the battle line for this struggle is the textbooks." Warning that "our children are being trained to deny their 200-year heritage," and that "most public school texts are nothing more than Soviet propaganda," Falwell urged his followers to "rise up in arms to throw out every textbook that does this to America's schoolchildren."[36]

Falwell's overt organization and amorphous membership reflects a significant consonance between the theologically inspired NODL with its later inclusion of "civic, fraternal and Protestant" groups and the CDL—a wholly secular organization based in civil conservatism. While the Moral Majority has claimed its "majority" on the basis of Gallup polls of those Americans who identify themselves as "born-again" Christians,[37] its civil influence and actions have been concerned with secular morality. The statistical equation of spiritual experience with membership in a political body is not only illusory but has been a source of insult to millions of Christians, whether "mainline" or born-again, who do not necessarily share Falwell's beliefs nor identify with his organized efforts.

Indeed, the notion that Christian philosophy must be equated with procensorship activities was often questioned in the course of the censorship debates, most effectively by religious leaders who opposed censorship. A case in point is the 1981 debate in Buncombe County, North Carolina, over the use of *The Catcher in the Rye, Andersonville,* and *The Grapes of Wrath* in the high school classroom. The request for removal of the books was made by Randy Stone, the pastor of the local Calvary Free Will Baptist Church. "The use of God's name in vain," Stone explained, "whether it be in a Pulitzer-prize winner or a book from an adult bookstore, is offensive to us and demands some sort of attention."[38] Stone's plea was countered by the argument of Fred Ohler, pastor of Warren Wilson United Presbyterian Church. Asking "why is immorality seen only as profanity and sexuality in Steinbeck, Salinger or Kantor, and the larger issues of grinding poverty and social misjustice, of adult hypocrisy, of war camp atrocities never faced," Ohler posed a cautionary parallel to the selective reading practices of the complainants; "To read the Bible as some folks read *The Grapes of Wrath* would be like going through the Gospels and only seeing tax collectors, winebibers and Mary Magdalene."[39]

The Stone-Ohler interchange occurred in February 1981. In April 1981, Reverend H. Lamarr Mooneyham, leader of the North Carolina chapter of the Moral Majority, responded with a twenty-eight page review of textbooks, curricula, and library materials allegedly used in North Carolina.[40] "In the past, coverage has been focused on objections to such books as *Brave New World* and *Catcher in the Rye*. The placement of these books on selective reading lists is not the problem, the problem is much deeper than this," Mooneyham worried in his editorial cover letter to the report. "Even those who found the above books acceptable may still question the textbooks and associated teachers' guides that are now in use in our schools." Hedging the theological debate, Mooneyham's reasons for censorship revealed less moralistic and more political concerns. "One recurring theme found running through all history and social studies texts is that they advocate an ever-increasing reliance on government to solve all of our problems. In so doing," he lamented, "they glorify the socialist societies and consistently find fault with our free society."[41]

Mooneyham's secular concerns were rooted in his fear of the increasingly godless direction in which he saw American society moving. In his extended statement he explained his opposition to "values clarification" as a "major thrust of the educational process" in which "the child is taught that there is no right—there is no wrong, that ethics is autonomous and situational." But it was more than the absence of a definitive standard of right and wrong that was disturbing to Mooneyham, leading him to close his argument with Arizona Representative John Conlan's classic statement against "secular humanism" as he agonized over the "significant trend in education today to teach children that there are no values—that there is no God—that man is his own God."[42]

A belief in the decline of "traditional values" has been increasingly significant to the religious right—a belief evident in the activities and arguments of the NODL since 1954, carried into the 1960s by the CDL and reaching full development with the emergence of the Moral Majority in the late 1970s. Whether a majority or particularly moral, it is clearly a community of common ideological concern and activity that is perhaps more aptly termed the "New Right." And in 1981 Richard Viguerie published its manifesto, *The New Right: We're Ready to Lead,* with the blessing of its spiritual shaman. "Mr. Viguerie has not detailed a new group; he has described the backbone of our country," Jerry Falwell proudly announced, "those citizens who are pro-family, pro-life and pro-American, who have integrity and believe in hard work, those who pledge allegiance to the flag and proudly sing our national anthem."[43]

Reminding the reader that "America was built on faith in God, on integrity, and on hard work," in his introduction to Viguerie's tactical text Falwell echoed Viguerie's call to conservative arms among "that group of citizens who love their country and are willing to sacrifice for her," emphasizing the necessity of "right" leadership in a time of great need: "At this present hour, there can be no questioning the retrogression of America's stability as a free and healthy nation. In the last several years, Americans have literally stood by and watched as godless, spineless leaders have brought our nation foundering to the brink of death. . . . The vacuum of leadership in America must be filled. Conservative Americans must now take back the helm and guide America back to a position of stability and greatness."[44]

Falwell was certainly correct in pointing out that the New Right is not a new ideological group. The rhetoric alone owes much to the tradition of the "American jeremiad," a ritual incantation that originated among the Puritan preachers of seventeenth-century New England. Decrying their secular iniquities and failings as a "chosen people," Puritan leaders then quoted biblical verse in a call for ever greater faith and more fervent commitment to God's errand: the creation and sustenance of true spiritual community.[45] Something more than "a mode of public exhortation," the American jeremiad was a cultural ritual "designed to join social criticism to spiritual renewal, public to private identity, the shifting 'signs of the times' to certain traditional metaphors, themes, and symbols."[46]

Traceable in public rhetoric from the seventeenth through the twentieth centuries, the ritualism of the American jeremiad is readily recognizable in the expression of the New Right: a spiritual sense of national destiny accompanied by an intense commitment to individualism and democracy, expressed in their hostility toward bureaucratic government, big business, and communism. The joining of public to private identity, evident in the rhetorical definitions provided by Viguerie and Falwell, effectively detracts attention from demographic consideration of who the "we" actually is. From the arguments of NODL to CDL to the Moral Majority, even the post–World War II perception of America's "retrogression" as a world power, this sense of internal instability and the corollary fears that the American youth is peculiarly susceptible to communism,

atheism, and immorality are not truly new. This tradition of detailing
of sins and transgressions to introduce protestations and affirmations of
faith belies the same "underlying desperation" and evasion of account-
ability that characterized Puritan New England: "a refusal to confront
the present, a fear of the future, an effort to translate 'America' into a
vision that works in spirit because it can never be tested in fact."[47]

What is "new," then, about the New Right is largely its location in
history. As documented in studies such as Riesman's *The Lonely Crowd*,
Whyte's *The Organization Man*, and Friedan's *The Feminine Mystique*,[48]
the lives of many Americans in the post–World War II period were
increasingly characterized by a sense of alienation and loss of individual
control and distinctiveness that lent new meaning to the merging of
public and private identity. The ideological refusal to confront the present and fear of the future take on a new cast when the present encompasses the use of atomic weaponry and the future threatens nuclear
world war. Similarly, ensuring that the vision is retained requires concrete actions in the historic present: censorship activities are necessary to
prevent the subversion of American youth and to "take back the helm"
of American education.

This meeting of ideology and ritual in the immediate social-historical
moment is the juncture of participation for many "concerned parents"
who embraced or followed the leadership of the New Right in the *Catcher*
debates. If the New Right participants emerged in the mid-1950s through
the censorship activities of NODL, by the 1980s the "New Right" had
come to include a much broader group of participants, linked primarily
by American jeremiad ideology. In the first two weeks of November
1980, censorship attempts reported to the American Library Association's Office for Intellectual Freedom increased fivefold, averaging three
to five attempts per day across the nation.[49] Even more striking was the
self-identification of the participants as reported by librarians: "The
complainants in many of the incidents identified themselves as 'members of the Moral Majority,' as 'Fundamentalist ministers,' or merely as
'moral Americans.' Many persons told the librarians to whom they
were complaining that their intent was to help the new President and the
new Congress move closer to a 'moral' America by removing materials
that were 'anti-family,' 'anti-American,' 'anti-Christian,' and 'morally
degenerating.'"[50]

The librarians, for their part, interpreted this increased activity as "a
warning that intellectual freedom, one of the foundations of librarianship in the U.S., may be the focal point of a strenuous, sustained attack."[51]

Indeed, when the New Right does attempt such inspired censorship, whether as individuals or as a group, they must immediately contend with the librarians, our next community of participants in the *Catcher in the Rye* debates.

Librarians at the Battlefront

Librarianship in the United States emerged as a professional community in 1876 with the founding of the American Library Association (ALA). At the time, Melvil Dewey lauded the place of libraries and role of librarians in American life: "Time was when a library was very like a museum, and a librarian was a peruser among musty books, and visitors looked with furious eyes at ancient tombs and manuscripts. The time is when a library is a school, and the librarian is in the highest sense a teacher, and the visitor is a reader among the books as a workman among his tools. Will any man deny to the high calling of such librarianship the title of profession?"[52]

Having been "called" to such a profession, librarians soon saw themselves as moral guardians protecting a naive reading public through proper book selection. "Books that distinctly commend what is wrong, that teach how to sin, and how pleasant sin is, sometimes without the added sauce of impropriety are increasingly popular," ALA president Arthur Bostwick observed in 1908, "tempting the audience to imitate them, the publishers to produce, the booksellers to exploit"—but, he wryly added, "Thank heavens they do not tempt the librarian."[53]

Bostwick's comment discloses, if not recommends, censorship by librarians in the selection of books to be purchased. However, by 1916 ALA president Mary Wright Plummer railed against librarian censorship in selection as much as public censorship. In the event of any censoring of books, "it is the library that loses, for some people begin to mistrust an institution that is afraid of a book, for a book cannot really and permanently damage truth," and she reminded her audience of librarians that "those who wish all argument for or against to have a fair field, need be everlastingly vigilant to keep the umpire's mind and to have courage."[54]

"Moral guardians," "called" to everlasting and courageous vigilance? Here the rhetoric and ritual of the American jeremiad is invoked again, this time in the service not of God or Christianity but of intellectual freedom, the guarantee of access to the "redemptive power of books." Consider the argument of Frances Clarke Sayers's 1964 keynote address to the California Library Association. Titled "If the Trumpet Be Not Sounded,"

Sayers's address opened with her call to librarians, asking, "Is there a chance that in addition to the librarian as teacher, censor, and umpire, the contemporary stance may be the librarian as inciter, arouser, as trumpeter and champion?" Warning that "if bigotry and hatred are to be pushed back, the arena of public debate and discussion must be open before the festering process of witch-hunting consumes the community," Sayers then asked rhetorically, "To carry the attack to the enemy, does this not seem necessary to the intellectual climate of the nation, even though your own community be calm and peaceful?"

Warming to her subject, however "trite and condescending for me to repeat what the character of our time seems to be," Sayers recounted the failings of post–World War II American society: "It is a time of such change. . . . You know the catchwords of the century: the Age of Anxiety, the Air-Conditioned Nightmare; the Failure of Communication, the Era of Nihilism." In a remarkable parallel to the concerns of the New Right, she continued, "We are no longer a Protestant, middle-class society, with fixed concepts of morality, religious beliefs, a world of fixed boundaries. Everywhere and everything is questioned, uncertain, and in ferment."[55]

However similar Sayers's perception of late-twentieth-century malaise was to that of the New Right, her solutions lay steadfastly in the secular realm of librarianship. "No other profession is as well equipped for the confrontation with the future as is our profession," she proclaimed, pointing out that as "an institution that functions above and beyond the profit motive, and pressure of competition," the profession of librarianship "attracts idealists to its ranks, people who believe in the perfectibility of man, and who find in service to others a gratification of the spirit." As professionals who "relish the stirring up of communities by the circulation of ideas, notions, facts, fancies, pleasures—all the hubbub and exhilaration of reading," Sayers proposed that librarians "hold to the redemptive power of books" and called them to take leadership because "we have books behind us, and we know them well enough to have acquired an historical perspective on the vagaries of men's minds."[56]

Sayers's challenge to librarians to confront censorship and lead their communities in protection of the freedom to read was consistent with changes occurring within the ALA in the 1960s. In the past, librarianship in the United States was a profession to which "values of neutrality and autonomy entail[ed] a tacit agreement not to be too critical of society."[57] The original Library Bill of Rights, written in 1939 and published for ALA adoption in 1948, was a short three-point document supporting unbiased book selection, balanced collection, and the open use of meeting rooms within the library for public discussions. In 1960 the Intellectual Freedom Committee (IFC) was formed as a standing committee within the ALA and quickly recommended revisions and amendments to the Library Bill of Rights. The amendments, adopted in 1961, expanded the document to six points designed to openly oppose censorship and promote intellectual freedom. These amendments were followed by a further revision in 1967, also sponsored by the IFC, which added the category of age to the existing guarantee of the rights of all individuals regardless of race, religion, national origins, or social or political views—an addition that reflected growing concerns about the censorship of youth materials.[58] The final change within the ALA in the direction of anticensorship activism was the formation of the Freedom to Read Foundation in 1969: founded as a separate corporation but housed in the ALA's Chicago headquarters and with ALA directorship evident in the makeup of its offices, board of directors, and trustees.

The manner in which censorship attempts were reported within the profession also changed in the mid-1960s. Beginning in the early 1950s, the ALA reported censorship activity to its membership primarily through occasional brief notices in the ALA *Bulletin* and the bimonthly *Newsletter on Intellectual Freedom*. Concurrently, the American Book Publishers Council (ABPC) published its own set of *Bulletins:* the sporadic ABPC *Bulletin,* the superseding *Censorship Bulletin* (1955–62), and the final *Freedom to Read Bulletin* (1962–65). The ABPC *Bulletins* were of interest to librarians and the ABPC encouraged their support in spreading the awareness of censorship. Significantly, up through the mid-1960s, neither the bulletins of the ABPC nor the ALA advocated a course of action or a line of response to censorship activity; just reporting the attempts was deemed sufficient.

In 1965 a marked change occurred as the ABPC's *Freedom to Read Bulletin* was subsumed by the ALA's *Newsletter on Intellectual Freedom*. In part, the move was precipitated by publishing difficulties experienced by the *Freedom to Read Bulletin,* but the change was also an explicit recognition of the common interests of the ABPC and the ALA in combating censorship. The *Newsletter on Intellectual Freedom* emerged as a fuller and stronger publication with a marked willingness to respond to censorship activity—although the response did not include the advocacy of specific actions and practices.

The nature of advice to librarians on the fight against censorship initially followed the assumption that familiarity and awareness of censorship tactics were their greatest resources. But in 1964 librarians were made aware of their "newly accepted role as defenders of readers against the censor himself" by books such as Everett Moore's *Issues of Freedom in American Libraries*, published by the ALA. Pointing out that "the battle to preserve our intellectual freedom has become such an enduring aspect of our lives as librarians," Moore acknowledged that "we may be surprised to find that it is only in recent times that we have been engaged in it."[59]

To prepare librarians for censorship conflicts, Moore offered a collection of censorship case studies (1960–63) culled from the "Intellectual Freedom Department" of the American Library Association *Bulletin* and serving to outfit the naive librarian with the tools and techniques which had proven successful in combating censorship. This case study approach to the battle against censorship was also propagated by the *Newsletter on Intellectual Freedom*. Occasionally editorials in the *Newsletter* advocated active resistance and defense against censorship but, as was commonplace in advice to librarians throughout the latter 1960s, the strategies and specifics were left to the reader to determine — in the *Newsletter*'s case, from the expanded reportage of censorship cases across the country.

In 1969, the ALA established the Freedom to Read Foundation as a nonprofit membership organization intended to "promote and defend First Amendment rights" and to do so by "foster(ing) libraries as institutions fulfilling the promise of the First Amendment for every citizen." However, it was not until the mid-1970s that explicit strategies for defense against censorship appeared.[60] In 1974 Arthur Anderson's *Problems in Intellectual Freedom and Censorship* took the existing case study approach a step farther by offering critiques of each incident, asking what was not done and what could have been done to either avoid or defeat censorship.[61] The year 1974 also saw the publication of the ALA's *Intellectual Freedom Manual*, a tactical text that applied the principles of intellectual freedom to library service. The manual included reproduction of various ALA legal and constitutional documents, including the Library Bill of Rights and a recommended form for librarians to give to potential censors.[62]

Titled the "Request for Reconsideration of Library Materials," the form required the name and address of the complainant as well as identification of any organizational affiliation pertinent to the complaint. The intent was to require individual responsibility for censorship action, ferret out New Right allegiances, and frame censorship complaints as nonconfrontational "requests" for the librarian's implicitly reasonable "reconsideration." The potential censor then was required to provide written responses to eight dispositional questions:

1. To what in the work do you object? (Please be specific. Cite pages.)
2. Did you read the entire work? What parts?
3. What do you feel might be the result of reading this work?
4. For what age group would you recommend this work?
5. What do you believe is the theme of this work?
6. Are you aware of judgments of this work by literary critics?
7. What would you like your library/school to do about this work?
   ____ Do not assign/lend it to my child.
   ____ Return it to the staff selection committee/department for re-evaluation.
   ____ Other. Explain:
8. In its place, what work would you recommend that would convey as valuable a picture and perspective of the subject treated?[63]

The ALA recommended that *full* completion of the "Request" form be required before any request for removal or restriction of a book be considered and therein lay the tactical support for the librarian. The eight questions reflected ALA study and consequent findings that lack of familiarity with the texts, literary criticism, and alternative materials were the weak points of most censors. Moreover, the tone of compliance through compromise and the implication that every library book holds value for some potential borrower were intended to defuse the censor's assumed stance of indignation and rigid rejection. This form, as will soon be shown in the *Catcher in the Rye* controversies, was widely embraced by librarians and proved to be an effective defense mechanism against censorship.

The ALA *Intellectual Freedom Manual* did not stop at the presentation of forms and documents. For the first time, the ALA presented a descriptive analysis of the sources and reasons for contemporary censorship activity as well as a composite profile of the censor. In general, librarians were instructed that "almost every such instance of censorship is motivated by fear" and is "an emotional response to a basically intellectual problem" (pt. 3: 6). Furthermore, the censor was described as someone who is afraid of books and materials that might "corrupt morals, cause actions jeopardizing an established order, or challenge a religious belief, a philosophical viewpoint, or a deep-seated prejudice" (pt. 3: 6).

The ALA's analysis of censorship sources was divided into two categories: external and internal "forces." External forces were defined in the

Manual as parents; religious, political, ethnic, and "patriotic" groups; and "emotionally unstable individuals" who "may focus on any of the above causes as outlets for their frustrations" (pt. 3: 8). Internal sources were defined as "forces" that generated pressure either directly or indirectly from within the institutional structure of the library. Trustees or governing bodies, library staff, management, neglect in selection, restrictive selection policies, circulation methods, and catalogs were singled out for attention in this category. The ALA advised that internal sources of censorship were a "delicate matter" (pt. 3: 9), best handled through regular programs of education as well as review and evaluation of staff, procedures, and materials within the institution to ensure the preservation of intellectual freedom. If internal sources of censorship were more insidious, external sources were more readily recognizable and could be addressed more concretely. Hence, all of part 4 of the six-part *Manual* is devoted to "The Censor: His Motives and Tactics" (pt. 4: 21).

Editorial discussion of "The Censor" began with a caution to the reader against stereotyping the censor as an "irrational, belligerent individual" and the recognition that most complaints were based in a sincere concern for the well-being of the community. Censors were described as most notably alike in their belief that "they can recognize 'evil' and that other people must be protected from it" (pt. 4: 21–22). The editors then delineated four "basic motivational factors" that, singularly or in concert, served as the impetus for censorship action: family values, political views, religion, and minority rights (pt. 4: 21).

The phrase "family values" referred to "changes in attitudes toward the family and related customs" that threaten the individual complainant. According to the *Manual*, censorship occurred when the complainant misunderstood the library materials to be directing the course of social change rather than reflecting it—in which case, banning the book was equated with removing the threat of change. The factor of "political views" was similarly defined, with the additional comment that books containing "less than polite language" would be easier targets for censors who wished "to formulate an attack on the grounds of obscenity in addition to—and sometimes to cover up—objections on political grounds" (pt. 4: 22).

Under the heading of religion, the ALA editors explained that sexually explicit or "politically unorthodox" works as well as antireligious writings were likely to generate complaints from censors using theologically inspired arguments. Again the editorial description of the censor contended that the complainant was actually less concerned about a direct threat to his religious beliefs than he was disturbed by the apparent affirmation of his own fears, noting that protested materials were considered damaging to religious beliefs when they stimulated "concern about a society he sees becoming more and more hostile to religious training, and buttress his belief about society's steady disintegration" (pt. 4: 22).

The final "motivational factor" defined in the *Manual* was "minority rights," which included censors who were not interested in the preservation of traditional values but in the representation of "special group values." The examples given by the ALA were ethnic minorities and women, who "[in] struggling against long-established stereotypes are anxious to reject anything that represents a counter-value" (pt. 4: 22).

What is significant about these four "motivational factors" is that they can be applied readily to the librarians themselves: societal changes in family and political values, challenge to religious beliefs and perceptions of "society's steady disintegration," as well as the struggle against stereotyping of various sorts, were each as much a part of the librarian's world as the censor's. The difference lay in the nature of response to the perceived threat, and on this point the ALA editors of the *Intellectual Freedom Manual* were quite clear as they contrasted their understanding of the censor's view of the library with their own implicit view: "Whatever the censor's motives, his attempt to suppress certain library materials may also stem from a confused understanding of the role of the library and of the rights of other library users. The censor's concern about library materials shows that he views the library as an important social institution. But he fails to see that the library fulfills its obligations to the community it serves by providing materials presenting all points of view, and that it is not the function of the library to screen materials according to arbitrary standards of acceptability" (pt. 4: 22).

If the censor responded to the perceived threats to his beliefs or changes in the social context with attempts to ban, suppress or excise the offending material, the librarian relied on the exchange of ideas and the "redemptive power" of books to insure stability. The introduction to the *Intellectual Freedom Manual* attested that "opposition to these [censorship] activities emanate(s) from the belief that freedom of the mind is basic to the functioning and maintenance of democracy," and the librarian as guardian of materials and free selection was also a guardian of democratic society, in which "educated, free individuals possess powers of discrimination and are to be trusted to best determine their own actions" (xii).

Hence the ALA *Manual* not only served to prepare the librarian for censorship but also offered justification for professional opposition to censorship activities. This implicitly redefined the role of the librarian from one of passive guardianship to a more activist status—a position that became ever more strident in the 1980s as censorship activity in the schools became more organized. J. Charles Park, a University of Wisconsin professor of education noted for his scholarship on the New Right, surmised that "librarians are never more important than when a society is undergoing change, frustration, and confusion," as it is "during such times that voices of fear and absolutism can be expected to increase."[64]

Recognizing that librarians themselves were subject to the same insecurities of rapid social change as their patrons, Park asked his audience in the *Newsletter on Intellectual Freedom* to "learn to examine how our fear can be used," and then challenged them to "learn to protect the basic freedoms in our society, to maintain our integrity and our compassion, and to adhere to the rules of evidence." Titled "The Censorship War: Librarians at the Battlefront," Park's essay resembled Frances Sayers's earlier "call to arms" as he reminded librarians that "the first line of defense for the protection of democracy lies in the rights of inquiry and access to information." And if librarianship was inherently a profession of civic responsibility, the role of librarians in "times of confusion" and societal upheaval was crucial. "You are more important than you may recognize," Park prodded. "You need to know it and our society needs to know it."[65]

Park was not alone in his use of the military analogy: author John Robotham dedicated his 1982 text, *Freedom of Access to Library Materials,* to "all the librarians on the front lines."[66] In fact, the perception that the profession of librarianship had become an embattled one was not inaccurate. In a 1982 study sponsored by the National Council of Teachers of English, Lee Burress surveyed high school librarians across the nation and found that 50 percent of all respondents had experienced censorship attempts—in escalating contrast to 20 percent of those surveyed in 1966, 28 percent in 1973, and 30 percent in 1977.[67]

As an organization, the ALA responded with the declaration of "Banned Books Week" in September of 1982, to be co-sponsored by the American Booksellers Association, the National Association of College Stores, the Association of American Publishers, and the American Society of Journalists and Authors, and endorsed by the Center for the Book of the Library of Congress. To "celebrate and publicize the importance of the freedom to read," books censored in years past were pulled from the shelves of participating libraries and displayed to gain public attention. The success of the 1982 program in attracting national as well as local media attention to the argument that "books and ideas aren't dangerous, but information restraints on a free people are" led to the continuation of the program in succeeding years. By the late eighties, "Banned Books Week" had become a part of the rituals associated with the opening of the school year, fostered by ALA direct mailings to librarians of suggested news releases, display ideas, possible activities, and an annually updated list of challenged books.[68]

The increasing incidence of censorship aimed at secondary school libraries spurred *The Book Report,* a bimonthly journal for junior and senior high school librarians, to devote its November/December 1982 issue to "The Challenge of Censorship."[69] Of the nine articles in the issue, six offered tactics and procedures for librarians confronting censorship. Two of these articles, "We Took Censorship to the Classroom" and "Parent Power," followed the earlier case study approach but additionally encouraged the direct involvement of students and parents, respectively, in avoiding as well as responding to censorship action.[70]

The remaining four tactical articles largely reviewed and discussed strategies outlined in the ALA's *Intellectual Freedom Manual.* Use of the "Request for Reconsideration" form was explained and its successful use cited. In the case of a confrontation, readers were reminded of the six steps advised in the *Manual.* Step one was to remain calm and treat the complaining group or individual with "dignity, courtesy, and good humor," while (step two) making the complaint known to the administration and governing authority. Step three was to "seek the support of the local press, when appropriate," and step four advocated enlisting the support of civic organizations. Defense of "the principle of the freedom to read and the professional responsibility of teachers and librarians" was step five, which further distinguished between defending an individual book ("rarely necessary") and the advocated defense of the principle of intellectual freedom. The final step was to inform the ALA Office for Intellectual Freedom: for support in the form of parallel case citations and advice, and for the ALA's tracking of censorship occurrence.[71]

The three remaining censorship articles in this issue of *The Book Report* dealt with internal sources of censorship—an increasing area of concern for librarians in the 1980s. As early as 1962, the National Council of Teachers of English had noted in their text *The Student's Right to Read* that the major American authors were often "represented not by their best work but by their safest" in school libraries.[72] A concurrent (1963) ALA survey found libraries in the southern United States to be lacking in balanced collections. These findings caused the editors of the fall 1963 issue of the *Freedom to Read Bulletin* to speculate on the relationship between the lower frequency of censorship in the South and their imbalanced collections, remarking that internal censorship appeared to be "the answer to the censor's dream; if you can't get the books, they can't hurt you."[73]

Some twenty years later, southern librarians addressed the problem in an issue of the *Newsletter on Intellectual Freedom* devoted to "Censorship in the South." "My main observation is that teachers, librarians, media personnel and supervisors practice self-censorship," a Louisiana librarian explained. "'Let's do it for them before they do it to us' seems to be the prevailing attitude." From this librarian's vantage point, the implementation of "self-censorship" was a circumstantially necessary practice (if not an admirable one) because "most of the time, the people doing the censoring do it out of fear [and] misinformation and they usually are very professional otherwise." Other librarians explained internal censorship more pragmatically, as did a Georgia librarian who felt "no qualms about avoiding books that are potential trouble" when faced with economic limitations: given "monetary and space constraints, some decisions have to be made regarding retention and purchase."[74]

The singling out of southern librarians by the ABPC and the ALA in their respective publications was perhaps unfair, reflecting their wish to view self-censoring as a regional problem rather than accept it as a professional one. Studies of censorship as well as the reporting of censorship in the *Freedom to Read Bulletin* and the *Newsletter on Intellectual Freedom* showed censorship activity to be almost equally distributed across the United States. However, an independent study of American censorship from 1966 to 1975 suggested that the reporting of censorship attempts by librarians in the *Newsletter* might be inaccurate, since "librarians do not necessarily report self-censoring to a profession that does not condone censorship."[75] While 53.2 percent of the censorship attempts included in the 1966–75 survey originated outside educational institutions, internal censorship attempts were nearly equal at 46.8 percent. Based on *reported* attempts, these figures led the study's author, L. B. Woods, to speculate that "if self-imposed censorship is not brought to public attention as often as censorship from outside sources, it may be that a significantly higher censorship rate within educational institutions is in fact a reality."[76]

Nor did Woods find southern librarians more at fault than librarians elsewhere. In a later article published in the *Library Journal,* Woods quoted two of the "more militant responses" to her questionnaire/survey—from Iowa and New York. The Iowa librarian flatly stated, "I'll select books on their usefulness to this community, not on the basis of your checklist." The New York librarian explained self-censoring as a consequence of professional "realism," maintaining that "intellectual freedom is a great idea," however "realism requires a librarian to apply her community's standards. For instance, I can just imagine the flak if we had *The Joy of Sex* here."[77]

Meanwhile, concurrent articles on internal censorship in *The Book Report* did not contain any disclaimers of regional bias, squarely placing the blame instead on individual biases that superseded professional ethics and on job insecurity. The location of bias in the individual librarian was explored in Marilyn Knop's "I'm Totally Opposed to Censorship, But ...." A largely autobiographical essay, Knop's reflections demonstrate how relevant reader response is to the question of censorship. "You and I may have the same text on censorship, and hear the same advice on book selection and nonselection, which is just as crucial to the question of censorship," Knop admitted, "yet, my attitudes are colored by factors in my childhood, some half-remembered or not consciously remembered at all," and then emphasized that "as a product of my particular background" these childhood factors were "still exerting their influences on my adult judgments. I can't accurately weigh them, but I must acknowledge them."[78]

If the individual perceptions of each librarian shape their selection of materials, their participation and review of materials in an actual censorship controversy are equally likely to reflect personal bias as well. In "Selection vs. Censorship: A Way to Cope,"[79] a companion article to Knop's in *The Book Report's* censorship issue, librarian Sara Aufdemberge advocated the development of strong selection policies as a means of avoidance of censorship confrontation as well as for controlling for individual bias in selection—yet Knop's preceding acknowledgment of the depth and impact of personal value systems challenges the effectiveness of such policies in restraining internal censorship.

A final article in the censorship issue of *The Book Report,* "The Enemy Within," addressed the political dimension of internal censorship. According to librarian Gary Joseph, school librarians fear that they will lack the support of or receive condemnation from school boards and administrators, and these fears contribute to their self-censoring activities. "The question foremost in my mind is why have librarians acted to censor books in either an overt or covert manner," Joseph asked. "Can it be that we really do not honor those high ideals of academic and intellectual freedom?" He answered, "I think not," but then candidly observed, "The cause lies in our desire for job security. Why else does a librarian forsake the ideals of intellectual freedom because of the complaint of one parent or the request of one principal?"[80]

The remainder of Joseph's article was spent reviewing the librarian's lack of political power and issuing a general call to activism. If Joseph's conclusions stopped short of defining the course of action and methods necessary to gaining autonomy for librarians, his sense of insecurity among librarians was accurate. According to a 1964 survey of school librarians in Nassau County, New York, half of the fifty-four head librarians interviewed believed they would not be supported by the school administration in the event of a censorship controversy.[81] Similarly, the explanation attributed to self-censoring librarians by John Robotham in his *Freedom of Access to Library Materials* was that "librarians, in fear of losing their jobs ... and being timid and wishing to avoid controversy, betray their professional responsibility to provide materials." Believing that many librarians "avoid acquiring certain materials, or remove those to which they feel certain members of their community might object," Robotham highlighted the exacerbated position of school librarians in particular, as "their patrons are all young and still, ostensibly, under the control of their parents." While Robotham agreed that parents should correspondingly have some input into book selection, the logical channel for parental input in Robotham's view was through the school board: "They are, after all, charged with running the school."[82]

If the school board and school administrators then appeared to be the source of jeopardy to the librarian's job security, Robotham contended that the problem lay not in the structural relationship between librarian and school administration but in the definition of educational purpose. He asserted that a lack of clarity about the meaning and intentions of education created a ready environment for censorship, arguing: "The difficulty arises because the word education is widely misunderstood; many persons confuse the storing of facts with education, or they confuse education with the indoctrination of orthodox ideas, and they don't condone a variety of ideas. And that's where the censor puts in an appearance."[83]

When the censor "puts in an appearance," it may be to complain to a librarian or teacher, who then turns it over to the school board or administration, or the complaint may be made directly to the school board or administration itself. In any case, censorship attempts quickly escalate into community controversies once the school officials are involved. These educators—loosely defined to encompass teachers, administrators, and lay members of school boards and advisory committees—form the remaining community of participation in *The Catcher in the Rye* debates to which I now turn.

Teach Your Children Well

In conceptualizing this final community of participants under the rubric of "the educators," I drew on the participants' own often-stated sense of purpose. Where librarians saw their participation primarily in terms of their professional position, and the New Right in terms of their moral ideology, public school teachers, administrators, and parent and citizen members of boards and committees claimed their primary allegiance was to education—and even more specifically, education "to the good of the child." Broadly speaking, each of these participants saw themselves in a custodial relationship to the child and viewed education as a primary expression of that responsibility, both of which are conditions of what has come to be known as "modern childhood."

Philippe Ariès, in his seminal work *Centuries of Childhood*,[84] has argued that cultural recognition of modern childhood in Europe began with the historic emergence of the middle class in the early seventeenth century. While there is scholarly debate over the applicability of his thesis to American childhood, his conceptualization of the general conditions that served to define modern childhood are widely accepted, and it is clear that by the nineteenth century those conditions had long been met in America. Social and economic changes tied to the development of a middle-class culture increased the separation of the family from the public world and decreased its dependence upon the labor of children. The conceptualization of childhood reflected these changes as the world of the economically dependent child was restricted to the protective realm of the home and school for ever-lengthening periods of time; fourteen, eighteen, twenty-one years.

Such "quarantining" of the child, as Ariès termed it, was an expression of belief in the innocence of the child as much as a recognition of developmental incompleteness. Importantly, it was through formal education and parental guidance that the individual supposedly became knowledgeable and strong enough to participate in the public world.

Thus the recognition of childhood required the equivalent recognition of adult responsibility for the education of the child and the deeper assumption that adults have valued knowledge to impart.

The nineteenth century was also "a turning point for children" in America and abroad, according to historian Stephen Kline, "because publishers risked staking out the ground for children's culture."[85] If the invention of the printing press was, as historian Neil Postman has argued, in itself of signal importance to the emergence of modern childhood, nineteenth century changes in the *contents* of books *intended* for children were its quite literal expression. What few books there were for children before the nineteenth century were thinly fictionalized (if at all) lessons in religiosity and morality, many of which "wove into their stories a finger-wagging parental voice that concluded in no uncertain terms by restating the moral lesson of the story."[86]

The middle of the nineteenth century was the "dividing line" between "soul-saving didacticism and the modern children's book" as more adventurous and imaginative fiction emerged. Eric Quayle, historian of children's literature, found that after 1855 "children's books contained characters who resembled real children in their attitudes to the family and the world." "They were no longer paragons of virtue with saintlike attributes," Quayle discovered, yet "neither were they black-hearted little sinners plunging rapidly to hell."[87] With an increasing trend in the publishing of stories "from the child's point of view, focusing on a child protagonist and addressing problems in the child's experience of daily life," the number of children's books published each year grew steadily.[88]

Even so, the conditions and assumptions of modern childhood as to the import and nature of adult guidance of children continued to form the context for both the selection and censorship of school reading materials "for the good of the child." In a survey of children's literature and censorship, Anne Scott MacLeod found little dissension among educators, writers, publishers, and parents regarding the boundaries of children's literature for school use between 1900 and 1965. In the "implicit code of values" endorsed by this community, "the extreme idealization of the latter nineteenth century had largely disappeared" and the fictional children of the twentieth-century stories "had faults, made mistakes, and strayed (mildly) from the paths of righteousness." Yet however wayward the child, these fictional characters "lived universally within a firm and supportive social and familial system." The message of children's literature in the first half of the twentieth century was, as MacLeod put it, "that American society operated according to a single moral code;

that adults were reliable sources of wisdom, justice, and caring," and finally, "that childhood and children were sheltered under the protection of responsible adults in a responsible society."[89]

If this implicit code was an expression of consensus in the community of educators, there was little external challenge to raise it to a conscious, more explicit level up through the 1940s. MacLeod argued that the field of children's literature was treated with indifference by most adults, existing as "something of an island in the larger culture" until it was pulled into the mainstream by the social upheaval generated in the multifocused counterculture movement of the mid-1960s. Consequently, by the 1970s, children's literature "had become a battleground for the personal, social, and political forces of a changing society."[90]

In response, educators, writers, and publishers shifted to an emphasis on increasing realism in the portrayal of family, society, and human failings as much as idealistic pursuits. The Council on Interracial Books for Children was founded in 1966 to evaluate and guarantee egalitarian as well as accurate portrayal of women, racial, and other minority groups. The result was an improved reflection of the pluralism of contemporary American society, and increased inclusion of divorce, single-parenting, and teenage sexuality, including homosexuality, in children's books. A subgenre referred to as the "problem novel" presented alcoholism, drug abuse, suicide, and teenage prostitution, among other issues, as topics for consideration by adolescent readers.[91]

While this shift toward greater liberalism in the *portrayal* of American life in children's books occurred in the mid-1960s, children's literature was perceived as a "battleground" for a changing society between the New Right and the librarians much earlier. Moreover, teachers in the late 1950s and early 1960s were expanding the range of novels considered for assignment in high school literature courses—to the consternation of more than a few parents and school boards. Results from a national survey of secondary school teachers of English for the years 1962–64 found censorship to be an increasing concern and experience nationwide. *The Catcher in the Rye* was the most frequently challenged novel, teachers reported, and parents were the complainant in half of all censorship incidents.[92]

Teachers further reported that the novels most often challenged were those "modern classics" published since 1940 and newly included in the curriculum of American literature. Indeed, a paradigmatic shift or challenge to the boundaries of the traditional English curriculum was evident in this survey. As modern American literature was first included in

the curriculum of university literature courses, graduates of these English programs then went on to teaching positions in the high schools.
Prepared to teach the modern American novels and believing them to be
valuable and at least as important as the traditional classics, these new
teachers "extend[ed] their use of literary materials beyond the standard
'safe' textbook collection."[93] Since established teachers often resisted using
the new materials in favor of the traditional curriculum, school boards
faced with a book complaint questioned whether the value of the "new"
literature necessitated their inclusion in the secondary English curriculum or was worth the risk of controversy.

Such shifting and slippage in the American literary paradigm was
also evident in the complaints of parents as reported by the teachers.
Teachers found the parents to be "distressed primarily by the use of real-
istic modern fiction in English classes," and the teachers attributed this
distress to the probability that "these works were not included in the
curriculum when they—the parents—were students in high school."[94]
If the distress of parents was due to a nontraditional curriculum in conjunction with the realism of modern American fiction, it may explain
the preponderance of parents as complainants and the peculiar fact that
some parents were challenging novels that they had not actually read.

In two articles published in the *PTA Magazine* in the mid-1960s, educators addressed parent-readers on the topic of censorship in the schools
in a manner intended to reassure parents of the value of a liberalized
curriculum more than to actually inform them of the nature of censorship activity. "A good teacher has to assume that he may be allowed to use
the tools of his trade. For most teachers the tools are good books," one
educator wrote. "Good books have something important to say about
important issues. They are bound to be challenging and consequently
are bound to offend someone." "At this point the problem of censorship
arises," he reminded parents with the condescending simplicity of an
elementary school primer. "The effect of so many voices complaining
about so many things has resulted in too many schools being afraid to
teach any ideas."[95]

The educator then explained to his assumedly naive parent-reader
that English teachers made their curriculum decisions on the basis of
their knowledge of the student's world and interests and the recommendations of "reputable critics." In defending the use of "sensational" texts,
he argued that "one of the tests of a great book is that it does face life
honestly," whether the depiction is pleasant or not. Books should be
judged "not so much on the basis of the world they portray as by the

judgments they make on that world," he intoned. "*The Catcher in the Rye,* to take an example, is calling for a good world in which people can connect—a key word in twentieth-century writing." Censorship, by contrast, was a way to disconnect, and the author's intention to defuse potential censorship activity among parent-readers of the *PTA Magazine* was evident in his conclusion, subheaded "Two-Way Trust," in which he told parents that the elimination of censorship is dependent upon the connection of trust between teachers and parents: "If the nation wants good teachers, it must let them teach."[96]

In *PTA Magazine*'s 1965 "Symposium-in-Print," "Should We Censor What Adolescents Read?" another educator encouraged the audience of parents to rely on the experts in the field: teachers and librarians who were qualified to select books for adolescents. The need for such guidance varied, however, depending on the age of the book in question. "Time destroys bad books and preserves good books," he asserted, implying that the selection of "new books" was the major bone of contention and that the censorship activity of parents reflected confusion and concern over new materials which they did not feel able to evaluate.[97]

Accordingly, challenge to or at least revision of the American literary canon at the secondary school level was evident in the publication of curriculum guides such as G. Robert Carlsen's *Books and the Teen-Age Reader.* Published in 1967 and subtitled "A Guide for Teachers, Librarians, and Parents," Carlsen's text was more attuned to the interests of the teenager than to the aesthetic or literary merit of books for secondary school reading. His predominant concern was engagement of the teenage reader, with a combination of traditional and modern classics to be introduced at the appropriate developmental stages in the student's reading. This was a departure from pre–World War II instructional beliefs that exposure to the traditional classics was necessary and valuable, irrespective of the student's interest.

This reader-focused shift was apparent in Carlsen's first chapter, "The Reading Experience." Carlsen advised his reader that "you can only hope by example, by interesting discussions of books, by making materials available," that the student would then "gradually discover for himself that reading 'maketh the full man' and the full life."[98] Chapter 2, "The Teen-ager and His World," even more clearly placed the interest of the reader first in the selection of reading materials. Asking "How do books fit into a teen-ager's world," and "How do they serve young people's needs," Carlsen told his reader that "if books are to have any meaning, they must be related to the young person's personal and social needs."[99]

Suddenly, it seems, secondary school teachers should "woo" adolescents to literature rather than mandate they read it. Changes in the social context of the student necessitated this change in instructional approach, according to Carlsen, and he offered his summation of the teenager's world, circa 1967: "The teen-ager's world is a highly stimulating world—of folk rock, the Supremes, pep rallies, TV, clothing fads, exams, and the draft. Because of his buying power, the teen-ager has been wooed by clothing manufacturers, cosmetic salesmen, automobile dealers, and a barrage of peddlers of self-improvement. To this high-pressured environment the adolescent brings the complex problems of any maturing young person."[100]

In addition to this "high-pressured environment" and the "complex problems" of maturation, Carlsen added that the contemporary adolescent "feels a sense of isolation and alienation because human relationships in our society are increasingly impersonal."[101] In his concern for the selection of relevant reading materials that would not further alienate the adolescent reader, Carlsen's third chapter delineated "the stages of reading development" and appropriate fiction genres. While the latter chapters of Carlsen's guide explored these genres and recommended some titles (*The Catcher in the Rye* is suggested in two chapters: "The Shocker" and "Significant Modern Literature"), the focus remained primarily on the appeal to the teenager.

Strikingly, the educator's understanding of the context of post–World War II American culture corresponded closely to the perceptions of the New Right, the librarians, and those who embraced the more traditional literary paradigm. Everyone, it seems, was in agreement as to the alternatingly bleak and superstimulating, value-free/valueless, alienating nature of mid-twentieth-century American society. The debate came about over what to do in response or to gain control. As the New Right and the librarians turned respectively to the security of moral ideology and the redemptive powers of free reading, the community of educators was divided over guided reading: traditional classics in order of chronology, geography, or study of a particular author, or traditional and contemporary novels in a topical order to reflect the student's interest and developmental stage.

The conflict over selection and order of materials was not the extent of the problem but merely an overt expression of a deeper confusion. The educators as a community lacked the clear sense of purpose and procedure shared by the New Right and the librarians. Indeed, they increasingly asked themselves, "what are we trying to do?" Carlsen raised the question as both parent and teacher: "As parents living at the end of the twentieth century, we seem to have a desperate need to force early maturity on our children. We want them to walk early. We hope they will say their first word before the books indicate they should. We try to teach them to read at two and three. We encourage early dating and adult clothing styles although the children are physically still in childhood. Why are we so eager to have our youngsters grow up?"[102]

Carlsen's unanswered question recalls the concerns of teacher and critic Donald Barr discussed in the opening of this chapter. Nor were Carlsen (1967) and Barr (1986) the only educators who expressed concern and confusion over their professional purpose. "Some English teachers may be satisfied to live in their white-walled, high-windowed classrooms, complacent about or indifferent to their lack of contact with the real world or their very real students," one confessed. "But most English teachers rebel instinctively ... sure in their knowledge that ... students can only learn about reality from literature which faces reality."[103] Yet the English teachers who chose the "white walls and high windows" had their own rationale. "Why expose sweet and innocent students to the filth of modern literature?" one less rebellious teacher asked. "They'll discover how ugly the world is soon enough. Let's protect them as long as we can."[104]

In practice, such "protection" functioned as another form of internal censorship. Other educators, however, explained their reluctance to use contemporary literature on the grounds of their professional knowledge and concern about adolescent development. Framing the question of purpose and selection of high school literature in a broader philosophical context, educator Anne MacLeod asked rhetorically if "children have the same intellectual rights that adults have?" "Should children be encouraged to make comparisons among intellectual and moral concepts freely available to them," she wondered, and, if so, did the "dangers of restricting children's access to the full range of moral, social, and political attitudes outweigh the dangers of exposing the young to pernicious ideas?"[105]

The confusion among the educators, then, is not only the consequence of a paradigmatic shift in the training of literature teachers affecting their choice of materials but of a deeper division about the intent of education: whether the child best "learns about reality" through a restricted reading of literary classics that develop and protect traditional ideals and values, or through broader reading of traditional *and* contemporary literature that develops the same ideals but exposes the challenges of their pursuit as well. Some teachers expressed a good deal of suspicion about the intentions of teachers who encouraged or assigned the reading of modern classics. "'We' as individuals want our children to grow up cheerfully," admonished Donald Barr in the *New York Times Book Review*, pointing out that current classroom reading lists were "chosen by a social 'we' in which our hopes, our intuitions, and our good sense — all those intimate responsibilities of parenthood — are mysteriously replaced." Positioned as headmaster of a prestigious private school, Barr somewhat ironically placed the blame for this disregard of parental guidance on the "invidious quest in schools for precocity and prestige," and the inappropriately "invasive desire on the part of teachers to 'discuss' the most private concerns of students."[106]

It is likely that one academic champion of contemporary literature had educators like Barr in mind in his more skeptical opinion of the motivation behind such "protectionism." "Protecting students may bore them or give them a distorted picture of the world or may seem totally irrelevant to their lives," he observed, but "safe, antiseptic, dull, irrelevant teaching which offends no one often insures a teacher's job, indeed his almost certain promotion or tenure," whereas "the English teacher who tries to bring life into his English classes" by using contemporary novels "risks his job and tenure, for some school officials, parents and other teachers may not share his enthusiasm for reality in the schoolroom."[107]

In response, a 1974 issue of the *English Journal* introduced a set of anticensorship tactics intended to prepare teachers who felt their academic freedom might be at risk. Titled "Censorship in the 1970's: Some Ways to Handle It When It Comes (And It Will)," the article opened with a discussion of the American ambivalence toward secondary education, expressed in the "almost superstitious reverence that somehow education is good for everyone" even as these sentiments were "mixed with a fear of intellectualism and a dread of teachers." This "fear of education and the inquiring mind and the search for truth" was manifest in "the attacks on books that are the most likely to relate to kids' lives and their world, today and tomorrow."[108] These central concerns of these censorship attacks were then outlined in eight subject categories:

1. SEX ("filthy" or "risque" or "not decent reading material")....
2. POLITICS OR AN ATTACK ON THE AMERICAN DREAM ("un-American" or "communist inspired")....
3. WAR AND PEACE ("un-American" or "pacifist propaganda" or "one-worlders")....

4. RELIGION ("un-Christian" or "violating the separation of church and state")....

5. SOCIOLOGY AND RACE ("based on racial matters" or "promotes violence" or "Do kids have to see all that ugliness?")....

6. LANGUAGE ("profane" or "obscene" or "unfit for human ears")....

7. DRUGS ("Don't contaminate children with dirty things" or "Haven't we heard enough of depressing things like that?")....

8. INAPPROPRIATE ADOLESCENT BEHAVIOR ("Can't we give them better models than that?" or "Kids should know better than to act that way").[109]

This list paralleled the "motivating factors" identified by the American Library Association in the *Intellectual Freedom Manual* (published in the same year), and the *English Journal*'s proposal of six tactical responses or preparatory steps for teachers to defend themselves and their schools against censorship was similarly reminiscent of the ALA's advice to librarians:

First, each English department should develop its own statement of rationales for teaching literature.

Second, each English department should establish a committee which will recommend books for possible use by the department.

Third, each English department should work hard to win community support for academic freedom and to win that support before censorship strikes.

Fourth, each English department should try to communicate to the public what is going on in English classrooms and why it is going on.

Fifth, each English department should establish and implement a formal policy to handle attempted censorship.

Sixth, each English department should expect its members to prepare rationales for any book to be taught in any class.[110]

The problem in carrying out the first two proposals was the internal confusion in the English profession over what books were worthy curriculum selections and what English teachers were trying to do in teaching them. This crucial tactical flaw had also been ignored in an even earlier article for educators on the subject of censorship in the schools. "How Censorship Affects the School," published in 1963 under the auspices of the Wisconsin Council of Teachers of English, defined censorship as "the use of non-professional standards for accepting or rejecting a book," and then referred teachers to "the traditional body of literature in English" and the "tradition of literary criticism explaining and evaluating the literature" to ascertain what professional standards might be.[111] Even as early as 1963, the notion that such a set of received truths about literature was readily isolable was willfully ignorant of challenges to English curriculum boundaries as well as changes and challenges to the practice of traditional literary criticism.

The fourth proposal, communicating English department practices and rationale to the public community, raised the question of whether or not the public community was likely to support the intentions of the English department—assuming a given department could come to an *agreement* on "what is going on in English classrooms and why it is going on." However noble and ethical such public presentation of specific educational intent might be, some teachers looked upon public interest as warily as they did the specter of the censor, realizing that public distance from the classroom had allowed them to enjoy a degree of quiet freedom. One teacher openly decried the notion of public hearings. "These are not suitable occasions for the evaluation of the merit of a book," he claimed, "nor are they a satisfactory substitute for the public manner of dealing with books characteristic of professional persons." Pointing out that "the evaluation of literature requires, as does the evaluation of medicines, the scholar's study or laboratory," he then left it to the school board to prepare for battle with the censor as the appropriate mediator between the professional determinations of the teacher and the views of the parent.[112]

School boards themselves wielded the weapon of censorship within the schools perhaps most effectively as they represented the concerns of their local community and impacted employment decisions. The fear of reprisal or lack of support from administration due to community and school board pressures sometimes led teachers to internal censorship. "The community objects to what … teachers consider mature literature. The administration and other teachers know that the objection exists," wrote one young teacher, however "we do not get fully backed in other areas, and since we are told to be careful how we express ourselves … I assume I should tread lightly in this area also." Caught without tenure in an atmosphere of "unhappy compromise," this teacher had decided it was "better not taking chances." "If the administration openly defended a teacher's choices, and if they let the new teacher know that she need not fear for her job in case of trouble over chosen books," she lamented, "I would be braver."[113]

If some English teachers were unable to face involvement in a censorship controversy, other teachers welcomed the encounters and, like the librarian and the New Right ideologue, brought a sense of heroism to the conflicts. "I have a frequently recurring fantasy in which I am called before a censorship committee and asked to justify my teaching of such-and-such a book," one teacher confessed to his peers. "As hero of my own dream, I see myself starting on page one of whatever book is attacked and reading aloud," he continued, "with commentary and discussion, page by page, day by day, until the censors either lynch me or confess to a conversion."[114] In a more explicit "fantasy," censorship of *The Catcher in the Rye* was the fabricated occasion for an exemplary vision of intellectual heroics: "An irate committeeman comes to me (I am a very young instructor in a highly vulnerable school district), and he threatens to have me fired for teaching *The Catcher in the Rye*. . . . I look him boldly in the eye and I ask him one question: 'Will you, before you fire me, do me one last favor? Will you read carefully a little statement I have made about the teaching of this book, and then reread the book?'"

The "little statement" was a six-and-a-half-page discussion of the value of literature, "steps for the good censor," and a detailed analysis of the meaning of "the catcher in the rye." Although it may have been an enlivening statement for an English teacher to read, the visionary teacher acknowledges it is hard to imagine a complaining parent or school board representative having either the interest or patience to consider it. "And since it is fantasy, he says, 'Well, I don't see why not. I want to be reasonable.' And away he goes. . . . Some hours later he comes back, offers his humble apologies for what he calls his 'foolish mistake,' and returns my manuscript."[115]

Anticensorship polemics in this sense are admittedly best understood by others opposed to censorship. This type of in-group parable teaching is reminiscent of certain religious and ideological traditions more than academic ones. The missionary zeal to defend education and guarantee a student's search for truth inspires English teachers in a manner that recalls the zeal of librarians — and of the opposing New Right. The same teacher who authored the fantasy sequences of combat with the censor opened his narrative with a very real jeremiad call to battle. "To convert any 'enemy,' we must show him not simply that respectability, or tradition, or the National Council of Teachers of English are against him," he exhorted, "but that he is wrong, wrong according to his own fundamental standards." Warning that "to tell him that he is wrong according to our standards gets us nowhere, though it may be great fun," he proposed that "the problem is to find, somewhere among his standards, at least one that is violated by what he proposes to do."[116]

This educator was not the only one who brought a sense of professional mission to the English teacher's search for textual truths and contradictions. Another educator closed his 1974 essay with a corresponding call to arms of his own: "If we are to have any chance as English teachers to tell the truth and to let our students explore the many visions of truth available in literature, we have to fight the censor. To fight the censor with any hope of success, we must prepare carefully before censorship strikes, not in the panic of battle."[117]

To Tell the Truth

As educators, librarians, and defenders of Christian perspectives share the view of post–World War II American culture as a time and place of chaos and alienation, so too do they share the belief that there is a certain truth to contemporary American experience—and that it is accessible as much as defensible. The nature or definition of that truth, of course, is the line of conflict in contemporary censorship controversies. Yet even in the conflict there is paradoxical agreement. Whether seeking to remove it from the classroom or defending its use as necessary to develop an understanding of contemporary American experience, each of the participant communities identified *The Catcher in the Rye* as a central novel. In an incomplete survey by the American Booksellers Association (1983), over 300 fiction titles were listed as the subject of censorship activity between 1955 and 1983, along with an additional list of over 200 titles "often cited as having been banned or challenged" but for which exact dates and locales could not be verified.[118] Out of these 500-odd titles, spanning a thirty-year period, one title has appeared more frequently and consistently than any other— *The Catcher in the Rye.*

In seven independent surveys of high school teachers and librarians, and of published accounts of censorship complaints, conducted between 1961 and 1982 and spanning the nation, *The Catcher in the Rye* was found again and again to be the most frequently censored title.[119] Additionally, a 1962 survey of California professors of American literature, repeated and expanded nationwide in 1982, asked respondents two questions: (1) What American works published since 1941 should be considered classics? and (2) What books should be taught to college students? In the 1962 survey, *The Catcher in the Rye* was the number one answer to both questions, and in 1982 it was number three.[120] Statewide curriculum guidelines for high school literature teachers developed across the country in the 1980s also identified *The Catcher in the Rye* as both a "core" reading and a recommended one.[121] Finally, in their 1996 retrospective *Outstanding Books for the College Bound: Choices for a Generation,* the Young Adult Library Services Association (YALSA) of the ALA identified thirty-five titles for their repeated selection as "outstanding books" since YALSA began publishing its annual list of recommended titles in 1959. *The Catcher in the Rye* was one of only twenty-one books to appear seven or more times on the lists "created (by YALSA) with the target audience of 12–18 year olds planning to continue their education after high school."[122]

While the juxtaposition of repeated censorship attempts and continued recommendations for classroom use is unusual in the experience of the high school literature curriculum, it is not unique to *Catcher in the Rye.* Eldridge Cleaver's *Soul on Ice,* Joseph Heller's *Catch-22,* and John Steinbeck's *Grapes of Wrath* and *Of Mice and Men,* as well as *Slaughterhouse Five* by Kurt Vonnegut and *To Kill a Mockingbird* by Harper Lee, are among other frequently censored yet frequently taught titles. *Catcher,* however, experiences this double-bind much more often: censored (1966–75) twice as often as *Soul on Ice,* four times as often as *Catch-22* and *Grapes of Wrath,* and at least five times as often as *Of Mice and Men, Slaughterhouse Five,* and *To Kill a Mockingbird.*[123] Of related interest here is the finding of the Chicago Public Library system that by 1985 more than 1,000 copies of *The Catcher in the Rye* had "disappeared" from their holdings since 1951. Although a last resort, theft and destruction of library holdings has not been an unknown practice among procensorship groups.[124]

The question thus remains, What is it about *The Catcher in the Rye* that maintains its position of such paradoxical centrality in contemporary American fiction? The answer lies in the interpretations of *The Catcher in the Rye* articulated by the participants in the censorship debates. Having examined the background assumptions, self-definition, and censorship stance of their communities of membership, I turn to the individual participant arguments for and against *The Catcher in the Rye.*

5

The *Catcher* Controversies
as Cultural Debate

Ask yourself, What do we want in this country, above all? People
want to be happy, isn't that right? Haven't you heard it all your
life? I want to be happy, people say. Well, aren't they? Don't we
keep them moving, don't we give them fun? That's all we live for,
isn't it? ... Burn the book. Serenity, Montag. Peace, Montag.
— Ray Bradbury, *Fahrenheit 451*

The arguments over *The Catcher in the Rye* lead a sort of rhetorical
double life: as the singular statements of individual participants in a
localized controversy and, synchronically, as repeated expressions of
particular themes and viewpoints in an overarching cultural debate. On
the level of controversy, varied and often impassioned statements of
opinion are addressed to a geographically specific community at large
or, on occasion, in challenge and retort to the statements of another
individual. Characteristically disorganized, the explicit intent of the
localized dialogue is simply to gain support for either the banning or
retention of the novel on any number of grounds rather than the establishment of a communal evaluation (pro or con) of the novel.

Consideration of the dialogue as a cultural debate requires a much
broader analytical perspective. In this view, the context encompasses all
localized controversies over *The Catcher in the Rye* across time, and participants are identified according to their position regarding the novel.
This brings the commonalities, parallels, and paradoxes entangled in the
arguments of the two broad "opposing parties" into high relief. If this
conceptualization was wholly external to the arguments over *Catcher*, it
would run the risk of reifying the dialogue: imposing a structure or a
reality on the arguments that is not apparent to the actual participants
and, hence, not genuine. However, the debate concept is rooted in the

106

participants' own sense of polemic, and as the participants themselves frequently remarked about the relationship of their local controversies to conditions outside their community, it is instead a mode of clarification. The following arguments over *The Catcher in the Rye,* then, are drawn primarily from local controversies that occurred in California (1960–61), New Mexico (1968), and Alabama (1982–83), yet are structured for consideration as a cultural debate.

I selected these communities for in-depth study on the basis of their extended controversy (minimum duration of two months) and because they represented different time periods and regions of the United States: Marin County, California (1960–61); Albuquerque, New Mexico (1968); and Calhoun County, Alabama (1982–83). Public dialogue was culled from local newspaper articles and opinion letters, school board minutes, and lengthy participant interviews. The participant interviews, conducted in 1983, range from those of recall, reflection, and evaluation of a time past (Marin and Albuquerque) to expressions of immediate concern in Calhoun County. On occasion, I have included dialogue from controversies in other communities, based on newspaper accounts as reported in the American Library Association's *Newsletter on Intellectual Freedom* (hereafter *NIF*).

Although censorship of *The Catcher in the Rye* began as early as 1954 through its inclusion on various lists of "dangerous" books,[1] it was not until the early 1960s that *Catcher* became the focus of extended localized controversies. From 1961 to 1982, seventy-six communities across the United States generated enough controversy over *The Catcher in the Rye* to warrant media attention and consequent reporting in the *NIF*.[2] For sixty of these controversies, accounts in the *NIF* were sufficiently complete to suggest the normative experience and boundaries of attempts to censor *Catcher*.

Fundamentally at issue was the status of the novel within the school system. At the point of initial censorship activity, *The Catcher in the Rye* was a required high school literature reading in twelve schools, and a recommended reading in thirty-six schools out of the sixty. In eleven cases, *Catcher* was simply identified as "in the school system" or in the school libraries; in one further case it had been previously banned as part of a "dangerous" list and was being reconsidered for return to the high school library.[3]

At the close of censorship activity, *Catcher* remained a required reading in only two high school literature classes, a recommended reading in twenty-two classes, and became a restricted book (student access subject to written approval by a parent) in four school libraries. While the final status of *Catcher* was either unknown to or not pursued by the *NIF* editors in seventeen cases, in a full fifteen cases *Catcher* was banned outright from the library as well as the classroom. Of these fifteen schools, *Catcher* had originally been a required reading in only two classes. The defenders of *Catcher* did achieve a small victory in the one case in which *Catcher* had been previously banned: it was reinstated as a library holding, albeit on a restricted basis. Overall, the trend was toward decreased access, as *Catcher* was "demoted" one level from its initial status (from required to recommended to restricted to banned) as the consequence of censorship activity.

In the media reports of the *Catcher* controversies, a pattern of guarded anonymity was evident—although whether this was the decision of reporters or the request of participants is unclear in most cases. Complainants initiating the censorship controversy were identified largely as they categorized themselves: as parents, citizens, ministers, educators, and—in two cases—students.[4] Reporting of the often heated public discussions also identified participants categorically, with some identification of individual parents and ministers among those seeking to ban *Catcher.* Among the complainants and *Catcher*'s defenders alike, the commentary of individual administrators was often cloaked in media attributions to "the school board" or "members of the school's administration" except for the occasional identification of a specific individual in the course of issuing a policy statement or a final decision. Meanwhile, actual statements in defense of the novel were most often quoted from the arguments of individual teachers and parents.

A procedural pattern for censorship activity was also evident in the controversy reporting, with common elements and conduct that varied in few cases. The typical scenario was as follows: an initial complaint to the school board or librarian, broadening into a community controversy through the web of personal relationships on both sides. Direct discussions with the teachers who assigned or recommended *Catcher* were generally evaded and their suggestions for individual alternative readings were ignored, as the complainants' interest was in a community-wide ruling. Indeed, they expressed their objections in terms of concern for all adolescents, not just the children in their charge.

An overview of the Marin County, California, controversy illustrates this pattern. The Marin controversy opened with a twenty-one-signature petition and letter of complaint against the use of *The Catcher in the Rye* as a recommended reading for high school students, filed on 15 November 1960 with the Marin County High School District by the Reverend Thomas Grabowski of Marin Baptist Church.[5] "I guess it began with a letter of protest," Michael Reed, a senior administrator for the district, recalled. "I went to see him [Rev. Grabowski]. One of his parishioners' children had brought the book home and it had come to his attention." Initially trying to find some ground for compromise, Reed found that Grabowski's position was "absolutely non-negotiable." "By that time he had made up his mind that this was a bad book and there was no way that I found to deal with the book effectively," as Reed understood him, "other than to accept his decision that it should be pulled from the schools, which, of course, our school district never did." When the school district refused to remove *Catcher* or restrict the use of the novel, Reverend Grabowski found an experienced ally for his side. "Mrs. Keefe joined the Reverend Grabowski one week later or three weeks later," as Reed remembered the chain of events, "and by that time she had identified a number of books also, so our controversy that year was really a four book controversy."[6]

Kristen Keefe was a concerned parent who had led a previously unsuccessful censorship attempt in the Marin County School District in 1954, circulating a list of fifteen books that included *The Catcher in the Rye*.[7] In December of 1960, Mrs. Keefe sent a twenty-one-page letter defending Rev. Grabowski's position to each board trustee. The Marin County School Board received nineteen letters supporting the retention of *Catcher,* and the controversy received frequent attention in the local press.[8] Consequently, on 19 December 1960 the regular meeting of the Marin County Board of Trustees was devoted in large part to the book controversy. Minutes of the meeting show that "approximately 250 citizens interested in discussion concerning a petition to remove certain books" were in attendance and "an overflow crowd had assembled to hear the book discussion." The "main room and foyer" were reported as "filled to capacity" and a public address system had to be installed because "a group of about sixty persons stood outside the open windows." In addition, representatives of a local radio station were recording the proceedings and "a press table had been set up for reporters representing local and San Francisco newspapers."[9]

The 19 December meeting was to be only the first of four Marin County District Board meetings to be dominated by the censorship controversy. Nearly twenty-five years later, the sizzling tensions among those gathered were almost palpable, as Michael Reed described "a number of very hot school board meetings ... people standing in the aisles ... people leaning through the windows ... and they were very hot and heavy."[10]

Shauna Butler, a secretary in the Marin County School District, took the minutes and recalled "some very impassioned statements" from the audience that captured the tenor as well as the heated climate of the crowded meetings. One statement impressed in her memory was made by citizen Linaus Tyla, "a very dramatic sort of man": "He said, 'I can remember the books burning in the streets of Berlin,' and, I mean, it just sent the chills over you; it was something."[11]

In the midst of the fracas, the board of trustees, itself far from unbiased, attempted to maintain an atmosphere of order and respect while resolving the issue. Michael Reed explained that the school board was "determined the books were not going to be removed from the shelves, at least not without study." The school board formed an adjunct committee of English teachers to review the books, followed by the appointment of a citizens' committee that "contained at least one minister on it, the Episcopal minister."[12]

The minister, Reverend Jonathon Menjivar, had previously written to the board in support of *The Catcher in the Rye;* the other members of the "citizens' committee" were the aforementioned Linaus Tyla, Michael Reed, two Marin County District English teachers, and Mrs. Matthew Hester, representing the Marin County High School PTA. After reading the books for themselves, the citizens' committee found them to be educationally sound and recommended their retention. Perhaps recognizing the lack of impartiality or balance on the committee, Michael Reed emphasized that "the Board succeeded in treating these people [complainants] with respect," acknowledging "they were concerned about their children" and reiterating the Board's effort to "treat their feelings, their concerns, their anger with respect. The people whose concern was religious and moral, I know it was our goal to understand and respect them."[13]

While the tone of *Catcher*'s defenders here may be patronizing, it did not go unnoticed or unreflected upon by the school board members themselves. Reed himself identified and struggled against the undercurrent of paternalism as he later discussed the school board's "protection" of students and teachers from direct involvement in the controversy:

The alert ones [students] were aware but we tried to keep the controversy away from the school. We were ... playing a role in the school district then that probably the school district would not play now. It was probably something that some teachers now would call paternalistic. But we felt strongly that this was an administrative problem, that the job was to keep teachers' names out of the newspaper, to put the focus on us as the party of ultimate responsibility.... We took the role that we have authorized the use of these books, we are responsible for the use of these books, we are responsible for explaining why these books are used or justifying whether to use them or pulling them out.[14]

Finally, there was the perception that forces beyond or outside the local community were the actual source of upheaval. Much of this perception was an outgrowth of the earlier 1954 censorship controversy led by Kristen Keefe. "It was as if they had procedures for doing this, they had lists and a way of going," said Shauna Butler of Keefe's initial attempt at censorship.[15] Yet in neither case, 1954 nor 1960–61, was an organized group ever actually identified or confirmed beyond the level of suspicion and rumor. Attendance lists for the 1960–61 board meetings did include a few individuals who gave addresses outside Marin County, but their reasons for attendance remain unclear. Verbal statements recorded in the meeting minutes, letters, and petition signatures were those of Marin County residents or individuals representing large organizations (i.e., the ACLU, Episcopal Diocese) or of special expertise (i.e., Dr. S. I. Hayakawa of neighboring San Francisco State College).[16] Nevertheless, Kyle Russo, another senior administrator at Marin County High School, saw a commonality between the 1960–61 Marin controversy and controversies elsewhere, and he believed that it "wasn't just a group of local parents before the school board. It was organized through basically conservative groups; you could see the same type of arguments being presented across the country."[17]

Indeed, the commonalities between controversies over *The Catcher in the Rye* across the country were numerous, but explanation of those commonalities did not depend on the presence or influence of "outside" organizations. Instead it was, as Shauna Butler remarked, "a rather classic thing that appeared to be happening elsewhere"[18]—"classic" in the focus on *The Catcher in the Rye,* in the quick association with a few other books, in the local and then widening media attention, the unusually high attendance at school board meetings, the impassioned discourse, and in the controlling power of the school board.[19] Furthermore, where the later controversies in Albuquerque and Calhoun County deviated from the normative process, their participants acknowledged that they were aware of an understood sense of appropriate order to the public protest and defense of a book.

Consider the Albuquerque controversy, which began in an unusual fashion, with participants quickly attempting to redirect its course into the standard channels. The Albuquerque controversy was initiated in mid-May 1968 by the complaint of a high school student who objected to reading *The Catcher in the Rye*. In the first place, students as complainants in school book controversies are highly irregular. More unusual was the fact that this concerned young man took his complaint not to his teacher, librarian, or an administrator (all of whom arguably had a relationship to the assignment of the book), nor to a parent who might understand his concern, but took it first to his minister. Reverend Bradley Parsons, pastor of Albuquerque Baptist Church, recalled that the student "came to me and said that he had a book he had been assigned and wanted me to take a look at it, that he did not want to read it or do a report on it. He had marked several sections with slips of paper."[20]

Next, Reverend Parsons's handling of the student's complaint went outside the typical procedure—to the immediate discomfort of those who later came to defend *Catcher*. Kathleen Reynolds, supervisor of the Albuquerque Public School Library, criticized Reverend Parsons's tactics when he "went to the newspaper" and "omitted all channels."[21] When I spoke with Reverend Parsons, he recounted the sequence of events in the Albuquerque controversy:

> I had a daughter in Albuquerque [high school] at the time, and knew Tim Yates, the principal, so I called him at home, and I told him I was surprised that *The Catcher in the Rye* was being assigned, and had he read it? He said yes, he had, and asked what's wrong with it, took the general line that kids are exposed to these things and it shouldn't be a problem. I said I was surprised at his attitude; he said I had caught him at an inconvenient time. I asked if I could meet him at his office in the morning; he said he would be very busy ... I said "I'll be there waiting," 'cause I was quite upset.
>
> Well, that night, during the services that evening, I made the simple reference to it, to my shock at the type of book assigned and at Tim's reaction, and that I was going down to the school in the morning. At the end of the evening services, several parents expressed their concern and their desire to go with me, and when I got there in the morning, there must have been, oh, thirty parents. Yates was quite jolted—someone had called one of the television stations and they came down and interviewed me. Things became very public from the television station getting into it.[22]

Responding to accusations by the school board and others in the community that he had evaded the "proper channels," Parsons first stated that he never could find out what the proper channels were for book removal. Yet in his own explanation of his refusal to complete the recommended American Library Association complaint form or address the Albuquerque Board of Trustees, he acknowledged that he was familiar with those "channels" but found them unsatisfactory: "I learned what the proper channels were — passing the buck until finally public interest waned; don't know that it was ever resolved. Never did really meet with any Board, finally just got disgusted with the whole thing; their channels put you at their mercy."[23]

Reverend Parsons's frustration was, of course, exactly the response that the American Library Association (ALA) had in mind when the approved book-complaint forms were designed. In this case, the school board was able to refrain from formal engagement in the controversy because of Parsons's circumvention of the process, with *The Catcher in the Rye* remaining on the shelves of the library and on the list of recommended high school literature. Nearly fifteen years later, in Calhoun County, Alabama, another minister publicly protested the use of *Catcher* in the classroom and also evaded the ALA complaint process — again to the probable detriment of his cause. The Calhoun County controversy was one of very few in which the school board staunchly supported the censorship of the books involved, fighting to keep them off the shelves.

The Calhoun County controversy began typically and quietly enough. School board member Bo Brackett explained that it began "because a child was assigned one of the books to do a book report on, and the parent got a hold of it, saw some of the things that was in it; that was a parent that was concerned enough to look at what my child is reading, and that's where it began."[24]

Unfortunately, from Brackett's perspective, the parents took the complaint not to the school board but to their pastor, Reverend Wesley Crane of Calhoun County Baptist Church. Reverend Crane then openly preached against seven books, including *The Catcher in the Rye*,[25] and, joined by two other pastors, led approximately fifty church members to petition for removal of the books. The problem, as Bo Brackett saw it, was not the potential removal of the books but the considerable media attention that had been drawn to Calhoun County over the matter before the school board was addressed:

> Now, we [school board] have a good working relationship with the church people. I think the pastors that got together and did all this,

really raised a ruckus, I think they went about it in the wrong way. They should've come to the board; we've got a policy on how to report something that you think is offensive and a means by which they could've come to us, instead of getting up in the pulpit, and holding the book up, and preaching a sermon on it. I think they erred there.... I think, had they come to us first, and said, "Hey, I don't like what's in this book, I don't like for my child to be reading that book, how about takin' a look at it," I think we would have done that objectively and probably have made the same decision that we made anyway.[26]

When Crane and his supporters did turn to the Calhoun County Board of Trustees, the board's actions paralleled those of the school board in Marin County: appointment of a citizen committee to review the books and give their recommendation. Once again, paternalism on the part of the school board was apparent in the board's selection and approval of the citizen committee. According to board member Brackett, the makeup of the committee was a "couple of school principals, couple of school teachers, someone that was on the PTA, you know, just a good mixture of people."[27]

Objective and balanced in appearance, the two principals on the committee had in fact voluntarily removed the books before the petition was actually filed, and only one of the two teachers came to the defense of even one of the seven books in question (Steinbeck's *The Grapes of Wrath*). Hence, the recommendations of the citizens' committee in Calhoun County, as in Marin County, reflected the values of the school board rather than the possible range of community opinion. The outcome in Calhoun County was the restriction of all seven titles to student use only with written parental approval. By the close of the controversy, however, four of the books (*Doris Day: Her Own Story,* Francis Hanckel's *The Way of Love, The Catcher in the Rye,* and Steinbeck's *East of Eden*) could no longer be located in the school library holdings and their replacement was not ordered.[28]

The most striking commonality that emerged in my interviews with controversy participants was the extraordinary level of passion and personal involvement. To some degree, the passionate atmosphere lent credence to stereotypical notions of censorship controversies. In her recollection of the 1968 Albuquerque controversy, Kathleen Reynolds described the private meetings in homes and churches where "offensive words" were listed and counted, and passages from *The Catcher in the Rye* were read aloud "to sort of get the steam up."[29] Shauna Butler of

Marin County had a similar memory of the California protesters. "There were things going on about this group where they met together in order to divide their strategies and so forth," she recalled; "there was a lot of talk about that they met together and read excerpts to one another to, you know, get ready."[30]

The minutes of the December 1960 meeting of the Marin County Board of Trustees supported Shauna Butler's recollection. "Someone has compiled a list for us and this ["God's name taken in vain"] is used 295 times in the book," Reverend Grabowski, leader of those protesting *The Catcher in the Rye,* stated. "The Board has received copies of this from Mrs. Kristen Keefe," he continued. "She has checked it all out. Someone has told me she has all this on a big chart."[31]

In Calhoun County, parent Jenny Thigpen described similar behavior at the censorship meetings held by local ministers. "There were two or three meetings, night-time meetings with sixty to seventy people each meeting and provided transportation," she said, gatherings where many of the participants "consulted lists of words, passed the marked passages, and went on, with screams about books and vile filth in classrooms."[32] A reporter for the local newspaper covered two of the meetings in Calhoun County and her articles supported Jenny Thigpen's observations. "Our object tonight is to get some opinions," a minister proclaimed to the crowd at one meeting, and the reporter recounted their response: "Several ministers and county residents took the floor to complain about school library books and were greeted with choruses of 'Amen!'"[33]

These images of the arousal and manipulation of public sentiment, however accurate, fail to convey the sincere engagement of most controversy participants whose level of personal commitment and involvement was genuine and extensive. In the Albuquerque and Marin County controversies, participants on both sides (in interviews given with little advance notice) were able to give detailed recitations of the order of events and often exactly "who said what to whom" from fifteen and twenty-three years before. Participants interviewed in all three controversies often had kept newspaper clippings or other documents, if not personal files, which they volunteered for my review. Only one of the interview participants had kept similar clippings or files on other topics or community events. Alabama participant Jenny Thigpen was typical: a housewife, mother, and entrepreneur with her own seasonal weed abatement business in Calhoun County, for her interview she brought out two boxes of clippings, letters, photocopied school board records, and a cassette tape of one of the public meetings.

The degree of personal involvement was costly for several participants. Michael Reed, a teacher and administrator during the Marin County controversy, was reluctant to be interviewed because "it was kind of a traumatic experience for all of us; I suppose I've put a lot of it behind, in my mind, I don't really have any desire to keep reliving it, that particular experience."[34]

Although he saw it as "behind him," Reed expounded on the 1960–61 controversy for an hour and a half in his actual interview, with little prompting on my part. Yet he had more than usual reason to put it behind him. He believed that the strain of the controversy led to his first heart attack—although even then his participation did not end. "Within a week after the completion of the citizens' reports I went to the hospital with a coronary," Reed explained, "and while I was recovering from this, a committee of three would meet at my house and developed a book selection policy."[35]

Adding to the cost to his physical health, Reed felt his reputation in the community suffered as well. He spoke of a neighbor's change of view: "This lady had read something in the *Independent Journal* that prompted her to say to my wife: 'I always thought Mr. Reed was a very nice person but this had really damaged me,' what she read in the paper about *The Catcher in the Rye*. I'm sure she never read the book, but, there must be something morally wrong with me."[36]

Reverend Bradley Parsons, leader of the movement to censor *Catcher* in Albuquerque, actively sought much of the public attention he received, but in one instance he also felt his personal reputation was damaged. Recalling a guest lecture at his daughter's high school, he said, "I was asked to come and speak to a double class at Albuquerque, as to why I objected to the book. After I spoke at Albuquerque, I received 15 to 20 unsigned letters from, I perceived, various students—the gist of which was, 'How could such a wonderful girl like Sally have such a crumb for a father as you,' which reflected to me that even if they knew Sally to be a wonderful person as she was, how that they could see me as a crumb when they didn't know anything about me other than my thoughts on the book."[37]

There were other consequences for those involved in the *Catcher* controversies. At one point in the Marin County controversy, *Independent Journal* columnist Dorothy Simpers closed her "I-J Reporter's Notebook" with the observation that "the book controversy apparently produced its share of family squabbles, too. The board received two letters on the subject from a man and wife. One was for banning the books; the other was opposing."[38]

Anticensorship parent Jenny Thigpen felt that her then eight-year-old son paid the price for her activism in Calhoun County. At a time when other boys in his mixed elementary/junior high school were caught with switchblade knives and simply had the weapons taken away, David Thigpen was given the choice of "a paddlin', 3 written pages, or a parent conference" for playing with a rubber band in class. On a second occasion, David's school file was "marked for gambling in school" when a teacher overhead him say "I bet" to another student.[39]

That David was persecuted for his mother's anticensorship position does not appear to have been paranoia on Thigpen's part. Barbara Beasley Murphy, author of one of the seven challenged books, *No Place to Run,* came to meet with the Calhoun County Board of Education in late January 1983. Fourteen "concerned parents" (against censorship) initially supported Murphy; however, all but one parent eventually dropped their support due to fear of retribution in loss of jobs or damage to their image in the community.[40] "Jenny Thigpen . . . was the only 'concerned' parent with me at the end of my stay when I finally confronted the Calhoun County Board of Education," Murphy later reported to the Authors Guild. "It was a few minutes before midnight and she and I alone heard the board members' silent response and took in their billboard expressions."[41]

~

What is it about *The Catcher in the Rye* that generates these controversies with their "steamed up" and personally committed participants? The mildest objections to *Catcher* cited in the censorship reports of the *NIF* were often oblique: "I got nothing from it. I felt I missed the point. This book isn't fit for our students," was the objection of a school board member in a 1971 Roselle, New Jersey, controversy.[42] The local sheriff in Camden, South Carolina, decided *Catcher* was "not fit for a 16-year-old to read" when a high school girl brought the book to his attention.[43] In other controversies, Salinger's novel was simply labeled as a "dirty" book or "smut." Regarding a 1964 controversy over *Catcher* and *From Here to Eternity* in Molalla, Oregon, the *NIF* reported: "The school board, at a meeting earlier this week with about 150 parents, clergymen, civic leaders and students, heard the two novels and four others branded as 'filth' and 'muck.'"[44] Similarly, in Coventry, Ohio (1961), Reverend Carl

Narducci led a drive to remove *Catcher* from the local high schools, stating, "I am grieved that my daughter [a high school senior] has to have this kind of thing in school from a teacher who tells her she must read this smut and be graded on it—or else.... [I] intend to see who in the world recommends this kind of smut for our kids."[45]

The claims that *The Catcher in the Rye* is "unfit," "smut," "filth and muck" are a likely reference to the language used by Holden Caulfield as the narrator of the novel. In all of the controversies that generated the more explicit objections to *Catcher,* "obscene," "profane," or "vulgar" language was a common and often central objection. From Marin County's Kristen Keefe, who counted 295 occasions in which "God's name was taken in vain," to the letter of complaint filed with the Shawnee Mission, Kansas, school board in 1972 noting 860 "obscenities"; and the 1978 complaint of senior citizen Anita Page from Issaquah, Washington, who counted 785 "profanities," to the simple complaint of Middlebury, Vermont, parent Donald Desrocher Jr. (1982) that "there's a lot of filthy language in it,"[46] Salinger's use of language in *Catcher* was regularly attacked as evidence of the novel's unfit character.

Objectionable language was in fact the precipitating challenge to the use of *The Catcher in the Rye* in the schools of Marin County, California; Albuquerque, New Mexico; and Calhoun County, Alabama. In Marin County, Reverend Grabowski stated the primary objection of his group of petitioners: "The use of God's name or the name of Jesus Christ used in a derogatory manner is offensive to a cross section of the tax payers of our district.... We do not believe it is right to spend the taxpayers' money to purchase books which use profanity and teach disrespect to God and Jesus Christ."[47]

Marin High School administrator Michael Reed recalled that parent Kristen Keefe had prepared an eleven-page document in which "she had gone through, page by page, and every time Holden had said 'shit,' she noted it, and I've forgotten how many 'shits' she had by the end of the book."[48] In a cover letter to the document, addressed to the Board of Trustees and retained in the files of the Marin County District Office, Keefe summarized her analysis of *The Catcher in the Rye:*

> I found no pages to be without objectionable material in "Catcher in
> the Rye." I found only 22 pages of "Of Mice and Men" to be free of
> objectionable material. No newspaper, radio or television station
> could duplicate any three complete pages taken at random from the
> first named book without being subject to fine and possible imprison-
> ment and removal of license. It is doubtful if they could use any one

complete page of this book without at least some expurgation. Yet this is assigned classwork in our schools. The common term now used for such type material is, I believe, prurient. Furthermore, blasphemies against God average a little over 3.1 per page.[49]

The initial complaints about *Catcher* in Albuquerque were comparable. "The book contained continuous blasphemy, the taking of God's name in profanity, oaths," Reverend Bradley Parsons said. Defining his objections, he explained that "the book followed a general course of seduction and adultery, with sprinklings of coarse vulgarity, saturated with profanity."[50]

In Alabama, Calhoun County board member and parent Bo Brackett was less specific than Mrs. Keefe or the Reverends Grabowski and Parsons, but the nature of his complaint was similar: "It's not the story, it's the words, the phrases used in the book to describe different things. People felt, and I do too, that you could use some other adjective. . . . The thing that gets people is what words and things are in there to describe things; even if they are everyday things of life, they could still use substitute words to get the story across just as well."[51]

Would the novel work "just as well" with "substitute words"? Consider for a moment the following passage—selected as one of the more mundane passages in my reading of *The Catcher in the Rye*. The conversation is between Holden Caulfield and Ward Stradlater, his roommate at Pencey Prep. Stradlater is behind in his homework and wants Holden to help him out by writing his English composition for him while he reads for history class.

> "*I'm* the one that's flunking out of the goddam place, and *you're* asking me to write you a goddam composition," I said.
> "Yeah, I know. The thing is, though, I'll be up the creek if I don't get it in. Be a buddy. Be a buddyroo. Okay?"
> I didn't answer him right away. Suspense is good for some bastards like Stradlater.
> "What on?" I said.
> "*Any*thing. Anything descriptive. A room. Or a house. Or something you've lived in or something—*you* know. Just as long as it's descriptive as hell." He gave out a big yawn while he said that. Which is something that gives me a royal pain in the ass. I mean if somebody *yawns* right while they're asking you to do them a goddam favor. "Just don't do it *too* good, is all," he said. "That sonuvabitch Hartzell thinks you're a hot-shot in English, and he knows you're my roommate." (28)

Arguably, the swearing throughout this passage could be deleted or replaced—gosh, darn, son-of-a-gun—and the content of the exchange between Holden and Stradlater would remain intact. However, in this passage as with much of the novel, Holden's language lends the authenticity that is a requirement of successful first-person narration. In an early study of *Catcher* for *American Speech*, one author defended the linguistic accuracy of Holden's narrative as "an accurate rendering of the informal speech of an intelligent, educated, Northeastern American adolescent" and argued that "no one familiar with prep school speech could seriously contend that Salinger overplayed his hand in this respect."[52] Another academic critic ventured even further in his support of *Catcher*: "As a matter of fact, Holden's patois is remarkably restrained in comparison with the blue streak vernacular of his real-life counterparts. Holden's profanity becomes most pronounced in moments of emotional tension; at other times his language is notably tempered—slangy, ungrammatical, rambling, yes, but almost boyishly pure."[53]

Even if the offending descriptive language in *The Catcher in the Rye* were to be replaced at the cost of authenticity, the passages most offensive to those protesting the novel would remain intact. Consider the following passage in which the phrase "Fuck you" is the object of Holden's concern and action: "I went down by a different staircase, and I saw another 'Fuck you' on the wall. I tried to rub it off with my hand again, but this one was *scratched* on, with a knife or something. It wouldn't come off. It's hopeless, anyway. If you had a million years to do it in, you couldn't rub out even *half* the 'Fuck you' signs in the world. It's impossible" (202).

The irony of censoring Holden's own frustrated attempts to "clean up" his environment was apparently lost on those who attacked *The Catcher in the Rye*. Yet it was clear in the interviews with controversy participants that the lack of recognition of such irony was not so much the result of differing readings of *Catcher* as the lack of complete readings by some of the objecting readers. In Marin County, Kyle Russo recalled that "the book was more condemned for language, words, than for things to do with the story per se." The Marin County school board, in the process of defending the novel, effectively made *Catcher* a required reading for censorship participants. "We did not allow the use of word counting or single paragraphs out of context," Russo explained, "but saw to it that the book was evaluated on its merits."[54]

Librarian Kathleen Reynolds remembered that the "kick off point" of the 1968 Albuquerque controversy "was the language."[55] Indeed, Reverend

Bradley Parsons, who led the protest against *Catcher* there, told the local *Tribune* that he had not read the novel: "I just glanced at the pages underlined by a sophomore at Albuquerque High School. It was so nauseating to me I didn't bother to read the book."[56] Reynolds brought up the *Tribune* article in her interview and, recalling her reaction to Parsons's statements at the time, she exclaimed, "My next impression was 'My God, this man says he's a youth pastor and he's never seen the book, never heard of it.' If he never read the book, how could he comprehend that voice!"[57]

Parsons actually had defended his lack of interest in comprehending Holden's "voice" when he told the reporter: "I don't figure there's anything worth wading through that filth for to see if I can get the good out of it to offset it."[58] The Albuquerque school board, like the board in Marin County, required a full evaluation of a protested novel from the complainant. Consequently, Reverend Parsons's refusal to read *The Catcher in the Rye* and file a completed complaint form with the school district allowed *Catcher* to remain in use.

In Alabama, parent James Seckington also spoke of the protestors' limited familiarity with *The Catcher in the Rye*. "They didn't try to read the book, they didn't try to understand it; they just, uh, page numbers were brought out at one of those meetings that the preachers led," he observed, and "they passed the book around and had the pages folded and the words underlined, and that's all they did, they just inspected the book."[59]

Reinforcing Seckington's observation, Calhoun County board member Bo Brackett somewhat apologetically told me, "the thing is that I, I have not read any of the books, I was going to but I just don't have the time."[60] Nor were any other complainants in Calhoun County able to say they had read even one of the seven challenged books—including the ministers Wesley Crane, Peter Walker, and Donald Langford, who led the protest. The Calhoun County Board of Education made its decision to restrict the seven books solely on the basis of the recommendation of the board-appointed Central Complaint Committee (CCC). The CCC, in turn, based its recommendation not on its own readings and evaluations but on high school librarian Annie Aldrich's negative evaluation of *A Clockwork Orange* and teacher Georgia Baldwin's positive assessment of *The Grapes of Wrath*. A negative (anonymous) evaluation of Barbara Beasley Murphy's *No Place to Run* was appended to the CCC minutes; the missing evaluations of *The Catcher in the Rye* and three other books were justified by the notation in the minutes that they could not be found in the county libraries at the time.[61]

By contrast, those controversy participants who defended *The Catcher in the Rye* often did so on the basis of their independent reading of the novel, occasionally offering their explication of the text. Albuquerque librarian Kathleen Reynolds explained that while "I am sure that *The Catcher in the Rye*, to some students, is, you know, 'gulp,' because it's not within their background," she believed that "Holden's just a typical person, in some ways a very typical human being and, in another way, he's a very caring person." Pointing out that "you know, the whole title of 'I'm going to be the catcher in the rye,' out here, protecting people—which, in a way, the censor is the idea to protect," Reynolds then referred to the passage in *Catcher* where Holden himself acts as a censor, attempting to erase the "Fuck you" he finds written on his sister's school building.[62] When Holden imagines his sister and "all the other little kids" getting a "cockeyed" explanation of the phrase from "some dirty kid" that would worry them, he tells the reader, "I kept wanting to kill whoever'd written it" (201). In Reynolds's opinion, the relationship between censorship and the protection of childhood innocence was clearly drawn in the text itself.

In the Marin County controversy, Michael Reed defended *The Catcher in the Rye* based on his own reading as a teacher and an administrator. Yet he recognized the genuine concerns of many parents and his argument implies that even if complainants gave *Catcher* a full and considerate reading, their objections would stand. "I'm sure his ... church followers would find it easy to support him in regard to the book," Reed said, referring to Reverend Grabowski and his flock. "I don't think they would have wanted a child like Holden, who used terrible words like piss, shit, things like that." Reed then listed his understanding of the parental protests. "They'd tell you that in the first place, you shouldn't talk like that; second place, you shouldn't use those kind of words in a book; third place," he continued, "remember that *children* are reading that book and they can't figure out the subtleties," then added sympathetically, "I'm not sure I would have wanted Holden to be my child."[63]

Reed's ranking of first-, second-, and third-order objections in his hypothetical construction of the censor's argument is, in fact, accurate. A common exchange in each of the *Catcher* controversies went something like this: the protesting participant objected to the offensive language in the novel, to which a defending participant responded that the language, while distasteful, was certainly not unfamiliar or particularly shocking to late adolescents and much less so to adults. Consistent with Reed's second-order objection, the protesting participant then countered with a distinction between the tolerance of offensive language "in the street" or "daily life" but the unacceptability of finding language "of that kind" in literature—or in libraries.

"Even though it's street talking that goes on and most people have heard all of the words, we didn't feel it needed to be in the library," Alabama parent and school board member Bo Brackett argued. "I've heard all those words, and more, but I just don't think they should be in our libraries, of our public schools, and I think that people around here don't want them in our libraries."[64] Brackett's comment reveals an assumption that libraries are the supposed repositories of "proper" cultural knowledge rather than collections reflecting the range of highbrow and popular materials. In a similar manner, protesting parent Kristen Keefe contrasted the language boundaries of the media and the dictionary with the boundaries of literature and classroom discussions. The Marin County District school board minutes recorded the following exchange between Mrs. Keefe and defending board member Courtney Dean:

> Mrs. Keefe spoke. "Do you honestly, in your hearts, feel that material that cannot be read on television or printed in newspapers because we have laws against so doing; do you believe that teachers should read these books out loud in mixed classrooms? That has been done. Are these the best books that can be chosen for students at this age level?"
>
> Mr. Dean responded. "In my personal opinion I think a book is written for a purpose and not just to be smutty, that if it is written to give information, to teach or to provide a moral, it is a good book."
>
> Mrs. Keefe asked, "How does a teacher explain to a mixed class words that are not found in the dictionary?"[65]

Dean's statement and Keefe's response raises the question of whether or not children can figure out the "subtleties" in a given novel—the third order of the censor's objections pointed out by Michael Reed. Although Kristen Keefe did not take the issue further in the preceding exchange, it is an argument she had already made at some length in her earlier letter to the Marin County School Board. "I do believe that young people SHOULD be informed as to the temptations and evils that life often sets before them," she wrote, "but there is a world of difference between enlightenment and advocacy."

Significantly, the relationship between the type of language used in a novel and the question of what was being taught in the novel, its "message" or impact on the reader, was the critical nexus of each controversy. While participants may have been unfamiliar, hesitant, or unable to articulate their interpretation of the novel, the language used in *The*

Catcher in the Rye was graspable, concrete. Consequently, arguments protesting the novel often exhibited broad leaps from the highlighting or counting of offensive words to the understood meaning of the novel. Based on her documentation of "foul" language in *Catcher,* Keefe argued that "our young people are not dogs to be trained by rubbing their noses in filth," and then jumped to ungrounded assertions that reading *Catcher* would damage adolescents "by destroying their desire and will to be good citizens or their faith in principles and the good character of others, by portraying evil as the norm." Angered by and staunchly refusing to consider counterarguments that reading controversial literature could "possibly be called education in the true intent of the word," Keefe concluded that "to shock a young person, who is passing through the most sensitive and idealistic years of his or her life into insensitiveness only defeats constructive ends."[66]

Indeed, the moral implications of the novel's message to students lay at the very marrow of the controversy. Speaking of the censor's arguments in the 1960–61 Marin controversy, high school administrator Kyle Russo explained that "the theme was that the use of such language would be weakening to the moral fiber of the students, making them susceptible to communism."[67] In a parallel example in 1978, a protesting participant in an Issaquah, Washington, controversy followed her listing of the number of "hell's," "chrissake's," and "horny's" with the conclusion that "it shouldn't be in our public schools ... [*Catcher*] brainwashes students [as] part of an overall Communist plot in which a lot of people are used and may not even be aware of it."[68]

School administrator Michael Reed recalled comparable interpretive leaps from specific language use to broader meaning in the Marin controversy, but he further distinguished between the basis of the arguments of two central participants. Generally concurring with Russo's assessment, Reed drew a distinction between the essentially civil concerns of Kristen Keefe, and Reverend Grabowski's defense of his faith. "Mrs. Keefe was the one with the communists under the bed. She saw *The Catcher in the Rye* as an attack," he recalled, "on American values, Christian values; un-American and unpatriotic, hence, the kind of things the communists would support and encourage to undermine the fundamental values of our country."[69]

By contrast, Grabowski, who initiated the Marin controversy, "was probably more concerned with the moral part," in Reed's judgment.[70] Actually Reverend Grabowski's concern was a spiritual one. "Words convey ideas and thoughts and you can't get away from what is implanted in you. What you take in you will give out," he held; "that is the type of experience you are going to use." Alluding to the 295 occasions in which Holden "takes God's name in vain," Grabowski warned, "If this continues, there is going to be a great disrespect for God, a personal God people believe in and honor and worship."[71]

The distinction between a spiritual concern and a moral one proved to be a fine point across the *Catcher* controversies. In a 1965 controversy in Waterford, Connecticut, Baptist minister Duane Sweet shifted from a position of spiritual concern over profane language to a secular one as he closed his protest against *Catcher* with the statement that "I feel truly sad. I think if people like this kind of thing, it indicates a breakdown of moral standards. . . . We're not concerned with trivial curse words, but the entire philosophy which prevails."[72]

In the same vein, Justine Pas (secretary in 1968 to Tim Yates, senior administrator at Albuquerque High School) recalled the objections of the protesting parents in New Mexico under the leadership of Reverend Bradley Parsons. "They were dead set against that book being available; they didn't see there was anything to learn from that book," Pas informed me. "I think that it was the language—that reading that type of book would make their children that type, that that kind of stuff was all right. They were concerned with the morals of it."[73]

Given the focus on language, and the leap from language use to the "message" or the meaning of the novel, it is difficult to determine exactly where or how the complainants found *The Catcher in the Rye* to be morally failing. In the Marin controversy, one parent simply stated that "speaking as a mother, reading books like *The Catcher in the Rye* is the same as feeding children poison in small doses."[74] School administrator Michael Reed was more expansive in his reflective discussion of the protesting participant's concerns yet equally vague. As he saw it, the moral concerns resembled arguments regarding "creeping socialism" at the time. "If something had some ingredient of socialism in it, you had to oppose it because that was creeping socialism, and pretty soon you'd wake up one morning and it would burst upon you that we're now a socialist country," he explained, and then drew his parallel to the attempts to censor *Catcher*: "Well, it went the same way with American values: you keep feeding the kids books that even though some people would say; 'oh, its not all that bad,' that fact that it was bad *at all,* that it was un-American, that it was unchristian, that it showed somebody doing something as a model—this was a subtle undermining of our kids' values; 'creeping' in that sense."[75]

Reverend Bradley Parsons, who led the protest against *Catcher* in Albuquerque, simply claimed that "school use of the book contributes to the delinquency of minors."[76] Kristen Keefe had made the same claim in Marin County, but was a bit more specific in her charge that *The Catcher in the Rye* was "subversive," containing "anti-religious material, immorality, slang, suggestive references to crime and delinquency."[77] Intending to clarify her point, Keefe quoted the juvenile delinquency statutes of the Welfare and Institutions Code, which "make criminal any act which makes a minor lead an idle, dissolute, immoral life"; *Catcher*, she argued, "could be said to be a teenage primer to debauchery."[78]

Across the nation, charges of *The Catcher in the Rye*'s moral reprehensibility resembled the claims of the complainants in Alabama, California, and New Mexico: "immoral," "risque," "scandalous lifestyle," "pretty sexy," "atheistic," "brainwashing and against religion," and "scarring to youth" were repeated complaints.[79] In the absence of participant explanation or exemplification of these claims against *Catcher*, the novel itself must be searched for the possible origins and explications of these complaints beyond the use of offensive language.

⌒

In a strict sense, it is not difficult to see narrator Holden Caulfield as leading "an idle, dissolute, immoral life" for the course of the novel. If we understand idleness to be the absence of engagement in economically or scholastically productive work, or work directed toward a specific end, Holden can be seen as idle. Holden leaves Pency Prep just before being formally expelled, explaining, "besides, I sort of needed a little vacation. My nerves were shot. They really were" (51). He decides to take the train to New York City, planning to stay in "some very inexpensive hotel" and "just take it easy till Wednesday. Then, on Wednesday, I'd go home all rested up and feeling swell" (51).

What exactly he will do while "taking it easy" is unclear to Holden himself. After his arrival in New York, the novel is a chronicle of Holden's activities across a 48-hour period characterized by an apparent aimlessness in which his only sense of boundaries or direction lies in the time and space constructions of other people's lives. The erratic and seemingly random manner in which Holden acts and makes decisions further suggests the absence of moral restraints.

Consider the following sequence of events in the short two-day period. Arriving in his hotel room, Holden's view from his window is into the window of one room in which a male transvestite is dressing and another room in which a heterosexual couple are laughing as they squirt water out of their mouths at one another. He leaves his room for the hotel bar, where he dances with and buys drinks for three women, then leaves the hotel bar for a nightclub in Greenwich Village, where he has three drinks. "If you were only around six years old, you could get liquor at Ernie's, the place was so dark and all, and besides, nobody cared how old you were," Holden observed. "You could even be a dope fiend and nobody'd care" (85).

Holden leaves Ernie's to return to his hotel, where the elevator operator sets him up with a young prostitute. When the prostitute arrives, Holden talks with her and finds that he is not really interested in having sex with her. He sends her away, after paying her for her time, at which point she disputes as to whether it is five dollars or ten dollars "a throw." The prostitute returns with the elevator operator, who threatens Holden, takes the additional five dollars, and then punches Holden, leaving him on the floor.

The next evening Holden is in yet another hotel bar, drinking with a past prep school student advisor. Their conversation focuses on male sexuality: how one can recognize a homosexual, and a rehashing of the heterosexual experiences of the student advisor. When the student advisor departs, Holden goes to visit his sister, sneaking into his parents' home so they won't know he is out of school. From his home, he telephones a past favorite teacher, Mr. Antolini, and arranges to stay with Mr. and Mrs. Antolini for the night. It is at the Antolinis' that Holden experiences what he understands to be a homosexual advance from Mr. Antolini, and Holden flees, eventually spending the night on a bench in Grand Central Station.

A reading of *The Catcher in the Rye* that focuses on Holden's involvement in circumstances that he in fact defines as "perverty" provides support for the claim that Holden is dissolute; hence the novel is in a sense a "primer to debauchery." The sustained attention to sexuality—in the experiential world or Holden's imagination—further supports the claims that *Catcher* is "pretty sexy" or "risqué" reading. A reading that emphasizes immorality is directly challenged within the novel itself, however, as Holden continually evaluates his observations and experiences in the accompanying narration based on his own moral conscience.

Regarding his initial observations from his hotel window, Holden tells his reader, "I'm not kidding, the hotel was lousy with perverts. I was probably the only normal bastard in the whole place," and even though he then admits, "and that isn't saying much.... In my mind, I'm probably the biggest sex maniac you ever saw. Sometimes I can think of very crumby stuff I wouldn't mind doing if the opportunity came up," this very admission leads Holden (and his reader) to a more complex evaluation. "It stinks, if you analyze it. I think if you don't really like a girl, you shouldn't horse around with her at all—and if you do like her," he determines, "then you're supposed to like her face, and if you like her face, you ought to be careful about doing crumby stuff to it, like squirting water all over it" (62).

The hotel bar scenes fare no better in Holden's eyes. The first bar he describes as "one of those places that are very terrible to be in unless you have somebody good to dance with, or unless the waiter lets you buy real drinks instead of just cokes" (75–76). With the benefit of "real drinks," Holden finds the second bar just as intolerable. "I certainly began to feel like a prize horse's ass, though, sitting there all by myself," he confesses, adding, "there wasn't anything to do except smoke and drink" (86). Nor does the company of a past female acquaintance improve his disposition. "I couldn't even stick around to hear old Ernie play something halfway decent," Holden says regretfully, because "I certainly wasn't going to sit down at a table with old Lillian Simmons and that Navy guy and be bored to death. So I left" (87).

In his incident with the elevator operator and the prostitute, it is Holden's morality rather than immorality that is emphasized. When the elevator operator asks Holden if he is "Innarested in a little tail t'night?" Holden says "Okay," and tells the reader, "It was against my principles and all, but I was feeling so depressed I didn't even *think*. That's the whole trouble. When you're feeling very depressed you can't even think" (91). The arrival of the prostitute only adds to Holden's misery, demonstrating a moral tension that is held constant throughout *The Catcher in the Rye*. "I know you're supposed to feel pretty sexy when somebody gets up and pulls their dress over their head," Holden acknowledges, "but I didn't. Sexy was about the *last* thing I was feeling. I felt much more depressed than sexy" (95).

Holden, in a sense as Everyman, is posed between what he is "supposed to do" and what he feels to be right. In the midst of post–World War II American society in which what is "moral" has become what is "*normal*"—what one is "supposed to do"—Holden is out of place. Significantly, Holden's beliefs and actions are based on his own moral conscience; embodying sociologist David Riesman's "inner-directed" individual of pre–World War II America, in which choices and decisions are made on the basis of one's own inner "moral compass." As a maturing adolescent, Holden's moral dilemmas are given the sharpest focus in matters of sexuality.

Midway through the novel, for example, Holden ponders his sexual virginity. "The thing is, most of the time when you're coming pretty close to doing it with a girl . . . she keeps telling you to stop," he says. "The trouble with me is, I stop. Most guys don't." Declaring that he "can't help" stopping, he is nonetheless confused about "whether they really *want* you to stop, or whether they're just scared as hell," reasoning his way to the question of individual responsibility, asking "whether they're just telling you to stop so that if you do go through with it, the blame'll be on you, not them" (92).

At a later point, Holden tries to discuss sexual morality with his prep school peer advisor, who was rumored to be widely experienced, "knew quite a bit about sex." The student advisor tells Holden of his current relationship with an older Chinese woman, explaining that sex is more "satisfying" in the Eastern world since "they simply happen to regard sex as both a physical and spiritual experience." Holden eagerly exclaims, "So do I regard it as a wuddaya-callit—a physical and spiritual experience and all. I really do. But it depends on who the hell I'm doing it with. If I'm doing it with somebody I don't even—." Shushed by his advisor, Holden lowers his voice and continues, "I know it's supposed to be physical and spiritual, and artistic and all. But what I mean is, you can't do it with *everybody*—every girl you neck with and all—and make it come out that way. Can you?" Finding himself caught in a discussion of ethics rather than sexual exploits, the advisor evades answering Holden and tells him instead, "Let's drop it" (146–47).

Although sexuality is the most developed expression of moral tension in *The Catcher in the Rye,* Holden faces the same dilemma between what one is "supposed to do" or what is viewed as "success," and his own sense of morality and social justice in other areas of his experience. In the course of the novel, Holden regularly routs out the "phony" aspects of American life and searches for the means of a genuine existence. In this sense, Holden can hardly be seen as idle; rather, in his quest for truth he is a contemporary Diogenes of sorts. That the nature of Holden's quest is missed by hostile readers may be at least partially explained by the untempered cynicism that occasionally dominates Holden's narrative. In the following passage, Holden ridicules the religious faith of a Pencey Prep alumnus who made a financial success out of the undertaking business:

The first football game of the year, he came up to school in this big goddam Cadillac, and we all had to give him a locomotive—that's a cheer. Then, the next morning, in chapel, he made a speech that lasted about ten hours. He started off with about fifty corny jokes, just to show us what a regular guy he was. Very big deal. Then he started telling us how he was never ashamed, when he was in some kind of trouble or something, to get right down on his knees and pray to God. He told us we should always pray to God … wherever we were. He told us we ought to think of Jesus as our buddy and all. He said he talked to Jesus all the time. Even when he was driving his car. That killed me. I could just see the big phony bastard shifting into first gear and asking Jesus to send him a few more stiffs. (16–17)

The problem here is that the reader has no reason to extend credibility to Holden's evaluation of alumnus Ossenburger: his own cynicism short-circuits his exposé of Ossenburger's insincerity. Passages of this sort—and there are many—may serve to rankle the readers who identify with any one of Holden's targets, rather than cause them to reflect upon or consider the critique. However, the uncontrolled passages are outweighed by others in which Holden's evaluations are more disciplined in temper and balanced by his more empathetic reflections. For example, the morning after Holden has fled the Antolini home, he agonizes:

But what did worry me was the part about how I'd woke up and found him patting me on the head and all. I mean I wondered if just maybe I was wrong about thinking he was making a flitty pass at me. I wondered if maybe he just liked to pat guys on the head when they're asleep. I mean how can you tell about that stuff for sure? You can't. … I mean, I started thinking that even if he was a flit he certainly'd been very nice to me. I thought how he hadn't minded it when I called him up so late, and how he'd told me to come right over if I felt like it. And how he went to all that trouble giving me advice about finding out the size of your mind and all, and how he was the only guy that'd ever gone *near* that boy James Castle I told you about when he was dead. I thought about all that stuff. And the more I thought about it, the more depressed I got. I mean I started thinking maybe I *should've* gone back to his house. Maybe he was only patting my head just for the hell of it. The more I thought about it, though, the more depressed and screwed up about it I got. (194–95)

One way to understand this passage is to see that Holden's confusion over the meaning of Mr. Antolini's actions is actually secondary to the

larger moral question of whether or not someone's sexual preference—
or, implicitly, any other single factor in the composite of social morality—ought to dominate evaluations of individual moral stature.
Holden repeatedly struggles throughout *Catcher* to identify and evaluate
individuals as unique, complex, and integrated beings, a struggle that is
most evident in his criticisms of the "phony" symbols and processes of
social stratification. Yet, as another passage demonstrates, Holden often
finds himself defeated.

Holden tells the story of an earlier roommate, Dick Slagle, who had
"very inexpensive suitcases" that he would hide under the bed instead of
putting them on the luggage rack next to Holden's Mark Cross suitcases.
"It depressed the holy hell out of me, and I kept wanting to throw mine
out or something, or even trade with him," Holden explains, leading him
to "finally put *my* suitcases under my bed, instead of on the rack, so that
old Slagle wouldn't get a goddam inferiority complex about it." The next
day, Slagle puts Holden's luggage back out on the rack because, as
Holden later determines, "he wanted people to think my bags were his."
All the while, Slagle keeps "saying snotty things" to Holden about his
luggage being "too new and bourgeois." "The thing is, it's really hard to
be roommates with people if your suitcases are much better than theirs,"
Holden concludes. "You think if they're intelligent and all ... and have a
good sense of humor, that they don't give a damn whose suitcases are
better, but they do. They really do" (108–9).

In other examples, Holden's own perspective is clear and solidly
defended even as he entertains oppositional arguments. On the question
of religion, Holden distinguishes between his spiritual needs and his
rejection of dogmatic theological explanations. At one point Holden
admits to the reader, "I felt like praying or something, when I was in bed,
but I couldn't do it. I can't always pray when I feel like it." "In the first
place, I'm sort of an atheist," he confesses. "I like Jesus and all, but I don't
care too much for most of the other stuff in the Bible." The Disciples, for
example, "annoy the hell" out of Holden because "they were all right
after Jesus was dead and all, but while He was alive, they were about as
much use to Him as a hole in the head. All they did was keep letting Him
down" (99).

In contrast to his earlier mockery of alumnus Ossenburger's faith,
Holden recounts an ongoing argument between himself and a past prep
schoolmate, Arthur Childs. Childs is characterized as a devout Quaker,
"a very nice kid," who relies on the interpretations and teachings of the
church for spiritual guidance, whereas Holden's position is one of personal quest and interpretation. Childs tells Holden that "if I didn't like

the Disciples, then I didn't like Jesus and all. He said that because Jesus *picked* the Disciples, you were supposed to like them." Agreeing that Jesus did pick them but "at *random*," Holden asks Childs "if he thought Judas, the one that betrayed Jesus and all, went to Hell after he committed suicide." "Certainly," Childs answers, and Holden sees his opening. "I'd bet a thousand bucks that Jesus never sent old Judas to Hell," Holden argues. "I think any one of the Disciples would've sent him to Hell and all—and fast, too—but I'll bet anything Jesus didn't do it." Here, Holden has the last word in a final aside to the reader: "Old Childs said the trouble with me was that I didn't go to church or anything. He was right about that, in a way. I don't" (99–100).

These passages could undoubtedly be used to support claims that *The Catcher in the Rye* is "against religion" or that it at least hints at the plausibility of atheism. That they have not been cited in the controversies may be a consequence of abbreviated readings; reading the phrase "I'm sort of an atheist," for example, because it has been underlined and isolated rather than reading it in the process of following the story. In his recollection of the Marin County controversy, high school administrator Michael Reed remembered Reverend Grabowski "calling the book immoral" because "Holden Caulfield was not their kind of a child, who a parent in his church would want to own." Holden was seen by the complainants as "kind of cynical, he had bad thoughts, got himself in an immoral situation in a New York motel," and in his interview Reed pointed out that "the fact that it was a *frustrating* situation and really could *teach* was more than Mr. Grabowski might be able to see."[80]

The general lack of textual exemplification in the *Catcher* controversies may be equally a consequence of Salinger's narrative style: the preceding segments from the novel *are* lengthy and awkward to manage. Even when reproduced nearly intact, the rambling quality of Holden's "voice" makes a clear line of argument difficult. Thus, while the reading of a text can be seen to generate an individualized interpretation, the burden of explication may be too great for any individual reader to carry out—particularly in the case of a reflexive narrative such as *The Catcher in the Rye*.

This is true as well of the broader complaints against the overall perspective or point of view maintained in *The Catcher in the Rye*: they demonstrate familiarity with the text yet exemplification and explanation remain absent. In 1972, a school board member in Shawnee Mission, Kansas, argued for the elimination of *Catcher* because "it has widened the generation gap and confused moral values within families."[81] Likewise, in a Fort Myers, Florida, controversy (1980), Reverend Jack Gambill told the local school board that *The Catcher in the Rye,* as well as Eldridge Cleaver's *Soul on Ice* and Joseph Heller's *Catch-22,* "should be banished from the library shelves so the teaching of morality and situation ethics will be removed from the classroom and returned home."[82] Somewhat more expansively, the *NIF* reported the following objection to *The Catcher in the Rye,* grouped with Orwell's *1984* and Huxley's *Brave New World,* in a 1964 Pennsylvania controversy: "The principal is quoted as saying . . . [that] the three books treat the society in which we live in such a way that students might tend to question it. For example, they tend to compare communism with democracy and atheism with Christianity in such a way as to cause high school students to question the values we as a society have set up."[83]

"To question the values we as a society have set up." Here we finally have the crux of the debate over *The Catcher in the Rye.* From the literary critics to nearly every participant comment on the message or meaning of *The Catcher in the Rye,* everyone agrees that Holden's narrative is a purposeful questioning of American values. Participants then divide into the oppositional camps for or against *Catcher* on the basis of whether such questioning is a valuable and instructive experience for adolescent readers, or a dangerous and destructive one. On the side of value for such "questioning," the Great Books, Little Institute at Franklin and Marshall Colleges, Pennsylvania, chose *The Catcher in the Rye* and *Growing Up Absurd* by Paul Goodman as the "topic books" for their annual meeting in 1964 because "both books follow the theme of the difficulties encountered by young people maturing in today's world."[84] Similarly, a school superintendent in North Kingstown, Rhode Island, argued for *Catcher*'s retention in a 1967 controversy because it "is about a 17-year-old youth trying to mature the hard way" and offered not only "a keen insight into the adolescent mind" but also "the American way of life."[85]

In the Marin County controversy, Dr. S. I. Hayakawa spoke of the value of *The Catcher in the Rye* for high school as well as college classroom use. While noting that "the effects of reading *The Catcher in the Rye* are usually negligible with girls," Hayakawa explained that male readers aged seventeen to twenty years old "often find it a great help in gaining insight into their own feelings of rebellion."[86] Correspondingly, Marin County District school board member Vincent Handy characterized Holden Caulfield as "a good boy but a confused and rebellious one," agreeing with Dr. Hayakawa's observation, and extending the range of the audience which might benefit from reading *Catcher*. "I don't swear and I don't smoke and I don't like to read books of this type, but I read both of them," Handy told those gathered at the Marin County meeting. "When I got through reading *Catcher in the Rye* I was a little bit disgusted." "What is the purpose of this?" he said he wondered at first, "and then it dawned on me suddenly that it should be compulsory reading for every parent. It is just presented in a rough way."[87]

Discussion of the value of *The Catcher in the Rye* was not limited to the formal dialogue of the school board meetings. In her retrospective interview, Marin County school secretary Shauna Butler recalled almost continual informal discussion in the staffrooms of one of the high schools and in the district office. As faculty and staff came and went throughout the day, they joined in the running dialogue. "We spent a lot of time discussing these brilliant kids," Butler said, referring to the adolescent characters in *Catcher* and in Salinger's *Franny and Zooey*, fictional adolescents who the faculty concluded "were capable of living in the world and understanding its complexities; that the search for truth and so forth is free."[88]

A comparable defense of *The Catcher in the Rye* was made by Tim Yates, as senior administrator of Albuquerque High School at the time of the Albuquerque controversy. "I think it's a case study in adolescent turmoil. I think it is a useful teaching tool to help kids see the pitfalls of adolescence," Yates told one reporter in an interview for the *Albuquerque Tribune*. Admitting "I don't think it's a literary classic," Yates felt that the use of *Catcher* in the classroom was nonetheless justified because "neither do I think there is anything in it that a kid won't face anytime he goes to the movies or turns on a TV set."[89]

In the Albuquerque controversy, editorial letters to the *Albuquerque Tribune* acted as a community forum in lieu of school board meetings. In large part favoring the retention of *The Catcher in the Rye*, letters ranged from those that classified *Catcher* as a literary classic (grouped with "all of our great American authors, Hemingway, Faulkner, Malamud") to those that defended *Catcher* particularly for its critical view of contemporary American society.[90] "Since it has taken the Reverend Bradley Parsons seventeen years to discover Salinger's '*The Catcher in the Rye*' (first published in 1951)," wrote Albuquerque resident Luke Benz, "perhaps he will get around to discovering some of the real obscenities of our civilization (e.g., racial prejudice, poverty, the war in Viet Nam) within the next seventeen years." "How frightening it is," Benz continued, "to realize that a clergyman so desperately out of touch still exists."[91]

As I surveyed the secondary discourse and interviewed controversy participants, seeking to understand their positions and involvement in the *Catcher in the Rye* controversies, those who opposed *Catcher* were not so much "out of touch" as they were focused upon consciously protecting their sense of American values, perceived to be under question and challenge. In a 1971 controversy in Hinsdale, Illinois, *The Catcher in the Rye* (along with Steinbeck's *Grapes of Wrath*, Hemingway's *Farewell to Arms*, and John Updike's *Rabbit Run*) was criticized as "pessimistic, morbid, and depressing," with the local PTA literature subcommittee asking instead for more books with "positive, optimistic, uplifting standpoints."[92] Parent Ginney Desrocher "objected to the negative point of view" in *The Catcher in the Rye*, and concluded her argument in a 1982 Vermont controversy with the statement: "We look at the positive side, that's what builds character."[93] Marin County parent Kristen Keefe had argued the same point at greater length in her 1960 letter of complaint to the Marin County District Board of Trustees:

> The mind of a child is an unchalked slate. If we who push the chalk do not by examples write beauty and portray the satisfactions of having principle and character upon that slate, we are guiltier than had we left the writing to happenstance. If we do not point the way to the best, the worst will follow as night follows day, whether through intent by evil-doers, or by creation of a vacuum. This is to say, that I am equally concerned about the shortage of fine books upon our school library and classroom shelves as I am about the examples in use and here protected. Young people do not yet know all of what they believe. In fact, the modern world and our school constantly forces them to question the beliefs of their parents. They accept the authority of the school and this trust should not be lightly viewed by any trustee.[94]

The notion of a modern or different world in which children are instructed in ways and materials that challenge their parents' sense of American values was also addressed by Reverend Wesley Crane in Calhoun County. Although he refused to be interviewed on any specific aspects of the 1982–83 school book controversy, Reverend Crane volunteered his personal view of what is at stake in book controversies in general:

> I will say this. I'm still shocked at what our children can have access to, it wasn't there when I was there. No morals in our schools anymore; the teacher doesn't lay the Bible on the desk anymore and say, "We're an—(pause and audible exhalation)." Do you know where this is, ma'am? This is America, ma'am; do you get my drift? It's just

communism; it's a movement that people don't care anymore, and I
do. We do. It's not just something I've dreamed up. We're still an
American people. People have forgotten the morals this country was
founded on. Let's go back to the Constitution and read it. If we don't,
then pretty soon it'll be rewritten and then that's the end of it.[95]

The statements of those who oppose the use of *The Catcher in the
Rye* in the classroom, then, reveal a primary concern over the protection
of children from materials that either expose them to unpleasant "negative" facets of American life or encourage the child to question the traditional set of values. Of further concern is the time and educational effort
spent on literature that takes a critical view of contemporary American
society: replacing the reading of "classics" (or the Constitution) and presented without corresponding works supportive of traditional American values. Participant arguments as to whether *The Catcher in the Rye*
is, or will be, a "classic" or is merely popular "pulp" fiction disclose the
assumption that classic literature—at least for school use—is literature
that supports the dominant cultural value system.

Both complainant Kristen Keefe and administrator Michael Reed,
opposing participants in the Marin County controversy, addressed these
concerns. In her 1960 letter to the Marin County school board, Keefe
stated: "I am concerned also over the growing acceptance of the idea,
that just because a book has sold well and popularly to the public, that
it abracadabra can be misnamed a classic, or necessarily be taken for
granted as a fit book for schools. There is and should be a vast difference
between public and private adult selection, and selection for educational
purposes for not yet adult minds. Few modern books will be remembered fifty years hence—unless they may be used to show the decadence
of the age."[96]

Twenty-three years later, Reed voiced the same concern in his retrospective interview:

> There was another argument, and possibly it is one with a kind of
> merit. And that is, what about all of the really recognized classics that
> aren't being taught because books, I don't know, in favor of contempo-
> rary books, junk, that probably will be long gone in five years; a "best-
> seller." School time is a very valuable time, homework time is very
> valuable time. [There is] a whole argument as to whether children
> benefit most from a work of literature if they enjoy it, perhaps stimu-
> lating a desire to read more, or if they labor through it like generations
> of kids labored through *Ivanhoe*. In one case, they're exposed to a

classic, or where they read something like *The Catcher in the Rye* which is more contemporary and something that they know they enjoy more.[97]

The question of balance in developing a critical perspective on contemporary American culture was repeated in a letter to the Marin County school board from Reverend Jonathon Menjivar, Director of Education for the Episcopal Diocese of California. "'Catcher in the Rye' has been found a most helpful description of our contemporary culture. It may, indeed, have real value in bringing college students and adults to grasp some of the religious issues of the day," Menjivar wrote in defense of *Catcher*'s retention, adding that "we are not fearful of books which speak unfavorably of the Church or depict people using God's name in vain." Menjivar then asked that equal time or more be devoted to contrasting materials, hoping for "an abundance of classical and current literature which portrays a richer view of life, suggesting the strength of the Church at its best and the fruits of faithfulness" to be included in the curriculum.[98]

Reverend Menjivar implicitly identifies the actions of those seeking to censor *The Catcher in the Rye* as rooted not in strength of values or certainty of position but in fearfulness. This is the central basis of the split between those who defend or seek to ban *The Catcher in the Rye*: given that *Catcher* presents an intentional and fairly thorough questioning of American values, are American readers—be they adolescents or adults—able to sustain a positive view of their culture in reading it? In a similar vein, parent James Seckington of the Calhoun County controversy summed up his evaluation of Holden's experiences in the novel and what readers would gain from *The Catcher in the Rye* by saying that "people sometimes come into contact with the bad to know what is good."[99]

While Seckington's statement may sound more extreme than Menjivar's, both statements express the belief that moral values and character are not damaged by criticism and exposure to oppositional beliefs and actions but are in fact strengthened through the development of a critical perspective in place of "blind faith." A crucial fact about *The Catcher in the Rye*—as opposed to interpretive readings of it—is that Holden does not criticize the historically central values of individualism, family, democracy, and equality: he critiques their faulty *enactment* in American society and lambasts the tautological replacement of morality with *normal*ity, and its corollary value for conformity. The painful irony is that the censoring participants, the very people who, as Michael Reed put it, would not "want to own a child like Holden," contribute to the chasm between American values and experience that Holden as an idealistic adolescent is trying so desperately to bridge.

Nor do the censors recommend contemporary literature for students to read in place of *The Catcher in the Rye*. For all the protest that *Catcher* was taking the place of more positive, valuable, or character-building literature, not one actual title was suggested by objecting participants for student reading on contemporary American society. Based on her seventeen years of experience as a lead librarian in the Albuquerque Public School District, Kathleen Reynolds commented that "usually we get very little of that: you know the standard NCTE form—usually they have nothing else to suggest that follows that theme."[100] In the broadest sense, the "theme" Reynolds speaks of is that of the process of transition from the world of childhood to adult society. In *Catcher* this process is viewed as a difficult and ambiguous one: the world of childhood is portrayed as one of idealism and innocence while adult society is characteristically "phony" and "perverty," concerned with expedience over ideals and social status over moral action. This portrayal is undoubtedly challenging to educators, ministers, and parents as they seek to guide adolescents through this transitional stage. Whether such a bleak or critical portrayal is "necessary reading" is a different question.

First of all, it is not particularly true that those who wish to ban *The Catcher in the Rye* are unfamiliar with other novels following the theme of adolescent transition into contemporary American society. Instead, the problem is that the great majority of novels on this theme take the same perspective as *Catcher*—although perhaps not as successfully. The ALA regularly publishes a pamphlet titled "Best Books for Young Adults," and in 1976 published a cumulative pamphlet, "Still Alive: The Best of the Best, 1960–1974," which listed seventy-two titles frequently checked out of public and school libraries across the nation. Eighteen of these books are novels of the adolescent struggle toward participation in adult society: fifteen of the eighteen present that transition as one of difficulty and tension in ways that parallel some or much of *The Catcher in the Rye*.[101] Two novels portray the transition as a positive and relatively straightforward gain for adolescents, albeit locating the sense of struggle or conflict in the context of nondominant cultural experience. The eighteenth novel portrays adult society as equitable and preferable to the childhood of the runaway heroine, characterized by neglect and victimization.[102]

As might be expected given the continual attack upon *Catcher,* thirteen of the fifteen "negative transition" novels have been censored at least once and some repeatedly.[103] This highlights a critical gap between what young readers select for themselves based on interest and credibility, and what concerned (censoring) adults believe adolescent experience and interest should be. Correspondingly, controversy participants who defended *The Catcher in the Rye* differed, at bottom, from those who sought to censor the novel, not so much in terms of their conceptions of what "should be" but in their unwillingness to shield adolescents from "what is."

Marin County controversy participant Michael Reed ended his interview with the statement, "We are talking about our children's morals, and things very close to our hearts: as we [the school board] understand the truth; as they [the protesting participants] understood the truth."[104] Reed here repeats the earlier refrain of the educators, the librarians, and the New Right proponents. Yet we are closer to the nature and definition of "the truth" of contemporary American experience only by implication. The actual dialogue of the controversies over *The Catcher in the Rye* has identified what is objectionable as well as worthy in the novel. It is, however, through the interpretive framework of a cultural debate that participants can be seen to share a certain understanding of post–World War II American society, even as they disagree as to what version of that "truth" ought to be shared with adolescents. That this disagreement is rooted in doubt about the strength of the American character, present and future, has been suggested in the *Catcher* controversies themselves: that it is so is the argument of the next chapter.

6

Conflict and Character

It is only through free debate and free exchange of ideas that government remains responsive to the will of the people and peaceful change is effected. The right to speak freely and to promote diversity of ideas and programs is therefore one of the chief distinctions that set us apart from totalitarian regimes. Accordingly a function of free speech under our system of government is to invite a dispute. It may indeed best serve its high purpose when it induces a condition of unrest, creates a dissatisfaction with conditions as they are, or even stirs people to anger.
—Justice William O. Douglas, *Terminiello v. Chicago 357, U.S. 1*

I speak of the American in the singular, as if there were not millions of them, north and south, east and west, of both sexes, of all ages, and of various races, professions and religions. Of course the one American I speak of is mythical; but to speak in parables is inevitable in such a subject, and it is perhaps best to do so frankly.
—George Santayana, *Character and Opinion in the United States*

The introduction to the American Library Association's *Intellectual Freedom Manual* quotes the opinion of Supreme Court Justice Potter Stewart that "censorship reflects society's lack of confidence in itself. It is the hallmark of an authoritarian regime."[1] The cultural debate over *The Catcher in the Rye* both affirms and challenges this evaluation. Clearly, the arguments of both those who defend the novel and those who seek to censor it express doubt and fearfulness as to the nature and future of contemporary American society. *The Catcher in the Rye* itself is the narrative of an idealistic American innocent who is filled with doubt, anger, and disappointment as he confronts the mature society he is soon expected to embrace.

Yet however much the act of censorship may generally indicate the existence of or desire for authoritarianism, the reality of the censorship experience of *The Catcher in the Rye* is that it has taken place in a context of open contest and debate that is itself the hallmark of democracy. Many participants in the *Catcher* debate expressed a consequential revitalization of their faith in the democratic process, even when they were disgruntled with the final disposition of the novel.

As we recall the participant arguments of the *Catcher* debates, two critical questions are evident: whether or not *The Catcher in the Rye* is a "good" book—in estimation of its "American" or "un-American" viewpoint—and, in either case, whether or not *The Catcher in the Rye* ought to be read by adolescents. It is doubtful that *Catcher* would have entered the secondary school system on any other than a recommended or advanced reader basis were it not for Holden's own adolescence. Debate participants who felt that *Catcher* in itself was "un-American" found it equally unfit as reading for children—even if it was about someone their own age.

Given the heated opposition to the novel, those who found *Catcher* a valuable book might have used less controversial works for student reading were it not for the particular student appeal of a tale of adolescent experience. Still others who appreciated *Catcher* as an adult novel but believed that it was too mature or negative for student reading found themselves in the awkward position of arguing that a narrative about adolescence was too mature for its real-life peerage. Excepting those participants who both valued the novel in itself and found it to be not only manageable but necessary reading for students, the position of most participants revealed an implicit desire to shield or protect adolescents from critical portrayals of contemporary American society.[2]

Such protectionism suggests a broad lack of faith in the character of postwar American society—and particularly in the unready precocity of adolescents who are its future citizens. This lack of faith may be unduly stirred by the confrontational tone of Holden's adolescent voice, but it is generated by a wizening of the American spirit that nearly all the debate participants shared and brought to their reading of *The Catcher in the Rye*. One of the greatest frustrations (and ultimately a source of revelation) in my interviews with debate participants was their difficulty in articulating exactly how or why *Catcher* was "American" or "un-American," and their contrasting ease and willingness to explain what was "wrong" with contemporary society—often, specifically, how it was failing.

Early on in many of the interviews, participants spoke of the dual failure of the schools and of parents in the instruction of adolescents.

Not surprisingly, parents tended to criticize the lack of guidance from the schools or the wrong-headedness of "value-free" academic instruction, whereas educators and school board members (often parents themselves) criticized the lack of parental guidance and involvement in their children's education. In Alabama, school board member and parent Bo Brackett emphasized the cultural implications of Calhoun County's local controversy when he explained that "the problem" was "not only just here, but all across the country. Parents don't take enough interest in their children at home and turn 'em loose." These parents "expect the school system to love 'em, educate 'em and get 'em a good job and all this," according to Brackett, at least "until you do something they don't like and then they're the first ones to crawl down your back."[3]

Albuquerque High School secretary Justine Pas's observation that the 1968 Albuquerque controversy was "a raindrop in a national storm" of censorship debate reinforced Brackett's perception. However, her explanation of the controversy in 1968 and the contrasting relative peace at the time of her 1983 interview differed from Brackett's understanding of parental censorship activity. Pas recalled that "back in 1968 there was much more parental care of children. . . . I would just call them concerned parents: they watched what their kids read, what they were doing." For Pas, if parent involvement led to censorship activity, it was less dangerous than the quieter disengagement she found in the 1980s among parents who simply "expect the schools to take care of everything."[4]

Perceptions of parental disengagement were not, however, a phenomenon of the 1980s controversies alone. At the first school board meeting of the 1960–61 Marin County, California, controversy, board member Vincent Handy challenged protesting parents to *guide* their children's reading rather than restrict it, and condemned the lack of parental involvement. "How many of you parents actually tell your children the facts of life," Handy asked rhetorically, and then answered, "Most leave it to the school or to what they pick up in the streets. If you are going to give the school this responsibility of training these young people you are obligated to help the school, to remain firm to the standards of this country of ours, to follow up whether we are doing the right thing or the wrong thing."[5]

Implicit in Handy's statement is a certain faith that the understanding of the "standards of this country" was one that was shared by those who run the school and by parents involved in their child's education. Yet in the immediate context of the Marin controversy the lack of such a common understanding was obvious. On one end, parent and school secretary Shauna Butler lauded the understanding of parents "who wish their children to be free, and they take the position that the freedom to read, training to read, training of critical thinking is invaluable."[6] From the opposing end of the spectrum, protesting Marin County parent Kristen Keefe argued that the distribution of power was everywhere imbalanced in the high school experience (between parent and child, parent and school board, student and teacher) and called into question the possibility as much as the desirability of developing critical thinking skills in adolescents. "Young people do not yet know all of what they believe," she wrote in her open letter to the Marin County School District Board of Trustees, "the modern world and our school constantly forces them to question the beliefs of their parents." Although the students appear to "accept the authority of the school," she argued, "students aren't fools. They know that to question an assignment is to put their grades in jeopardy much less to leave them vulnerable to possible embarrassment before their classmates."[7]

In the Albuquerque controversy, Reverend Bradley Parsons echoed Keefe's sentiments, recounting the explanation of Principal Tim Yates that although "the type of influences expressed in *The Catcher in the Rye* are not beneficial influences to anyone," the reading of books like *Catcher* was "a matter of academic freedom" in that "students should have the opportunity to be exposed to them." From Parsons's viewpoint, Yates's explanation "reflected to me the kind of powerful, powerful mental programming in the school systems" that ultimately led to Parsons's founding of Albuquerque Baptist Academy in 1978 as an alternative educational institution. Parsons claimed that "this is the primary reason behind the Christian school movement: where morals are concerned, they [public schools] simply don't teach any."[8]

It is, then, not only a perceived failure of parental or educational guidance—who should do the teaching—but a confusion as to what adolescents should be taught, the absence of a shared moral standard, that is the critical factor in the *Catcher* debate. Reverend Wesley Crane, leader of the Calhoun County protest, saw this confusion to be a specifically mid-twentieth-century problem. In trying to explain why the attempt to censor *Catcher* had developed into a community controversy, he believed that the causal deterioration of individualism, family, and community was self-evident to any and all who reached maturity in the post–World War II period. Asking abruptly in the middle of our interview, "How old are you?," my answer (thirty-one at the time) led Crane to spell out this assumption in an attempt to rally my support. "Well,

I'm a good few years older than you but surely you've seen the increase in divorces in your time, people just don't seem to care anymore." "Neighbors aren't neighbors anymore, people are too willing to compromise," Crane informed me, "people don't take the time to think about what they should and shouldn't do."[9]

Reverend Crane here invokes a vision of post–World War II American society as faltering: failing to allow or to inspire a sense of purposeful engagement and personal commitment among its citizens to either the local community or the larger nation. This decline, according to Crane, was brought about and sustained by the increasing vulnerability of the individual to impersonal and often distant bureaucratic sources of power which he perceived to have come about with the end of World War II. Initially refusing to be interviewed for fear that his statements and opinions would either be misrepresented or in some way render him liable to action by "the Alabama ACLU or somebody," he told me that he had nothing to talk about with "outsiders." Crane explained that "I'm not afraid of those people [the ACLU]," but the Calhoun County controversy was nevertheless a "closed case" as far as he was concerned because "I'm afraid of the money behind them, of going to court. The books are in the libraries, with parental permission required, and as far as I'm concerned, the whole thing is over."[10]

Interestingly, another Calhoun County participant on the opposing side of the controversy also spoke of the fearfulness of local citizens in speaking out in the censorship meetings or in granting interviews. Sharing Crane's perception of individual vulnerability, pro-*Catcher* parent James Seckington observed, "Here in this area people are afraid. People who should be speaking out don't speak out." "People are concerned about their security, their jobs, and so they don't speak out—the very people who should speak out, the librarians, the English teachers," he explained, noting that because of fear of reprisal in the workplace, "most people just stay away from it."[11]

The fear of some sort of institutional retribution, whether one is inside or outside the institution, seems odd in the type of communities that make up Calhoun County. In city water district manager Bo Brackett's description, his own community appeared to be a Norman Rockwell township, given the face-to-face intimacy of membership and the cozy integration of school, church, and family among its small communities. "Everybody knows everybody, just about, by the school communities; every little school community has its own church," Brackett claimed, offering in evidence the daily life of his own family and community where "my daughter plays the piano, teaches Sunday school, plays tennis with the preacher."[12]

Calhoun County also prided itself on the success of its own public radio talk show, "Speak Out," and the local newspaper titled its daily segment of letters to the editor "Star Readers Speak Out." And speak out the listeners and readers did, although with an agreed homogeneity that frustrated citizens like James Seckington, who sought a more open exchange of ideas: "Most people that call in are very conservative, I'd say radical, I'd say 98–99 percent of the calls are very conservative so I believe it's very important for an opposite viewpoint to be brought out, to sort of balance it but they get around this. They try to drown you out because they then try to limit you to three minutes, each one of the conservatives have their three minutes and then one person who's trying to be a moderate, they like to call them a liberal. They tend to identify people in opposing ways, but I think it's important to balance it out."[13]

As the contradictory descriptions of Calhoun County mounted — Brackett's friendly neighbors or Crane's alienated residents; citizens afraid to "speak out" in a school controversy yet lauding their mass-mediated democratic forums — I began to wonder what lay behind these apparently schizophrenic perceptions of the semirural, small industrial community that for many participants had been their hometown for several generations. It seemed that although in population, size, and permanence of residency Calhoun County was a collective of close-knit communities, the residents identified with and felt their lives to be directed equally (if not primarily) by social institutions of industry, politics, religion, and consumerism on a national scale.

Two sets of examples serve to illustrate my point. First, in a county with several small churches of various (predominantly Protestant) denominations in each community, churches with congregations as intimately engaged as Bo Brackett correctly described them, participants in the censorship controversy rarely cited their personal faith or their minister's guidance in explaining their position but instead repeatedly referred to and relied upon "The Church." This voluntary reliance on an abstract amorphous institution for support and identity instead of upon local relationships and personal understandings was highlighted when participants "spoke out" in the controversies: verbally and in letters to their school boards and local newspapers, they introduced themselves in terms of their job and educational status ("as management," "as a non-management employee," "given my education," and "I'm not an educated man") rather than their actual role in the community. The second example of this external locus of identification was more simple: in the attempt to gauge the success of their community in handling the censorship controversy, participants researched and made repeated, continually updated comparisons to media accounts of controversies in other areas of the country rather than evaluating the controversy and its impact in Calhoun County itself.

Reflecting back to the controversies in Albuquerque and Marin County, we see the same privileging of institutional and national associations over either personal or community expressions of local identity is apparent. The downplaying of local identity was less surprising in these controversies given the decentralized and more fluid relationship of these residents to their geographically defined "communities": Marin County is primarily made up of suburban bedroom communities and Albuquerque, historically a shifting and underpopulated city in the midst of several tribal communities on reservation land, had only recently emerged as an "urban center" in the sprawling Southwest. The controversies themselves transpired in specific communities of place and regional identity but the primacy of institutional and national membership in the participants' sense of identity often separated them into distinct avenues of distant allegiance even as it signaled their engagement in a cultural debate.

If this reliance on external institutions for identity and validation contradicts the sense of vested local interest that participants displayed in engaging in the controversies in the first place, both sets of allegiances were in fact secondary to another, more amorphous, constituency. The largest group of participants in the *Catcher* debate identified themselves in a manner that bridged the divisions of place and social structure: as parents of potential readers of *The Catcher in the Rye*. Individual incidents of censorship "activity" translated into community debates most often because of the parents who were motivated to protest and defend their viewpoints regarding the education of their children; parents who were willing to articulate the often extravagant, unselfconscious, and painfully honest claims as to whether *Catcher* was "American" or "un-American." In experience, individuals in this group were most closely bonded in the intimacy of their local geographic communities, something which by residency they felt the right to define and protect. In identifying themselves, they highlighted their status as parents and then relied upon their institutional memberships and professional affiliations for credibility. But in their arguments, they spoke "as Americans," calling upon broad American ideals which they saw to be failing in the larger experience of contemporary society, not the least of which was democratic freedom.

"We believe we are a free people. We have been told this is so since childhood, and it is one of our most cherished convictions." These are the words of librarian John Robotham, arguing in 1982 for the freedom of access to library materials. "Freedom" is here placed at the very heart of American enculturation, a faith that traces back into a personal state of innocence, and consequently becomes a framing concept that shapes the adult perceptions of many Americans. In exactly this sense, the bittersweet power of this statement lies in the implication that contemporary freedom exists as an article of faith (we are free if/because we believe we are) more so than as a course of action. As to the actuality of democratic experience, Robotham went on to describe his fellow Americans as "something resembling automatons, obeying [institutional] dictates and saluting mythical freedoms."[14]

To the contrary, in the cultural debate over *The Catcher in the Rye* the unifying factor among participants was not their salutation to mythical freedoms but their attempt to enact the belief that we are a free people. Each participant entered into the debate in the first place because of their individual allegiances to an "American way of life" that they wished to sustain and perceived to be endangered. Putting aside for a moment their differing explanations of the source(s) of endangerment, it is significant that in the face of their expressed alienation from the leadership of institutional powers and the federal government, and their parallel experience of regulation and constraint by these very forces, these participants felt called upon and able to act, to seek expression and representation of their beliefs in a public forum. Nor was the significance of their actions missed by the participants themselves: at the conclusion of many controversies, participants were less concerned with the final status of *The Catcher in the Rye* than they were pleased with their own participation in and renewed sense of a democratic community.

Consider first the suspicions of opposing participants Bo Brackett and James Seckington. Bo Brackett believed that "everybody's entitled to state their opinion, but most people don't get involved until it becomes something that's goin' to affect my child or my thing" yet wished that when people did get involved they would have done so through bureaucratic channels and not "raised a ruckus."[15] In this instance, Brackett expresses wonder at the apathy or self-concerned involvement of members

of his local community at the same time that he implicitly supports a
paternalistic authoritarianism in local government. This contradiction
was not missed by James Seckington, who spoke of his lifelong experience as one of Calhoun County's few outspoken, and hence identifiable,
liberals. In a moment of self-reflection, Seckington told me that although
"the main thing to me is respect; tolerance for someone else's viewpoint,
other than their own," he felt this was a belief that his fellow citizens did
not share: "I've been asked why I don't leave the country and stuff like
this, where I would always protect their viewpoints whereas they're not
willing to protect mine."[16]

Even so, it was Bo Brackett who expressed most fully the realization
of many participants, for and against *Catcher*—and in nearly every controversy—that respect and tolerance are the necessary requirements of
a democratic society. Prefacing his remarks with the defensive caveat
that "I'm not an educated man," Brackett summarized his observations
of and his feelings about the Calhoun County controversy:

> Personally, if it was my decision and it was going to be a final decision,
> I'd have a bonfire. But, you know, I know, I don't have a final decision
> and I've got to use some reason too, and a parent wants their children
> to read things I consider vulgary or trash, that's the parent that'll have
> to answer, that'll have to watch that child. The Constitution gives cer-
> tain rights and you can't just sweep those things under the mat. That's
> why I said, you know, if I had to be objective I'd get rid of 'em: if I had
> the final say, they wouldn't be here but I know that's not the final say
> and I don't say it, that's not the way it's going to be. So, the only solu-
> tion I know is what we did. It's, aaah, they're still available. The parent
> wants to do it, go read 'em.[17]

Such successful realizations of the democratic process might be
heartening, but they do not soothe or answer the deep concern that generated the striking degree and range of individual participation in the
Catcher debate. Bearing in mind the view of American society as declin-
ing and deeply contradictory, as examined in *The Catcher in the Rye* and
as shared by both protesting and defending participants, the question
remains: what version of adult society do we wish to share with our children if we are to pass on our ideals and beliefs and equally prepare them
for the complex experience of membership in contemporary American
society? On this level the debate remains, like *The Catcher in the Rye*
itself, unresolved.

The opening chapters of this book examined the perceptions of a number of social critics and historians that American "innocence" was threatened, if not wholly lost, in the post–World War II period. Literary critics expressed a strong sense of identification and purpose within their own community, however, as they generally refrained from engagement or concern with the public readership—appreciative or hostile— few literary analyses of *The Catcher in the Rye* acknowledged the controversial reception and history of the novel. The interest for literary critics clearly lay in the work of art itself and perhaps in the writer as artist, which left them at once integrated as a professional community yet alienated from the concerns of the broader American public.

Indeed, contemporary American society appears divided against itself as Americans have come to define themselves in primarily subcultural avenues. Each community of participants expressed frustration with the felt gap between the internal coherence of their own group beliefs and the apparent incoherence of broader public beliefs as well as the seemingly monolithic dominance of institutional rulings which governed them. In the fourth chapter, the parallel arguments of those who led the participant communities of the *Catcher* debate have demonstrated that the New Right, the librarians and the educators equally shared the perception of contemporary American society as chaotic, alienating and, at best, confused as to moral standards—a "value-free" society. At worst, they perceived American society as utterly failing. Spokespersons for each group challenged their membership to lead the quest for the reinstatement of "the truth" of American experience but a lack of clarity as to what that truth is, much less agreement as to how it ought to be carried forward, has tempered the success of all.

Religious and local community leaders approached the debate with positions appropriate to their own commitments—moral guardianship and civic responsibility in terms of the necessary censorship of materials such as *The Catcher in the Rye* which might undermine the character of the American youth. Social activists, such as representatives of Common Cause and the American Civil Liberties Union (both anticensorship) and Citizens for Decent Literature (procensorship), equally expressed a profound sense of purpose rooted in both democratic and Christian ideals, albeit with a vastly different interpretation and focus on those ideals. The "liberal" or anticensorship activists saw their social responsibility to be one of maintaining equal value and balance between the often opposing interests of individual freedom and social tolerance of the rights of others. The "conservative" or procensorship activists argued that individual rights and social tolerance alike were secondary consequences of "American freedom," expressed in terms of the primacy of Christianity and capitalism. Given their very definition as either local leaders or outside representatives, participants from each of these communities (religious, civic, social activist) essentially stood outside the community of place.

Educators and librarians participated in the debates over *Catcher* primarily from the perspective of their respective disciplinary communities—both relying heavily upon the First Amendment in the argument for intellectual freedom. Like the literary critics, these participants enjoyed a stable source of identity and expression through their membership in their respective professional communities. However, they also expressed an equal, if not primary, allegiance to the interests of their community of residence. The consequence was that, structurally speaking, these participants were at once the most fully integrated members of American society to participate in the debate and often the most deeply conflicted.

Nor are these perceptions limited to the intellectuals, or the leadership and articulate membership of religious and professional associations. That the tradition of the American jeremiad is so evident and suasive in the political rhetoric of our own time indicates the chasm between "what is" and "what ought to be" in American society—a chasm recognized by politician and potential voter alike. Somewhat paradoxically, I find the marked apathy of the near-half of American voters who have relinquished their vote throughout this period to suggest that the jeremiad has become so credible as to lose its power to inspire action: we recognize the failing mission and no longer believe it can be saved.

Even in the immediate postwar period of the 1950s, American thought and action expressed not the confidence of the victorious but the introversion of the frightened. Here, the feelings of Manhattan Project physicist and Nobel Laureate Isidor Rabi are paradigmatic: "grateful for the bomb and its success," upon Japan's surrender he still "could not bring himself to open the bottle of Johnny Walker Black he had laid away for a victory toast."[18] As individuals and as a nation, we found security in adjustment, accommodation, and conformity; we took comfort in isolation and self-focused contemplation.[19] When we looked up again in the early 1960s we experienced, in historian Laurence Vesey's words, "a new sense of flatness as we viewed the world scene and our place in it."[20]

Historians and social scientists of the post–World War II period have attributed this leveling of the ever-hopeful American vision to several factors. Some scholars privilege a single factor while others see many factors working in concert: in any case, there is common recognition of their impact upon American ideology and experience. As a review of these factors will demonstrate, their recognition has been inescapable, if unpleasant, for much of the American public and particularly for the primarily white, Anglo-Saxon, Protestant, middle-class participants in the debate over *The Catcher in the Rye*.[21]

~

The triple "discoveries" of poverty, racism, and sexism in the 1960s challenged the idealized vision of postwar America as a society of equality and opportunity for all. Certainly this was no surprise to the poor themselves, nor to Americans of color—nor particularly to those who wielded even moderate power in American life. If "America" was shocked at the incontrovertible evidence of inequality and injustice, it was the insular WASP middle class of America for whom the shock was perhaps genuine. The consequential activism of young middle-class Americans, rooted more in the persistence of American idealism than in rejection of it, was understood as open rebellion by many of the mature middle class and contributed to the sensation that America was "coming apart."

This renewed recognition of American pluralism and the growing political strength of the more organized subcultures (particularly those of black Americans and women) led to significant gains in the battle against poverty and discrimination by the 1970s. However, the accompanying acknowledgment of the divided or segmented nature of contemporary American society raised the question of in what way were we unified as a nation, and whether there was, after all, such a thing as "mainstream" America. This question was highlighted in the peace marches and antiwar protests generated by America's involvement in Vietnam.

Questions of conscience as to the morality of war and practical questions as to the reasons for and expectations of military involvement were not unknown in past American experience nor deemed necessarily unpatriotic. Yet in the Vietnam era, these questions at once flourished and appeared especially threatening in the context of the broader question of the relationship of any given individual to the nation he was being asked to risk his life for. At least partly in response to this question, President Richard Nixon declared that there was indeed a heartland deserving of patriotic service, a majority of America of common experience and value: they were merely silent. Less than fifteen years later, New Right leader Jerry Falwell claimed to speak for the "moral majority" of America as he reaffirmed that America was indivisible through its pledged unity under God.

If the claims of unity among either a silent or a moral majority remain unsubstantiated, a different sense of unity is evident among contemporary Americans: in the postwar period, we can be said to share equally in what I have referred to earlier as a wizened view of American culture, in which our status as a unique society or even a very moral one is uncertain. In external contrasts, our standard of living remains high but is not unknown among other nations; our military strength, technological development, and industrial production are no longer without parallel; in education and the provision of social services we are surpassed by not a few nations.

Internally, Vietnam, Watergate, and the continuing succession of national political and institutional scandals throughout the 1980s and 1990s have taken a tremendous toll upon public confidence in American leadership.[22] Sissela Bok has argued in *Lying: Moral Choice in Public and Private Life* (1978) that "deception is taken for granted when it is felt to be excusable by those who tell the lies and who also tend to make the rules."[23] Noting that a 1975–76 Cambridge Survey found 69 percent of the respondents in agreement with the statement that "over the last ten years, this country's leaders have consistently lied to the people," Bok further summarized a 1976 Harris opinion poll: "The loss of confidence reaches far beyond government leadership. From 1966 to 1976, the proportion of people answering yes to whether they had a great deal of confidence in people in charge of running major institutions dropped from 73 percent to 44 percent for medicine; for major companies from 55 percent to 16 percent; for law firms from 24 percent (1973) to 12 percent; and for advertising agencies from 21 percent to 7 percent."[24]

While we might not expect to place our trust in advertising, we did previously expect to do so in regard to political and professional leadership. And our confidence in our fellow man seems not to have fared much better: in the popular journal *Psychology Today,* a critic of social science ethics argued that "these tricks (of social science research methods) simply strengthen the growing conviction that you can't trust people that you don't know. If a mugger doesn't hit you, a credit checker doesn't spy on you … a social scientist will dupe you."[25]

If Americans, then, can be said to have little confidence in their fellow men, much less in their leadership, our depressed confidence in ourselves as individual participants in society has dealt the greatest blow to the vision of American exceptionalism. The size and diversity of the American population, geographic mobility and the rapidity of social change in combination with the post–World War II "unifying" factors of bureaucratic organization and the mass media have called the meaning of individualism into question. Individual freedom and independence of thought and action are meaningful only when one has a grasp of the world one seeks to understand and act in as well as a sense that one's thoughts and actions are of consequence beyond the self. That this is not the case in postwar American society is evident in the commonplace expressions of apathy and alienation: that we cannot manage the barrage of information available to us, trustworthy or not; that we lack power or influence in the machinations of society; that, as individuals, we simply do not matter. The following image of contemporary America conjured by librarian John Robotham is most effective in its clichéd familiarity and its location in a middle-class context: "Concurrent with the disbelief in reason is the belief that individualism is no longer possible — even, perhaps, not desireable, that society so molds us that we merely run with the herd.... It is also easy to share this view of our society.... The suburban street with the blue spruce planted squarely in the middle of every front yard, and with every television set turned on and tuned to the same situation comedy, is only the most obvious sign that mass communications and mass consumerism are turning us into a country of think-alikes."[26]

The point here is that even as the costly loss of individualism furthers perceptions of the dwindling vitality of American society, it contributes to a behavioral unity in which there is an identifiable "mainstream" experience. In a similar vein, historian Laurence Vesey has argued that if "the hefty shadow of the bureaucratic organization" has dwarfed the solitary figure of individualism in the postwar period, it has also guaranteed "that American society does not suffer crucially from a lack of form or structure." Vesey then cautioned those writing consensus history as to "how little we can say about growing up in America, beyond the elementary fact of the need to come to terms with big organizations, that will apply to nearly everybody."[27] It is the fragmented nature of postwar American experience that is once again highlighted even in the attempt to credit its structural unity.

Vesey sought to define the "national character" of postwar Americans by isolating "what it presumably meant to grow up here rather than somewhere else."[28] His assumption that the American character could be isolated in a study of the early phases of the developmental process is not unusual in American historiography; it does suggest why novels that focus on adolescence and young adulthood such as *The Catcher in the Rye* are a potential source of concern and dispute. In fact, as Vesey located postwar idealism in the "youth scene" and equated maturity with "settling down" and accommodation, it was a characterization of American experience that was shared—and rejected—by J. D. Salinger via Holden Caulfield. Yet historical accounts of the post–World War II period such as Vesey's are rarely the target of controversy and censorship. Aside from the obvious distinction between the reading and writing of descriptive history and of arguably proscriptive fiction, a reconsideration of *The Catcher in the Rye* as a primary cultural document sheds further light on its controversial status.

~

The Catcher in the Rye was discussed earlier as an exemplary novel within the tradition of the cultural mythology of the American Adam. Where Holden is readily recognizable as the classic Adamic character, "the individual going forth toward experience, the inventor of his own character and creator of his personal history; the self-moving individual who is made to confront that 'other'—the world or society,"[29] *Catcher* also reflects the impact of the historical conditions of the post–World War II period upon the Adamic tradition. The sense of absurdity and futility of any contemporary quest is evident not only in Holden's near continual confusion and frustration as he seeks the genuine enactment of American ideals of liberty, justice, and equality but also in the Sisyphusian circularity of the novel: it ends as it begins, with no resolution. Any hopefulness exists simply in Holden's sustained resolve to continue the circuit. This confrontation with the hopeless contemporary condition of the hopeful American character is both unavoidable and truly bothersome for those readers who reject *The Catcher in the Rye*—and particularly so because Holden as hero is not a juvenile delinquent, or a "sorry little worm" but "a normal specimen of his age," a familiar adolescent.

I speak here not only of reader familiarity with adolescence based in the experience of adults responsible for the guidance of real-life adolescents. While the American Adam has generally been characterized in a somewhat more mature state, perhaps the most familiar and cherished Adamic hero is yet another adolescent: Mark Twain's Huck Finn. In celebration of *Huckleberry Finn's* 1985 centennial, *Newsweek* commentator George Will wrote that the tale "resonates in America's heart because it is about freedom understood in a distinctively American way, as the absence of social restraints, and obedience to the promptings of a pure heart." "To be free" in Twain's America, Will noted, was to be "footloose in a pathless wilderness, unbounded by geography or history, utterly unconstrained by social bonds."[30]

The resonance of Huck's story in the heart of Holden Caulfield is evident in Holden's dream of hitchhiking West, escaping society by living in an isolated cabin as a voluntary deaf-mute. There is however, a greater parallel between the two novels, apparent in Will's characterization of Huck in postwar terms. Arguing that "pessimism about the ability of Americans to measure up to America's promise is, in a way, Twain's theme," Will pointed out that "authenticity" and "self-realization" are achieved outside or against society, not through it: "Huck is—dare I say it?—an 'alienated' 14 year old."[31]

This statement could stand equally as well for Salinger's theme and characterization of Holden Caulfield in *The Catcher in the Rye,* and it is significant that the "alienation," as well as the action, in both novels is rooted in the attempt to maintain idealism in the face of maturity. When R. W. B. Lewis wrote of "the American habit of resistance to maturity," he described it as a series of "repeated efforts to revert to a lost childhood and a vanished Eden, and issuing repeatedly in a series of outcries at the freshly discovered capacity of the world to injure."[32]

The adolescent, then, would seem to be particularly suited to the embodiment of the American Adam: passing through a developmental stage that allows idealistic rebellion against mature society, in full literary exploitation of this peculiarly American resistance, yet implicitly reassuring the reader that the Adamic character will in fact "grow up" and perhaps carry his idealism forward into society. This is certainly true in the case of *Huckleberry Finn.* Even as Huck wishes to "light out for the territories," he is not only moving forward in time and space but he has already matured in the course of the novel with his idealism ultimately strengthened through the challenge of experience.

The Catcher in the Rye is quite another case, and differs in ways that at least partially explain its controversial status. Holden, like Huck, is "an Adamic person, springing from nowhere, outside time, at home only in the presence of nature and God, who is thrust by circumstances into an actual world and an actual age,"[33] but where Huck is thrust into being in the expansionist nineteenth century, Holden is a child of the contracting mid-twentieth. The consequence is that for all the parallel nature of their quests, Holden is only able to fantasize about escaping society, his idealism is the cause of his downfall, however staunchly he seeks to defend it, and perhaps most importantly, he is unable to resolve what his future course of action should be.

In this sense, Holden has much more in common with the mature characters conceived by Salinger's contemporaries such as Saul Bellow and John Updike. Writing of the essentially static quests and contexts of frustration that characterized the work of American writers following World War II, literary historian David Madden asked—and answered—"What was left in the fifties? A dominant school of personal sensibility and superior entertainment … writers who are always leading up to something that never happens and never can happen."[34] While adult readers could assumedly appreciate if not "enjoy" the nightmare version of the Adamic struggle carried out by their fictional peers in contemporary literature, the awareness of Holden's adolescence—which the reader was constantly reminded of *by his use of adolescent slang and profane language*—was jarring and unnerving to adult readers of *The Catcher in the Rye*.

Among those who have ventured to comment on the nature of postwar America—scholars, critics, artists of both popular and elite productions, politicians, and citizens alike—the phrase "American Nightmare" (and its gentler expression "American reality") has become nearly as commonplace as the generative phrase to which it corresponds, "American Dream." These phrases have so come to represent a dualism in the cultural imagination rather than a singularly understood vision that even when not explicitly paired, the use of one implies tacit recognition of the existence of the other. In one sense, these phrases appropriately distinguish between cultural ideals and realities which in the post–World War II period have become increasingly distanced. In another sense they encapsulate particular understandings of American culture: two opposing mythologies of American experience, coexisting as expressions of past and present contexts.

The originating vision, generated in colonialist hopes for both spiritual and secular gain, is the mythos of American exceptionalism. Ideologically valuing liberty, justice, and equality above all, in this telling of "the dream" America began and remains ethnocentrically superior and destined to guide the world as a democratic nation of regenerative innocence, selfless individualism, and consequent ingenuity.[35] The presentist vision is the horrific storyline of the immediate historical moment: a long-standing alternative mythos with period-specific revisions and emphases, it is a commonly explicated understanding of American experience in which reality is viewed as a "nightmare." In the postwar period, the presentist vision has focused on extremes of social order and chaos, individual alienation and increasing conformity, monolithic unity and

fracturing multiculturalism, and the threat of impending nuclear annihilation wrought by our own technological ingenuity. The presentist
mythology is necessary to maintain cultural sanity as the gap between
ideals and realities, belief and behavior, widens instead of drawing closer.
Our repeated exclamations of the awfulness of our present historical
moment serve as reassurances that it is, after all, just that: a terrible
moment in an exceptional history to which we will return or go forward
as we have always done.

Herein lies the crux of the cultural debate. Do we hold "the dream,"
the originating myth of exceptionalism, as a nostalgic vision of an idealized time that we might somehow recover if we only have faith enough
and wait out the aberrant present, or do we see it as an inspirational
vision cut short by waking realities, a dream that we might still achieve
if we use it as the critical standard by which we evaluate our past as well
as our present actions? In this context, *The Catcher in the Rye* serves as a
cultural Rorschach test for much of middle America by actively engaging the originating and presentist visions: the dream and the nightmare
and both their nostalgic and inspirational readings. As the debate is
resolved, over and over again in each discrete controversy, we find that we
are not in fact cultural schizophrenics. We respond with nearly uniform,
shared understandings of both cultural myths, and what appeared to be
psychosis becomes instead a set of coping behaviors: oppositional courses
of action undertaken in the common effort to manage both visions.

"Interpretation is not an isolated act," wrote Frederic Jameson in the
preface to *The Political Unconscious: Narrative as a Socially Symbolic Act,*
"but takes place within a Homeric battlefield, on which a host of interpretive options are either openly or implicitly in conflict."[36] So it is that
the censorship controversies over *The Catcher in the Rye,* with their
opposing interpretations of its significance conceptualized here as a cultural debate, have taken place in the context of numerous other struggles
and contests in American public life. In *Habits of the Heart,* Robert Bellah and his colleagues chronicled the struggles of individual American
citizens "devoted to defending the moral beliefs and practices of his or
her community in the face of a permissive therapeutic culture" and captured the angst of these "concerned citizens" when they were faced with
"the decisions of administrators and managers that do not understand,
and are not answerable to, local community feeling." However heartened
by the individual displays of independent citizenry found among his
interviewees, as he concluded the text in 1981 Bellah remained fearful

of "the erosion of meaning and coherence" in contemporary American life. For as long as the American sense of individualism remains rooted in "biblical and republican traditions of which we seldom consciously think," those traditions are in danger of being crushed between "the upper millstone of a fragmented intellectual culture and the nether millstone of a fragmented popular culture," and along with them, the civic-minded individualism they inspire.[37]

Bellah's text arguably exposes the philosophical and experiential underpinnings of what has come to be referred to as the "culture wars" of post–World War II America. "America is in the midst of a culture war," according to James Davison Hunter: a war between "the impulse toward orthodoxy and the impulse toward progressivism" and one "that has had and will continue to have reverberations not only within public policy but within the lives of ordinary Americans everywhere." Profiling six representative case studies of individual struggle, Hunter argued that "the nub of political disagreement today on the range of issues debated" falls outside of historic differences of religious authority. These disagreements, in Hunter's view, are actually debates over "the matter of moral authority," which he clarified to mean "the basis by which people determine whether something is good or bad, right or wrong, acceptable or unacceptable, and so on."[38] If Hunter's sweeping sense of the contest between orthodox and progressive impulses here parallels the differing perceptions of American experience as held in the exceptionalist and presentist visions, other recent studies have drawn more specific outlines of both the opponents in these culture wars and the objects of their struggle—and the education of children is found to be the primary battleground.[39]

In illustration, consider cognitive scientist George Lakoff's analysis of the divisions in contemporary American politics. Lakoff's study began as a response to a friend's suggestion that how people answer the question "If your baby cries at night, do you pick him up," might be "the single best indicator of liberal vs. conservative political attitudes." Lakoff's resulting argument in *Moral Politics: What Conservatives Know That Liberals Don't* was that political commitments could best be understood in relation to parenting styles. "Conservatism . . . is based on a Strict Father model, while liberalism is centered around a nurturant model," wrote Lakoff, and the fundamental differences between the two are most evident in their definition of a moral educational system.[40]

A moral education in conservative or "Strict Father" terms was identified by Lakoff as one that teaches "the conservative notion of character, starting with self-discipline," and that sets standards "based on the classics of Western culture that are tried and true and have withstood the test of time." For the liberal or "Nurturant Parent," Lakoff found that a moral education "requires honest inquiry" into the "dark side" of American history as much as into the "bright side." "We must learn the dark side partly so that we will not repeat it," Lakoff explained, and "partly so that we will not be self-righteous."[41]

It is not hard to imagine here which of Lakoff's political parenting categories correspond to which sides of the controversies over *The Catcher in the Rye*. As we have seen, among those who wished to censor *Catcher*, Salinger's characterization of Holden Caulfield has been criticized for his lack of self-discipline whereas those who fought against censorship took appreciative note of his "honest inquiry" into postwar life—including his exposure of its "dark side." That the education of children continues to be a primary site of cultural contest is in itself evidence that American adults are unable to reach agreement as to who we are as a culture: what we believe and have believed about ourselves, what we have done and what we should raise our children to do.

The position of participants who opposed the adolescent reading of *The Catcher in the Rye* was, at bottom, an attempt to manage the split between cherished ideals and behavioral reality by housing them in distinctly separated developmental phases, each with its appropriate mythos. As adults we may experience disappointment, alienation, and cynicism as to the meaning of our membership in contemporary American society, laboring under the presentist vision, but we sustain ourselves through the knowledge contained in our heart of hearts, established in the innocence of childhood: that we, the American people, are just, free, and equal because we believe we are. This split allows the accommodation of the idealistic individual to the "adulteries" of post–World War II American society, and hence, is the model that is seen by many to be "the American way." *Catcher*, then, is "un-American" in its open recognition and criticism of this split, and censorship is as much an attempt to protect the sanctity of the originating myth as to protect adolescents from premature exposure to postwar realities.

By contrast, those who defended adolescent reading of *The Catcher in the Rye*—and not simply on the basis of the First Amendment—sought an avenue for the integration of belief and action, even at the cost of change or rebellion against the established contemporary order. Equally troubled by the increasingly horrific vision of postwar America, they believe that we may take the originating mythos as instructive, a source of inspiration through which the errors of the past and present might be recalled and judged and the future redirected toward a reconciliation of ideals and behavior. In the struggle to comprehend our contemporary morass in the unforgiving light of our stated ideals of liberty, justice, and equality, *Catcher* appears as a paradigmatic tale for adults and as a preparatory text for adolescents who embody the future.

Jane Tompkins, in her acclaimed text *Sensational Designs: The Cultural Work of American Fiction, 1790–1860,* asked that scholars seeking to understand literature as a cultural document pay attention to "the way a text offers a blueprint for survival under a specific set of political, economic, social or religious conditions." In doing so, she argued, scholars would find that "an entirely new story begins to unfold" as "the text succeeds or fails on the basis of its 'fit' with the features of its immediate context, on the degree to which it provokes the desired response."[42] I believe that *The Catcher in the Rye* succeeds in its portrayal of post–World War II American society: the "catcher in the rye" itself is, after all, only another of Holden's escape fantasies, and the lack of any real resolution in the novel seems an appropriate recognition of our apparent willingness to walk right over the "crazy cliff" of innocent idealism, plunge into the realities of adult experience, and survive through the killing adjustments of the late twentieth century.

However, if the novel can be said to fail, it is for Salinger's persistent and eloquent appeal for the restoration and genuine enactment of liberty, equality, and justice through individual engagement in the democratic process to continue to be read as an "un-American" narrative. This failure indicates not a lack of "fit" but rather a fearful limitation of the contemporary American imagination. The nature of that limitation, as initially revealed by the participants in the debate, is the subject of the final chapter: a meditation on the cultural impact of America's development and first use of the atomic bomb.

Afterword
In Cold Fear

"Every hour so many things in the sky!" said Montag. "How did those bombers get up there every single second of our lives! Why doesn't someone want to talk about it! We've started and won two atomic wars. Is it because we're having so much fun at home we've forgotten the world?... I've heard the rumors about hate, too, once in a long while, over the years. Do you know why? I don't, that's sure! Maybe the books can get us half out of the cave. They just might stop us from making the same insane mistakes!"

— Ray Bradbury, *Fahrenheit 451*

Among other things, humankind is distinguished by the imaginative ability to develop abstract conceptualizations of desirable states, reason them into a course of actions, and consequently "progress" toward a future in which reality comes to ever more closely approximate the ideal. In the Second World War, America reached and has since passed a point of disjuncture where imagination for a moment exceeded reason, and ingenuity allowed an expedient course of action that was in fact at odds not only with ideals of liberty and justice but with deeply held beliefs in the innocence and regenerative nature of the American spirit. Our general unwillingness, out of guilt and fear, to acknowledge this excess has created an expanding rupture between our ideals and our continued actions which is the antithesis of progress.

These conclusions were reached with the unintentional guidance of my interview participants, as their words redirected my initial understanding of my research materials. As participants in the cultural debate over *The Catcher in the Rye* share (although with very different responses) in the dual mythologies of past exceptionalism and present tribulations, so do they share a vague yet pervasive sense of fearfulness regarding the present and future of American society, if not all of humankind. When asked what he thought was at the root of the 1960–61 Marin County controversy over *Catcher*, former high school principal Kyle Russo simplified the repeated response of numerous participants in each controversy when he answered, "I think it just stems from fear."[1]

Russo's response was also typical of other participants in his inability to expand upon or articulate the actual nature or source of this fear. Instead, he fell into a meditative silence for a few minutes and then abruptly began to speak of how the specific issue of *Catcher*'s status had been resolved—or, as he put it, "controlled"—by the school board. While the statements of many debate participants suggest that they were more comfortable speaking of the ways they manage their uneasiness regarding the fate of present and future American society rather than the basis or origin of their disquiet, a few participants either directly specified or alluded to the threat of nuclear annihilation—often in seemingly incongruous contexts. Midway through his interview, pro-*Catcher* parent James Seckington of Calhoun County suddenly stated that there were "so many other areas of concern, that censorship is just a small part of it, because there is the nuclear, the school prayer, [long pause/sigh], all that goes together."[2] Some twenty years earlier in Marin County, pro-*Catcher* parent Linaus Tyla connected education and free speech to survival "in these perilous times," arguing in the open school board and community meeting that "it is not just a case of war and peace but a question of the survival of mankind and our ideals. We have to educate our children to become responsible citizens."[3]

If many of the participants in the *Catcher* debate were unable or unwilling to explain their perceptions, their behavior does not make the context of fearfulness any less real or significant. Fearfulness was the common denominator and often the dominant characteristic of every interview I conducted. Sometimes vague and at other times specific in their responses, with fears that were either narrowly focused or expressed in a more general anxiety as to "the future," the participants I talked with came across as a frightened people, silent as a consequence of their perceived impotence in influencing their future more than of true apathy. Indeed, it is in the persistent shadowed perception of "these perilous times" that the juxtaposition of "the nuclear" and school prayer—of education, annihilation, and a yearning for faith—becomes logical. Whether through an education including active reevaluation as argued for by the defenders of *The Catcher in the Rye* or through sheer faith and prayer as embraced by many who challenged *Catcher*, "all that goes together" in the common perception of a dire future for America and the world should we continue as we have since the development and first use of the atomic bomb in 1945.

That it is the threat of nuclear annihilation that looms large in the American imagination is evident in the arguments of those who have sought to define or describe contemporary American experience, whether broad-gauge or in terms of the specific context of censorship. In addition to the nuclear imagery of literary and social historians addressed in the first chapter of this text, passing references in the works of many scholars to the omnipotent presence of "the bomb" suggest its indelible impact upon the American psyche. Writing on American culture in the 1950s, social historian Stephen Whitfield noted "the incessant peril of the bomb" and referred later to "its ominous presence."[4] Historian Laurence Vesey, writing of the organizational bureaucracy that structures contemporary experience, argued that the "military side" of the government bureaucracy "reminds everyone who nowadays emerges into consciousness that we live in a world whose rhythms may at any time be roughly broken into or obliterated in an instant flash—even if we had better not let our minds become too depressed by this possible scenario."[5]

Vesey's argument appeared in Leonard Dinnerstein and Kenneth Jackson's 1979 historical survey *American Vistas: 1877 to the Present*. In the introduction, Dinnerstein and Jackson revealed the assumed preeminence of the nuclear threat by distinguishing themselves as members of "the first generation to have lived under the threat of atomic holocaust."[6] Such qualifying phrases are frequent in scholarship on contemporary America. Their presence suggests that even as we may not be able to define and discuss the impact of nuclear developments in any specific form, their magnitude demands acknowledgment before the scholar can address more manageable material and arguments. Tellingly, the very language of contemporary scholarship reflects a nuclear consciousness among critics such as Irving Howe, who, in *A World More Attractive* (1963), used the term "atomized" to characterize the mass experience of post–World War II American society.[7]

Equally common is the notion that Americans who have come to maturity since World War II form a crucial generation. In "The Prospects for the Future," an essay written in 1970 for the American Library Association, publisher Dan Lacy argued that while "every generation has felt that it lived at the very hinge of time, when all civilization was changing and entering a brave new world," Americans in the postwar period "have, perhaps, more reason to feel this than any other."[8] Lacy's justification of the unique status of contemporary Americans was based upon the condition that the "human capacity to determine fate has never been anything remotely as potential as it is now." The critical nature of our moment lay, for Lacy, in the imbalance between positive advancements such as space exploration and the lethal capacity "to poison the atmosphere so as to destroy all life on earth." Lacy's own share in the fearfulness and hopelessness of the nuclear conscience was made clear when he pointed out that the benefit of space exploration was "to escape the whole prison of the earthly planet."

When he wrote his essay, Lacy was the senior vice-president of the McGraw-Hill Book Company. Not surprisingly, his position was reflected in his reliance "at such a hinge of time" on his reading of post–World War II scholarship and "the liberal education of those of us who share the power of decision, which now means most of us," as sources that have "assume[d] a peculiar importance" in posing solutions and offering sheer sustenance.[9] This relationship between education and annihilation was echoed by librarian Charles Park in his essay "The Censorship War: Librarians at the Battlefront." Here, the need for a liberal education in this critical period first parallels Lacy's statement, with Park writing that "the freedom to learn, to have access to information, is being threatened today." In the very next sentence, however, Park puts ambiguity to rest as he draws a specific picture of the threat: "The stakes are higher, higher than ever before, for we are all very much in the shadow of a mushroom cloud."[10]

Park's invocation of the specter of nuclear annihilation in the circumstance of censorship is unusual only in its frankness, and his depiction of a pervading atmosphere of nuclearism is accurate. In his 1988 treatise *Nuclear Fear*, historian Spencer Weart argued that while in general "the images we cherish have a greater role in history than has commonly been thought," with America's development and use of atomic weapons, mythic images of cultural annihilation "acquired a new power because hardware had been purposefully brought into realms once inhabited only by myth."[11]

As noted in the introduction to this study, historian Paul Boyer shares these sentiments, and his book, *By the Bomb's Early Light*, is invaluable in its documentation of the pervasive impact of the bomb upon the cultural imagination as he seeks to understand how "a people react[s] when the entire basis of its existence is fundamentally altered."[12] In his argument detailing the reactive cycles of activism and apathy, Boyer found

American reaction to the use and continued development of nuclear weaponry to sway or cycle from periods of active promotion and protest to periods of "sharp decline in culturally expressed engagement with the issue"[13] and back again. To explain the apathetic periods, Boyer offered four prevailing reasons: (1) "the illusion of a diminished risk" (based in the appearance of control through arms-limitation negotiations and treaties); (2) "the loss of immediacy" of concern as the existence of nuclear weapons has become an assumption and other concerns such as the war in Vietnam have taken precedence; (3) "the promise of a world transformed by atomic energy," emphasizing the positive uses of nuclear energy; and (4) "the complexity and comfort of deterrence theory" in which security has lain in maintenance and advancement of our nuclear superiority.[14]

Important as these cycles of overt reaction to the bomb may be, I believe they draw attention away from the more significant aspect of Boyer's work: the impact of the bomb upon the cultural imagination, including the generation of a new category or structuring of human experience. Boyer himself explained the difficulty of American writers in coming to terms with the bomb in literary expression, a difficulty in which "silence may have signaled not a failure of imagination, but an intensity of imagination—a recognition of the folly of too quickly trying to assimilate this monstrous novelty."[15]

Actually, an "intensity of imagination" is required for the public's very extension of credibility to the four illusions that allow the apathetic phases of nuclear response. I say four illusions here because although Boyer identified only the first notion of diminished risk as an illusion, the second, "loss of immediacy"; third, "promise of a world transformed"; and fourth, "comfort of deterrence theory" can be seen as illusions that require a willing if not desperate imaginative state to gain plausibility in the first place. In this vein, Stephen Whitfield's earlier take on the conformity and cynicism of the 1950s as a period of "recoil from innocence" can be seen as an attempt to explain the same recoil from activism that Boyer has identified while sustaining, indeed relying upon, the bomb's imaginative impact. "To recoil from innocence was to have ventured, at least vicariously," Whitfield argued, "to the edge of the abyss, to be burdened with images and ideas which were shaped by the perception of inscrutable evil."[16]

The imagery of Whitfield's statement once again recalls the central passage in *The Catcher in the Rye,* which gives title to the novel. In his innocence, Holden Caulfield has ventured up to the "crazy cliff" at the end of adolescence—the moment where one's idealistic stance suddenly appears groundless in the view of the bottom reality of adult society. Yet Holden's response is not a recoil from the innocence in which his ideals were founded but a recoil from the maturation process, the killing adjustments of twentieth-century life, through which they would be broken. By the mid-1980s, cultural critics Robert Bellah and Christopher Lasch were documenting the erosion of meaning and coherence in post–World War II society, the uncertainty as to how to preserve or create a morally coherent life, and the absence of a shared moral standard. "The hope that political action will gradually humanize industrial society has largely given way," Lasch wrote in his 1984 study *The Minimal Self*, "to a determination to survive the general wreckage or, more modestly, to hold one's life together in the face of mounting pressures."[17]

Meanwhile, the precise nature of the "inscrutable evil" of the abyss had already been given definition by American poet Robert Lowell. In a 1965 interview, Lowell reiterated the role of the mythology of American exceptionalism in widening the chasm between long-standing ideals and contemporary actions in the Cuban missile crisis: "We were founded on a Declaration, on the Constitution, on Principles, and we've always had the idea of 'saving the world.' And that comes close to destroying the world. Suddenly it is, [the] really terrible nightmare has come true, that we are suddenly in a position where we might destroy the world, and that is very closely allied to saving it. . . . It is the Ahab story of having to murder evil: and you may murder all the good with it if it gets desperate enough to struggle."[18]

In an even earlier recognition of this grave cultural contradiction, Manhattan Project physicist and Noble Laureate Hans Bethe had questioned President Truman's announcement in early 1950 that development of the "hydrogen superbomb" would proceed. Emphasizing the disparity between the fundamental basis of American ideals and the current course of nuclear action, Bethe asked, "Can we, who have always insisted on morality and human decency between nations as well as inside our own country, introduce this weapon of total annihilation into the world?"[19] This was, however, a contradiction that could be resolved within the paradigm of America's manifest destiny as a world force: it simply required understanding the bomb as a necessary, if awful, blessing in the hands of Americans to protect and insure the principles of democracy and Christianity.

Widely shared in the years following the bomb's use, this resolution is still effective.[20] A case in point was the 29 July 1985 issue of *Newsweek*, devoted to the fortieth anniversary of the bombing of Hiroshima and Nagasaki. In the lead article, "Living with the Bomb: The First Generation of the Atomic Age," Peter Goldman first wrote of the dramatic change in human experience wrought by the bomb's use: "In a flash of cosmic light, mankind had entered the atomic age and has lived at risk ever since, hostage to the bomb and to ourselves."[21] Goldman then addressed the inevitability of the bomb's invention and its consequent use. In true paradigmatic fashion, he explained that as a moral force, the justification of America's use of the bomb was self-evident—"neither was it likely that America, having the means to end the bloodiest war in human history, would not employ it"—and described the atomic holocaust in terms suggesting divine inspiration: "Seen from a distance, the nuclear dawn had a certain Biblical beauty, like a vision out of Genesis."[22]

The metaphoric substitution of an atomic Eden in place of the hellish nightmare of Japanese experience is perhaps most reassuring in its implication that the nuclear age is not the beginning of the end of the world but another new beginning led by America. Yet the strain on the imagination required to maintain this illusion quickly becomes obvious in the difficulties of locating and defining the Adamic character and his course of action in the radioactive Garden, setting a wholly new context for the meaning of American individualism. In *Advertisements for Myself* (1960), author and critic Norman Mailer wrote of the new American character as "the hipster" or "the American existentialist." In a world in which nihilism rather than optimism is the context of action, the fictional hero of contemporary American literature becomes "the man who knows that if our collective condition is to live with instant death by atomic war ... or with a slow death by conformity with every creative and rebellious instinct stifled[,] ... if the fate of twentieth century man is to live with death from adolescence to premature senescence, why then the only life-giving answer is to accept the terms of death, to live with death as immediate danger, to divorce oneself from society, to exist without roots, to set out on that uncharted journey into the rebellious imperatives of the self."[23]

Hence, when Holden Caulfield sets out on the "uncharted journey" traditional to fictional narratives of the American Adam, it is ultimately an inward journey of self-doubt and accusation ("I'm crazy, I swear I am") as he seeks to fend off immobilizing despair. This painful awareness of the endless double-bind—the "catch-22"—however paralyzing to sincere action and forfeiting resolution, is the literary contribution made by much of contemporary American fiction. Termed "the nuclearist frustration" by psychiatrist and eminent nuclear critic Robert J. Lifton, it is the awareness that "one holds the power of the deity in one's hands but is none the more powerful for it."[24] The adventurous image of Huck on a raft becomes safe and almost domesticated when it is juxtaposed against the highly charged image of Holden atop a nuclear warhead, but it is Huck's escape route that portends the sense of adventure inherent in a new beginning where Holden's fantasied "escape" is consciously suicidal: "I'm sort of glad they've got the atomic bomb invented. If there's ever another war, I'm going to sit right the hell on top of it. I'll volunteer for it, I swear to God I will" (141).

Bearing in mind that Holden's alternative fantasies are the escape to Thoreau's mythic cabin in the woods and the central fantasy of protecting other innocents from his own despair—both wishful attempts to maintain a sense of a viable future—Salinger was able to sufficiently manipulate the contemporary context of nihilism into a credible environment for an Adamic hero. In a comparative analysis of *Huckleberry Finn* and *Catcher*, critic Edgar Branch noted that "neurotic or not, Holden's criticism often hits home"[25] and this is nowhere so evident as in the reader response of a high school student who wrote, "I accept *The Catcher in the Rye* as part of myself."[26] Sixteen years old at the time, Sandra Christenson argued that "Holden's perambulating thoughts and abusive language help paint the picture of bitter confusion that surrounds this boy as he gropes about for stable bearings, wondering if there are any," and then explained her identification with his bitterness:

> The bitterness is derived in part from the uncertainty of the future. It is the fear that you are looking forward to something that won't exist that makes you acrid and spiteful. Maybe the future will consist of rehashed memories; you are only closer to dying each day as you wallow in your rut remembering how you and the gang played kick-the-can when you were twelve. When you are sixteen, you wait until your life becomes miraculously transformed into something worthwhile, and you can become cynical about the future and life in general in order to protect yourself from the let-down.[27]

While Christenson's interpretation may be shared by adult readers, the central identification of an adolescent with the theme of bitterness, a theme explained by "the uncertainty of the future," may well be the aspect of *The Catcher in the Rye* that is most threatening to adults. Where Christenson and, suggestively, her peers take comfort in the sheer congruence between their own perceptions of postwar American society and Holden's, adults respond to the novel either by seeking to protect adolescents from such recognitions or by encouraging them in the hope that they will develop a critical perspective that will stir them to seek change.

Perhaps even more disturbing to adults is the implication that Christenson's sensibility of resigned cynicism precedes her reading of *The Catcher in the Rye:* as a reader, she "accept[s] *The Catcher in the Rye,*" because it fits a pre-existing self-constructed frame of bitterness that then shapes her understanding of *Catcher.* Here, a look at a 1985 bestseller touted as "this generation's *Catcher in the Rye*"[28] is instructive as to the perspective embraced by late adolescents. Written by 18-year-old Bret Easton Ellis and embraced by his "Generation X" peers, *Less Than Zero* is a novel about 18-year-old protagonist Clay's return to the company of his high school friends when he comes home from college during winter break of his freshman year.

In a postpublication interview that was remarkable in itself for its odd combination of extreme passivity and arrogance, then 20-year-old Ellis spoke of his intentions in writing *Less Than Zero.* Responding to the interviewer's comment that, "certainly the message [of *Less Than Zero*] is relatively dispiriting," Ellis stated, "That is a conscious decision on my part," and then added, "I guess if you took the two books, *Catcher in the Rye* and *Less Than Zero,* and compared them, you would get a pretty interesting sociopolitical commentary on how America has changed."[29] Explaining that "this is where Holden would have evolved to, he would have become blond and drugged," Ellis emphasized that all idealism is intentionally absent from Clay's narrative account: "There is none. There is solipsism and self-involvement, yeah, and a weirdly huge need for material things and sensations."[30]

Set in Southern California and written when Ellis himself was on break from Bennington College in Vermont, *Less Than Zero* was summarily indicted by the interviewer as "bleak, morally barren, ethically bereft and tinged with implicit violence."[31] Ellis's response to this charge was the simple acknowledgment that "Yeah, it is a bleak book" and to point out that although "it's warped," his characters "have this desperate need to feel something, anything. There's a real pathetic need, but it is the way they feel it." Although set in the particular context of the affluent beach culture of Southern California, Ellis pointed out its broader applicability to contemporary adolescent experience, stressing that "in terms of universality, there is the weird aimlessness that seems almost purposeful. I think it's symptomatic," Ellis concluded, "of what is happening among youth in general."[32]

By 1999, an ever more extreme incarnation of "where Holden would have evolved to" was given voice in the Web page diary of Littleton, Colorado's adolescent assassin Eric Harris, posted not long before the shootings at Columbine High School. Writing in apparent "Holdenese," the pages contain what one reporter called "the musings of a cyber-age Holden Caulfield":

> You know what I hate? (People) ... that cut. Why ... can't you wait like every other human being on earth does? If you cut, you are the following: Stuck-up, self-centered, selfish, lazy, rude and. ... You know what I really hate? Liars! Oh Gawwwwd I hate liars. And living in this ... neighborhood there are thousands of them!!! Why the fuck must people lie so damn much! ... You know what I love? Zippo lighters!!!! ... You know what I love? Freedom of speech!!![33]

If Eric Harris was intending to echo Holden Caulfield here, there are signal differences (the least of which is that Holden himself never used the word "fuck" expressively) between Holden's pacifist musings as a fictional character and Harris's stark terrorist threats. Recalling that the only time we see Holden actually "take aim" is in a mock pose targeting his "people shooting hat" and that Holden *at his most alienated* wishes to *remove himself* from society (only to later find himself "missing everybody"), Harris's last writings went unrecognized as the plan of action they proved to be:

> Well all you people out there can just kiss my ass and die. From now on, I don't give a fuck ... unless I respect you, which is highly unlikely. ... For the rest of you, you all better hide in your houses because I'm coming for EVERYONE soon, and I WILL be armed to the fucking teeth, and I WILL shoot to kill and I WILL fucking KILL EVERYTHING! ... God DAMMIT I AM PISSED!![34]

If Harris's willingness to take aim at "everything" is an active as well as violent reversal of the passivity in Ellis's "weird aimlessness," which is in itself reminiscent of Christenson's "bitter uncertainty," and all three identify with Holden's own adolescent crisis of purpose, it is a spiraling phenomenon that was predicted much earlier by historian Lewis Mumford. In his 1947 essay "Social Effects," Mumford envisioned four possible scenarios as the consequence of America's nuclear developments.

The third scenario assumed a "drawn out period of nuclear proliferation and intensifying danger" in which, as Mumford envisioned it,

> The young who grow up in this world are completely demoralized: they characterize themselves as the generation that drew a blank. The belief in continuity, the sense of future that holds promises, disappears: the certainty of sudden obliteration cuts across every long term plan, and every activity is more or less reduced to the time-span of a single day, on the assumption that it may be the last day.... Suicides become more frequent ..., and the taking of drugs to produce either exhilaration or sleep becomes practically universal.[35]

With incredible prescience, Mumford understood at once the "breakdown in man's sense of symbolic unity and impairment of his sense of immortality," attributed only as late as 1979 by Robert Jay Lifton to the "quantum mental leap" from prenuclear to nuclear forms of destruction.[36] Furthermore, even as Stephen Whitfield pointed out in his 1977 essay that "symbolic of the political posture of the era [the 1950's] was the school child crouching under a wooden desk during a mock atomic attack,"[37] it was not until the 1980s that social scientists began to seriously consider the impact of the nuclear bomb and nuclear education upon the American imagination. In 1982 psychologist Michael Carey argued that "this generation's unique encounter" should not be "written off" but rather should be the focus of increased research, that the postwar generation "had America's only formal and extended bomb threat education in its schools, and that education—along with the lessons about the bomb from government, the media and the family—[was] well learned. This generation has a collection of memories, images, and words that will not disappear, even for those who profess not to be troubled."[38]

Memories and images: a 1985 anniversary article in *Time* magazine, "Living with the Bomb," contained an interview with Manhattan Project physicist Hans Bethe, who has "found his own seven-year-old grandson tortured by waking nightmares of nuclear war." The authors went on to point out that "such nightmares have become part of the common lot of mankind," citing a 1983 Harris poll which found that "two thirds of America expected a nuclear war sometime in the next twenty years."[39] While Americans "profess not to be troubled," the rates of depression and suicide in America increase—and the increase is greatest among the young.

In the late 1980s, the National Institute of Mental Health reported that the average age of first onset of clinical depression had dropped from pre–World War II normative onset in late middle age (50+) to contemporary onset among Americans in their mid-20s to early 30s, with the highest frequency of onset occurring among 25 to 44 year olds. Researchers could not explain this demographic shift and were search-ing for an identifiable "Agent Blue," "some cultural or environmental factor that might account for the change" in which "coming to maturity in the period from 1960 to 1975 seems to have had a profound adverse impact on the likelihood of depressive illness." A possible explanation offered by one psychiatrist at Cornell University Medical College was that the "unprecedented social upheaval" of the 1960s–70s was the causal effect of "a new age of melancholy." A peculiar sort of blindness is at work here when the possibility is overlooked that both "social upheaval" and the increase in depressive illness are symptoms of a deeper cultural malaise.[40]

An equally troubling indication of this contemporary malaise is the equally "unexplainable" and dramatic escalation in the number of teen-age suicides in postwar America. In 1960, teenage (ages 15–24) suicides numbered 1,239; 3,100 in 1970, and 5,200 by 1980. And the 5,000-plus completed suicides represent only a fraction of the estimated 100,000 annual teenage attempts.[41] In response to growing public concern, a 1987 segment of the topical *Phil Donahue Show* was devoted to "Teen Sui-cides." Early on in the program, Donahue listed eight "signs of suicide," based on the research of psychotherapist and program panelist Karen Blaker, a specialist in the area of teenage suicide.[42] While awareness of these "signs" may be important to the prevention of a suicide attempt, the program significantly omitted any discussion of why teenagers try to commit suicide—and with an increasing frequency. The question of motivation was not overlooked by members of the studio audience, however, as is clear in the following interchange between a female audi-ence participant who appeared to be in her mid- to late fifties, psycho-therapist Blaker, host Donahue, and program panelist Jan Perrine, whose son committed suicide at age 16.

> **Audience participant:** What is different in this day and age than, for instance, when I was growing up? A lot of the factors are very common to any child growing up.
> **Karen Blaker:** I think you're asking, too, why so many more teen suicides [cites more statistics showing increase].... We've got a real big problem on our hands here ... can I just say that I think it's because people don't hear the cries for help....

Phil Donahue: We didn't speak to the question of what it is about today? Does anybody on the panel have any insight?

[long pause]

Jan Perrine: I think that the threat of total annihilation has got to be a real biggie. I mean, I'm 49 years old and I did not grow up with that threat. I think that's pretty frightening.[43]

This interchange, in its very simplicity, provides an outline of cultural dialogue that I found in the dialogue of the *Catcher* debate. In the pervasive and widely shared recognition that American society is failing the task of enculturating its youth—a recognition forced by signs as wide-ranging as depressive illness, "social upheaval," suicide, and the fictional characterization of alienated adolescence in *The Catcher in the Rye*—the American people seek an explanation of "what is different in this day and age" from professionals who can only answer in terms of further description and then suggest possible methods of prevention. Significantly, the only attempt at an actual explanation in this case was made by a parent whose immediate confrontation with the problem had given her the courage to risk the explanation of nuclear consciousness, recognizing that the development and potential use of nuclear weapons and the increase in adolescent suicides are both trends of self-annihilation that are at odds with the moral origins of a nation explicitly dedicated to "life, liberty, and the pursuit of happiness."[44]

I say *risk* here because the challenge faced by those who believe that nuclearism explains various forms of contemporary malaise is two-fold. First, there is little hard evidence, a lack of "social facts," to support such a conclusion; not because such evidence does not exist but because it has not been documented in a form that is readily accessible to social science methodology. This first challenge I find to be in actuality a consequence of a second difficulty inherent to the nuclearist explanation: nuclearist explanations, in a manner that itself reflects an unwillingness to face the consequences of nuclear development, are written off as "kooky" or too far-fetched to deserve credibility, much less scholarly attention.[45]

Perhaps as a consequence of increasing cultural strain, the resistance to nuclearist explanations is weakening. In 1977 the American Psychiatric Association created a task force explicitly charged to "bring psychological understanding to bear on various aspects of nuclear arms and nuclear energy, and the threat they pose to human mental and emotional life."[46] One of the early studies generated through this commission was the 1978–80 questionnaire survey of 1,000 grammar and high school students conducted by Harvard professor of psychiatry John Mack. Mack's general conclusion was that "children are aware of the threat of nuclear war and live in fear of it."[47] That this is a cautious understatement is clear in the revealing representative student statements presented by Mack. Culled from the detailed responses of 100 10th–12th grade students, when Mack asked "Have nuclear advances affected your way of thinking about the future, your view of the world, and time?" typical student responses were as follows:

(A) I am constantly aware that at any second the world might blow up in my face. It makes living more interesting.
(B) I think that, unless we do something about nuclear weapons the world and the human race may not have much time left (corny, huh?).
(C) It gives me a pretty dim view of the world and mankind but it hasn't really influenced me.
(D) Everything has to be looked at on two levels: the world with the threat of ending soon, and life with future, etc. The former has to be blocked out for everyday functioning because very few people can find justification for living otherwise. But [it] is always there—on a much larger scale than possibilities of individual deaths, car accidents, etc.—even though the result to me personally would be the same.[48]

In a parallel study, Phyllis La Farge, child development professional and former managing editor of *Parents' Magazine*, documented similar responses of alternating fearful awareness and concerted denial in the drawings and written work of children from kindergarten to high school. One of the many representative responses she included in a 1987 article, "Learning to Live with the Bomb," pointed out the apparent irrelevance of the enculturation process to adolescents who waiver between denial and acknowledgment of the nuclear threat to their future: "I'm angry because I feel I won't have a future like most people and I ask myself, why do I take classes I hate, such as science and math when maybe I won't live to use my knowledge from those classes in college. I feel helpless. I keep trying to kid myself and forget about any possibilities of a nuclear war."[49]

The expression of awareness and justifiable fear of nuclear developments by children and adolescents is not unique to the 1970s and '80s. Paul Boyer, writing of the 1945–50 aftermath of America's use of the atomic bomb, noted the response of children among the "tantalizingly fragmentary" early evidence of the bomb's psychic impact: "the child who, in a prayer shortly after Hiroshima, asked God to let his family die altogether; the little girl who, when asked what she wanted to be when she grew up, replied 'alive.'"[50]

An alternative response, requiring apparently some brief distance from the actual historical moment of the bomb's development and use, is denial of the nuclear threat. A helpful reminder at this point is that the middle-aged adults of the late 1970s–1990s were the children of 1945–50, a fact that I believe has shaped their experience as parents and, correspondingly, the development and expectations of their children. In a 1988 interview, 1960s cultural radical Abbie Hoffman spoke of the baby-boomer generation as a "tribe," born "on August 6, 1945, when the atom bomb was dropped. So that during the '60's we were all young. The whole world was going through its youth, its atomic youth." In a similar vein, historian Mark Gerzon wondered, "Why does the possibility of nuclear war haunt me? I was born in the year 4 A.H. (after Hiroshima)," and then speculated that "these memories flood me because my son Shane is now the same age" as Gerzon was when he first learned about "the bomb's awesome power" in school. Noting that "some things have changed after a generation. He has no air raid drills; they are out of fashion. Civil defense is apparently considered futile," Gerzon closed off his train of thought with a final grim comment: "In case of war, he will just die at his desk."[51]

While the place of the bomb in the adult conscience in the 1980s and '90s has not yet been studied, the very reliance of contemporary American children and adolescents on denial as a mode of psychic survival is very likely a learned response. "The experience of powerlessness of children and adolescents, the sense that they have that matters are out of control, is not different from the way most adults feel in relation to the nuclear arms race," John Mack concluded in his study of adolescent response. "Little can be done to help our young people unless adults address the apathy and helplessness that we experience in relation to the arms race and the threat of nuclear war."[52]

Phyllis La Farge came to a nearly identical conclusion in her explanation of the paradoxical expressions of nuclear awareness and denial in the student work she studied. Arguing that such expression was a learned response and reflected a gap between knowledge gained in the home and from outside sources, she explained that "as the child absorbs the vocabulary and images of power, destruction, and vulnerability, he learns who talks about them, who does not, and how they talk." Noting that "in the case of nuclear weapons, they are just about never mentioned by anyone in his family, yet are referred to on the nightly television news," La Farge concluded that "this 'not talking'—out of a desire to protect our children—is in itself a message, suggesting that the subject is taboo or beyond our power to deal with."[53]

That children grasp the condition of adult paralysis and helplessness in the face of a nuclear threat is starkly evident in the following responses from children. The first is the letter from a grammar school student to President Reagan in which the recognition of parental powerlessness is managed by the belief that power to insure the future lies within Presidential authority:

> Dear President Reagan,
> I am sure that my parents don't like knowing that I may never reach 21 or even 12 since I'm only 11. You may not be causing it but you can control it in the U.S.[54]

As children mature and authority figures become increasingly human or "real" to them, the recognition of adult powerlessness becomes harder to avoid, leading to the angry suspicion that it is not powerlessness as much as adult complicity that has sustained their jeopardy. One "scornful adolescent" reportedly challenged his "exasperated father" by arguing that "if we stay up all night and do the twist, whom do we hurt? It's you who made the bomb that's going to blow us up in the end." And in the words of another high school student, reminiscent of the narrative of Holden Caulfield: "It [nuclear advances] has shown me how stupid some adults can be. If they know it could easily kill them I have no idea why they support it. Once in a while it makes me start to think that the end of my life might not be as far off as I would like it to be."[55]

If it seems at this point that we have run far afield of the *Catcher* debate, I believe instead that we have here come to the heart of it. The lack of faith in the American character that is expressed in the dialogue of the *Catcher* controversies as a cultural debate is rooted not in doubt of the strength of adolescent character so much as recognition of the powerlessness of American adults to provide a genuine sense of future and hopefulness for the adolescents in their charge—as parents, professionals, and community leaders. *The Catcher in the Rye* is an indictment of adult apathy and complicity in the construction of a social reality in which the American character cannot develop in any meaningful sense beyond adolescence.

This is an indictment that, however much adult readers recognize its accuracy, many adults wish their children to avoid as long as possible. Phyllis La Farge ended her study of adolescent response to the nuclear threat with the statement that "never losing hope is what all parents fervently want for their children," a yearning that leads them to "try to encourage hopefulness by keeping silent about the nuclear weapons, the arms race, and other issues."[56] *The Catcher in the Rye* confronts the adult not only with the impossibilities of this wishful protectionism but with its dysfunctional consequences: in its "very American" embrace of the right to the pursuit of life, liberty, and happiness and the embodiment of the American Adam in the radical idealism of Holden Caulfield, it is mature American society that is "un-American" in its apathy, denial, and pursuit of superficial comforts in the shadow of nuclear annihilation.

If America's development and use of nuclear weaponry, however much for a "just cause," has rendered the ideology of American innocence finally untenable, I believe it is fiction such as *The Catcher in the Rye* that can reach the American imagination and, in doing so, generate action. Paul Boyer concludes *By the Bomb's Early Light* by stating his belief that "there are always novel twists [in the history of man's experience], in the interstices of which one may sometimes find reason for hope."[57] I believe that the cultural debate over *The Catcher in the Rye* is an example of an interstitial moment that indeed gives reason for hopefulness as it has renewed public faith in democratic participation. As American culture has come to the point where we celebrate instead of expect the exhibition of democratic action and the achievement of tolerance in a local school-book controversy, it is at least a step toward the broader enactment of liberty and justice. If we are to ensure a future for ourselves and future generations, it will require the active engagement of individuals willing to assert their ideas of what that future should be and then act to bring about their realization—in short, making full use of the democratic principle in American government. The continuing cultural debate over *The Catcher in the Rye* indicates the growing willingness of the American public to face criticism, question both ideals and realities, and to "speak out." This in itself I find to be hopeful.

Coda: 1999

Where I had once managed to end on the above hopeful note, the school shootings in Littleton, Colorado, have eclipsed Holden Caulfield's centrality as a fictionalized "troubled teen," but the immediate and panicked public cries for censorship on national levels in response to the shootings, with little evidence of thoughtful discussion, certainly allow less optimism. The role of "the media," "the Internet," and "video games" all have come under fire as causal forces, as if these arenas or resources for cultural expression had a life of their own—tacitly acknowledging that many teens find them fascinating and choose to access them while simultaneously repressing questions of *why* the particular narratives of these expressive texts might engage or fascinate them. Public discourse once again centers on censorship, but this time it is far afield from discussions of democracy or tolerance or any discussion of why this is happening: all we need or want to know, it seems, is *how to stop it*. Censor films, censor rock music, video games, censor access to the Internet: "just say no" rather than ask why. Not a hopeful situation.

There is little doubt that each of the adolescent assassins discussed in the introduction to this book were and may still be "troubled teens." Yet until the moment they acted out, they were more often than not perceived as "normal" teenagers or at least harmless; having trouble "finding their niche" maybe, but "not dangerous." Their interests in video games, in popular if alternative rock music, in commercial films, and in establishing artificial social relations on the Internet were far from unusual. In each incident, these young men were defined by some of their peers as "outcasts" and "misfits" or "slackers," yet none were entirely without a social network, and most were noted for "running with a (particular) crowd of students."

Nor is it likely that tensions among "high school cliques" or even particular types of cliques create or identify troubled teens. Much has been made of the fact that Eric Harris and Dylan Klebold of Littleton were members of Columbine's "gothic"-inclined "Trenchcoat Mafia" and harbored hostility toward "jocks," for instance; yet Kip Kinkel, the trenchcoated assassin in Springfield, Oregon, was a member of Thurston High School's junior varsity football team. Different schools, different cliques: not one of the strengths of high school life in America but there is nothing new here. In a *Los Angeles Times* interview just after Littleton (when apparently any kid, anywhere, who dressed in gothic fashion became an instant expert on troubled teens), a local "goth participant" didn't think that Harris's and Klebold's rampage had anything to do with their supposed gothic interests. "They did what anybody else wanted to do. They just got to their snapping point," he said. "If it had been the jocks, there would have been a witch hunt after jocks."[58]

Indeed, as stressed by an anonymous member of the Trenchcoat Mafia on a Web site created in memoriam of Harris and Klebold,

> It is entirely possible that the killers' parents had no idea that anything was wrong with their teenage sons. They were smart, they got good grades, and they behaved more or less like other kids who drive BMWs to school every day. Their parents gave them everything an American teenager could possibly want: cars, computers, pocket money, clothes, you name it. Their suburban community was peaceful and full of fun stuff for teenagers to do. At the core of all the hysterical bullshit that has appeared in the Denver press and on national TV, it is indeed frightening that the only difference between Eric Harris and most other suburban teenagers was intelligence. Eric was extremely intelligent.[59]

So how to tell the "troubled teens" from "other kids who drive BMWs to school?" Maybe "parents should be concerned about a sawed-off shotgun next to the bed," as the owner of Necromance (a Hollywood shop catering to "gothic" tastes in clothing and accessories) told the *Los Angeles Times,* "not a bottle of black fingernail polish."[60] Yet the shotgun next to the bed more likely indicates the individual teen who has moved beyond troubled and is reaching his "snapping point." And whereas the shotgun in the hands of a teenager at his "snapping point" was, until recently, likely to result in suicide at worst, the result now may be the multiple deaths of select and random others.

"In the old days, kids would walk away from a fight with a few bruises," stated Ronald Stephens, executive director of the National School Safety Center. "Now it's a body count."[61] Stephens, it seems to me, is entirely missing the point here. While both may involve a sense of settling a score, schoolyard fights are typically one-on-one or group-against-group engagements while school shootings are individuals blasting away with lethal intention at others: these are assassinations, not fights. These are troubled teens who, having reached their snapping point, take aim at their larger social environment.

We should have seen it coming. Each of the assassins from 1993 to 1999 talked about their plans and/or wrote murderous poetry and short fiction for their English classes. At Columbine High School, Dylan Klebold and Eric Harris filmed a video project in which, as students later told reporters, "Harris and Klebold pretended they were gunmen and had their friends play athletes." After the real shootings, school officials in possession of the tape declined to comment on the video but turned it over to the police. "They walked around in this video and they acted out what they eventually carried out," said Lt. John Klekbusch.[62]

Even so, how do we tell the emergent assassins from the normative troubled teen? Speaking of his own experience with high school students in the privileged suburbs of Thousand Oaks, California (where there have not been any school shootings to date), one school administrator said, "If you read some of their poetry and some of the things they write, it's basically dealing with the macabre and the dark side of our existence."[63] In an interview following Kip Kinkel's assault in Springfield, Oregon, Governor John Kitzhaber "bristled at suggestions that this was a 'school problem' and said it was time to seek out the reasons for adolescent pain." "I think we need to ask ourselves: what kind of despair drives children to this kind of violence? What kind of lack of hope or sense of abandonment," wondered Kitzhaber, "drives them to make this kind of terrible choice?'"[64]

Instead of compiling a laundry list of innumerable indicators signifying troubled teens, this is where I believe the discussion should begin. I believe that the "killing adjustments" of life in postwar America discussed in this chapter and earlier offer a broader explanation for the peculiar morbidity and nihilism evident in late-twentieth-century teenage angst as expressed in teens' increasingly commonplace interests and activities. Nuclear fears answered with mediated images and activities serve only to blur the boundaries between the fantastic and the real: "playing" the video game "Doom" is a cold comfort against an uncertain future. "I just have sorrow that some children out there feel they have no future, or anything to live for," one Springfield resident said helplessly after the shootings in Oregon. "I'm just afraid there will be more."[65]

Hope upon hope that I am wrong, but if all we know how to do in response is to censor and deny rather than acknowledge the fears that our teenagers are playing out in their games and their musings, I too fear there will be more. "When adults treat the worst dangers young people face as taboo topics because they are impolitic to raise," wrote one social critic in 1998, "they dismiss young people themselves as unimportant."[66] If many teens are troubled, by their fears and their dismissal, some will demand that their fears be confronted. As Eric Harris wrote in a song he created by mixing lyrics from three different songs performed by the commercially successful alternative rock band KMFDM:

I AM YOUR APOCALYPSE
I AM YOUR BELIEF UNWROUGHT
MONOLITHIC JUGGERNAUT
I
SHOCKWAVE
MASSIVE ATTACK
ATOMIC BLAST
SON OF A GUN IS BACK
CHAOS-PANIC
NO RESISTANCE
DETONATIONS IN A DISTANCE
APOCALYPSE NOW
WALLS OF FLAME
BILLOWING SMOKE
WHO'S TO BLAME....
WATCH OUT.[67]

Notes

Introduction

1. "Alabama," *Newsletter on Intellectual Freedom* 32, no. 1 (Jan. 1983): 7.

2. This finding came out in the interviews of postmaster Bo Brackett and parent Jenny Thigpen, opposing participants in the Calhoun County debate. Interviewed in August 1983.

3. Based on my review of the *Newsletter on Intellectual Freedom,* published by the American Library Association (ALA), from 1953 to 1985. The peak year for censorship attempts on high school literature during this period was 1972 with 60 attempts, although 1964 (56 attempts), 1971 (57 attempts), and 1975 (57 attempts) were close to the peak. Modal frequency for 1955–85 was 42. In a 1982–96 survey of censorship attempts, *Catcher* was the second most frequently censored novel over the fifteen-year span (see the People for the American Way online publication "Attacks on the Freedom to Learn '96" <www.pfaw.org/ attacks/96appen2.htm>). In 1996 *Catcher* ranked fifth on the ALA's annual review of censored titles reported to the ALA's Office for Intellectual Freedom (see the *Intellectual Freedom Action News,* April 1997, 3–4).

4. For example, Peter Jennison and Robert Sheridan's *The Future of General Adult Books and Reading in America* (Chicago: ALA, 1970). Even in the case of censorship survey texts, authors tend to collect case studies of different types of censorship actions rather than look at the content of or commonalities among the texts in question. A 1974 censorship controversy in West Virginia generated two such case studies, both using interviews and participant statements to understand the processes and reasoning behind the censorship activity but with limited discussion of the texts involved. See George Hillocks's "Books and Bombs: Ideological Conflict and the Schools—A Case Study of the Kanawha County Book Protest," *School Review* 86 (Aug. 1978): 632–54, and also James Moffett's later book on the same controversy, *Storm in the Mountains: A Case Study of Censorship, Conflict, and Consciousness* (Carbondale: Southern Illinois UP, 1988). An exception to this approach is James Francis Symula's doctoral dissertation, "Censorship of High School Literature: A Study of the Incidents of Censorship Involving J. D. Salinger's *The Catcher in the Rye,*" (Ed.D. diss., State Univ. of New York, Buffalo, 1969). Symula's study provides an in-depth

description of the early controversial history of *Catcher;* however, the focus of his analysis and argument is aimed at the problem of censorship in the schools. Evelyn Geller's *Forbidden Books in American Public Libraries, 1876–1919: A Study of Cultural Change* (Westport, Conn.: Greenwood P, 1984) also treats censorship in relationship to socioeconomic contexts and explores the cultural significance of censorship. However, her work does not address the post–World War II period and is helpful primarily as a model for understanding the relationship between censorship and cultural tensions.

5. USIS selection as quoted in Warren French's literary study *J. D. Salinger, Revisited* (Boston: Twayne Publishers, 1988), ix. The other eleven novels were *Another Country* by James Baldwin, *The Adventures of Augie March* by Saul Bellow, *The Grass Harp* by Truman Capote, *The Wapshot Chronicle* by John Cheever, *Catch-22* by Joseph Heller, *On the Road* by Jack Kerouac, *The Naked and the Dead* by Norman Mailer, *New Life* by Bernard Malamud, *Letting Go* by Philip Roth, William Styron's *Lie Down in Darkness*, and John Updike's *Poorhouse Fair*. In 1977, *Catcher* was one of seven documents (and of only two novels — the other being James Farrell's *Studs Lonigan*) selected for review in the *American Quarterly*'s special winter issue "Reassessing Twentieth Century Documents." *Catcher*'s 1981 teaching and censorship status is cited in Adam Moss's retrospective essay "Catcher Comes of Age," *Esquire* 96 (Dec. 1981): 56.

6. See the ALA's retrospective of their College Bound Committee's recommendation lists since 1995: ALA/Young Adult Library Services Association, *Outstanding Books for the College Bound: Choices for a Generation* (Chicago: ALA/ALA Editions, 1996). Censorship studies of educators in Utah (1963), Wisconsin (1964), and Arizona (1965) and a joint committee of the National Council of Teachers of English and the American Association of School Librarians (1966) consistently found *Catcher* to be the most frequently censored or "controversial" book — censorship incidents based on the protests of parents, school administrators, teachers, and clergy. See Nyla Herber Ahrens, "Censorship and the Teacher of English" (Ed.D. diss., Teachers College, Columbia Univ., 1965). See also Lee A. Burress Jr., "How Censorship Affects the School," *Wisconsin Council of Teachers of English, Special Bulletin* 8 (Oct. 1963), and L. B. Woods, *A Decade of Censorship in America: The Threat to Classrooms and Libraries, 1966–1975* (Metuchen, N.J.: Scarecrow P, 1979).

7. Moss 58. See also the television series *Sixty Minutes,* CBS, 1 Nov. 1981, and *Archie Bunker's Place,* CBS, 21 Feb. 1982, as well as popular novels ranging from contemporary romances such as *Oliver's Story* by Erich Segal (New York: Harper and Row, 1977) to "teen fiction" such as Michael Bowen's *Can't Miss* (New York: Harper and Row, 1987), and reaching the literary realms of detective fiction in Julie Smith's *New Orleans Beat* (New York: Ivy Books, 1994).

8. As read aloud by Chapman from J. D. Salinger, *The Catcher in the Rye* (New York: Bantam Books, 1964), 173. See profiles on the arrest and court trial

of Chapman in the *New York Times,* 9 Feb. 1981, sect. B12, and *Time Magazine,* 7
Sept. 1981, 14.

9. Moss 56.

10. Gerald Rosen made exactly this point as early as 1977 in his essay "A Retrospective Look at *The Catcher in the Rye,*" in *American Quarterly* 29 (Winter
1977): 547–62. "The radical nature of Salinger's portrayal of disappointment
with American society, so much like Twain's in *Huck Finn,*" wrote Rosen, "was
probably as much of the reason that *Catcher* (like Huck) was banned from
schools and colleges as were the few curse words around which the battle was
publicly fought" (548).

11. Raymond Firth, *Symbols: Public and Private* (Ithaca, N.Y.: Cornell UP,
1975), 26.

12. Betty Friedan, *The Feminine Mystique* (1963; New York: Dell Publishing,
1974), 174.

13. See also Elaine Tyler May's recent book *Homeward Bound: American
Families in the Cold War Era* (New York: Basic Books, 1988), in which she makes
a similar argument regarding "domestic containment."

14. Abbie Hoffman, *Soon to Be a Major Motion Picture* (New York: G. Putnam's Sons, 1980), 7.

15. I take the term *culture wars* from the title of James Davison Hunter's
comprehensive text *Culture Wars: The Struggle to Define America* (New York:
Basic Books, 1991). See also George Lakoff's more recent study *Moral Politics:
What Conservatives Know That Liberals Don't* (Chicago: U of Chicago P, 1996).
While explicit discussion of the contest over cultural authority reached popular
as well as scholarly audiences in 1992 with the publication of William Bennett's
conservative polemic *The De-Valuing of America: The Fight for Our Culture and
Our Children* (New York: Simon and Schuster), the liberal critique was given
voice as early as 1985 by Robert Bellah et al. in *Habits of the Heart: Individualism
and Commitment in American Life* (Berkeley: U of California P).

Hunter argues, "The divisions of political consequence today are not theological and ecclesiastical in character but the result of differing worldviews ...
(revolving) around our most fundamental and cherished assumptions about
how to order our lives—our own lives and our lives together in this society."
Hunter refers to these opposing worldviews as "the impulse toward orthodoxy
and the impulse toward progressivism," with orthodoxy understood as "the
commitment on the part of adherents to an external, definable, and transcen-
dent authority," whereas for adherents of progressivism "moral authority tends
to be defined by the spirit of the modern age, a spirit of rationalism and subjec-
tivism.... [W]hat all progressivist worldviews share in common is the tendency
to resymbolize historic faiths according to the prevailing assumptions of contemporary life" (42–45).

Lakoff frames the opposing forces in more familiar terms of conservatives
versus liberals but identifies the construction of the family as the basis for their

different worldviews: "Deeply embedded in conservative and liberal politics are different models of the family. Conservatism ... is based on a Strict Father model, while liberalism is centered around a Nurturant Parent model. These two models of the family give rise to different moral systems and different discourse forms, that is, different choices of works and different modes of reasoning." See Lakoff 12, 35, and 170–73, for expanded discussion of these two models.

16. June Sochen, "On Writing Cultural History," *American Studies Association Newsletter,* June 1985, 4.

17. Paul Boyer, *By The Bomb's Early Light: American Thought and Culture at the Dawn of the Atomic Age* (New York: Pantheon, 1985), xviii.

18. See Tom Engelhardt, *The End of Victory Culture: Cold War America and the Disillusioning of a Generation* (New York: Basic Books, 1995), and Alan Nadel, *Containment Culture: American Narratives, Postmodernism, and the Atomic Age* (Durham, N.C.: Duke UP, 1995).

19. Engelhardt 10.

20. Nadel xi-8. It should be said here that Nadel's reading of *Catcher,* specifically his interpretation of Salinger's characterization of Holden Caulfield, is one that I do not share. Nadel argues, for instance, that "in thinking constantly about who or what was phony, Caulfield was doing no more than following the instructions of J. Edgar Hoover, the California Board of Regents, *The Nation,* the Smith Act, and the Hollywood Ten, to name a very few" (75), and that as narrator of the tale, Holden "spoke for the cold war HUAC witness, expressing existential angst over the nature and meaning of his 'testimony'" (181).

While Nadel's reading fits in the context of his larger argument as to the symbolic performance of Cold War narratives of containment, I believe that at best—*supposing* Salinger did intend the "red-hunter" parallels that Nadel finds throughout the novel—he is failing to appreciate Salinger's use of quixotic irony. At the very least, Nadel's reading suggests the dangers of claiming cultural meaning based on a singular intellectual reading, however thoughtfully contextualized. The numerous procensorship participants in the *Catcher* controversies who defined Holden *as a Communist* would certainly be taken aback at Nadel's interpretation. My own intellectual reading of *Catcher* in chapter 2—contextualized there in intellectual discourse but equally contextualized by and consistent with the readings of debate participants throughout this study—is that at least at one point, Salinger is *critiquing* McCarthyism.

21. My sentiments here echo those of Robert Bellah in his preface to *Habits of the Heart,* as he wrote of his interviewees: "We found them eager to discuss the right way to live, what to teach our children, and what our public and private responsibilities should be.... These are important matters to those to whom we talked, and yet concern about moral questions is often relegated to the realm of private anxiety, as if it would be awkward or embarrassing to make it public. *We hope this book will help transform this inner moral debate, often shared only with intimates, into public discourse*" (vi; emphasis added).

However similar our perspectives, this last line points to the signal difference between my study and Bellah's. I believe that these moral debates are present in public discourse, albeit in "transformations" that are difficult for scholars to identify, much less to render. Where Bellah sought out the privately held aspirations and beliefs of Americans by asking direct questions of his interviewees — "How ought we to live.... Who are we as Americans? What is our character?" (vi) — I was able to follow the voluntary discourse of participants responding to issue-generated questions: what is meant by the adjective (and hence characterological) use of the terms *American* and *un-American?*

22. As only one example of the many labels generated by a rapidly increasing number of social scientists studying the school shootings, the term *fledgling psychopath* was coined by University of Kentucky psychologist Donald Lyman in an interview regarding his ongoing study of "the spectre of a new type of student-criminal." See Terence Monmaney and Greg Krikorian, "Violent Culture, Media Share Blame, Experts Say," *Los Angeles Times,* 26 March 1998, sect. A16. I have identified four incidents of school shootings with multiple fatalities and injured from 1993 to 1995: *18 Jan. 1993, Grayson, Ky.:* Scott Pennington (17/senior) shoots and kills an English teacher and a janitor, holding twenty-two classmates hostage at East Carter High School; *26 May 1994, Union, Ky.:* Clay Shrout (17/senior) kills his parents and two younger sisters at home before going to school and taking a math class hostage at Ryle High School; *23 Jan. 1995, Redlands, Calif.:* John Sirola (14/8th grade) wounds the school principal, shooting him in the face with a sawed-off shotgun, and then accidentally shoots and kills himself when he trips while fleeing Sacred Heart School; *15 Nov. 1995, Lynnville, Tenn.:* Jamie Rouse (17/senior) kills a teacher and a student and wounds another teacher, shooting them in the head, at Richland School. Given that these shootings were understood as isolated cases and media coverage was consequently isolated and limited, there may be more (or earlier) incidents that I am not aware of. As three out of four of these cases occurred in the southern states, one of the earliest and continuing (if eventually insufficient) explanations offered was the South's "culture of honor." "Recent research suggests that Southerners are more inclined than Northerners to react aggressively if insulted, perhaps because they have historically placed a high value on personal honor," reported two writers for the *Los Angeles Times,* noting that "homicides associated with a personal grievance are four times more common in Southern states than in Midwestern states." See Monmaney and Krikorian, "Violent Culture."

23. All school shootings resulting in fatalities that have received any national coverage from 1993 to 1999 were committed by white adolescent males of at least middle-class background who used guns to carry out their clearly premeditated assaults upon their classmates and, in most cases, teachers or school staff as well. While some of the following elements were represented in the 1993–95 shootings, the adolescent assassins of 1996–99 all shared a majority of these elements, if not evidencing every single one: identified as unusually or exceptionally

intelligent; identified as social "misfits" or socially "on the fringes"; involved in video war-gaming and role-playing; fans of alternative rock music, specifically Pearl Jam's "Jeremy" and Marilyn Manson; familiar with film *The Basketball Diaries* (unclear familiarity with the autobiographical novel of the same title by Jim Carroll, on which the film was based); wore long black overcoats ("trench coats") at the time of the shooting; and were armed at levels more than sufficient for the killing/injuries that occurred.

24. My position here is argued more fully in the afterword. After Loukaitis in 1996, the school shootings are as follows (in chronological order): *19 Feb. 1997, Bethel, Wash.:* Evan Ramsey (16/sophomore) takes a rifle to Bethel Regional High School and kills the principal and a student, wounding two other students; *1 Oct. 1997, Pearl, Miss.:* Luke Woodham (16/sophomore) slits his mother's throat at home and then goes to Pearl High School, where he kills two students and wounds seven others; *1 Dec. 1997, Paducah, Ky.:* Michael Carneal (14/freshman) walks up to an on-campus student prayer group at Heath High School, puts in earplugs, and takes a "marksman's stance" as he pulls a .22 caliber handgun from his backpack and kills three students, wounding another five; *24 Mar. 1998, Jonesboro, Ark.:* Andrew Golden (11) and Mitchell Johnson (13) stand in the woods bordering Westside Middle School, clad in hunter's camouflage and carrying two handguns and two hunting rifles, shooting at their classmates as they filed onto the school grounds in response to a false fire alarm. Four students and one teacher are killed, with nine more students and another teacher wounded; *25 Apr. 1998, Edinboro, Penn.:* Andrew Wurst (14/8th grade) kills one teacher and wounds two students and another teacher at a school dance; *21 May 1998, Springfield, Ore.:* Kip Kinkel (15/freshman) kills his parents at home and later walks into the cafeteria at Thurston High School wearing a trench coat, climbs up on a table, and "shoots from the hip" with his rifle across the room. Kinkel is also carrying a pair of handguns. Two students are killed, twenty-two injured; *20 Apr. 1999, Littleton, Colo.:* Eric Harris (18/senior) and Dylan Klebold (17/senior) enter Columbine High School wearing dark glasses and trench coats, tossing pipe bombs and "cackling" as they calmly execute students, some selectively and others apparently at random, with handguns and shotguns. The toll is twelve students and one teacher killed, with twenty-three wounded, before Harris and Klebold commit suicide via self-inflicted gunshots.

Based on my preliminary survey of national media coverage, the Paducah, Springfield, and Littleton shootings exhibit all of the ritual elements (except in Paducah Carneal's clothing received no mention, although upon his arrest he did explicitly name *The Basketball Diaries* as his inspiration). However, the Paducah, Springfield, and Littleton shootings received extensive national media coverage (print and televised), Pearl and Jonesboro received immediate abbreviated national coverage, and very little coverage was given to the shootings in Bethel, Wash., and Edinboro, Penn., outside of local news media, so it may be that upon further localized research more common elements may become evident.

Finally, there have been at least two additional school shootings that, while causing injury, (luckily) did not result in any fatalities, and hence did not receive any in-depth coverage. Based on this limited coverage these incidents appear to be more disorganized and less ritualistic beyond their demographic indicators plus the not-inconsequential act of shooting at their classmates. Even so, their very existence may evidence a poorly performed ritual attempt. For the record, these are the incidents: *15 June 1998: Richmond, Va.:* a 14-year-old male student (unnamed) at Armstrong High School opens fire in a hallway during final exams, wounding a basketball coach and a volunteer aide but missing the student(s) believed to be his target(s); *20 May 1999: Atlanta, Ga.:* one month after Littleton, a 15–year-old male student (unnamed) begins firing both a rifle and a pistol at his classmates at Heritage High School in a "wild" and "panicked" manner, wounding six students before tearfully turning the weapons over to the assistant principal.

25. J. R. Moehringer, "Littleton Killings Strike at Heart of U.S.," *Los Angeles Times,* 29 Apr. 1999, sect. A1.

26. Bellah et al. vii. It is likely that Bellah may also have been sadly unsurprised at the bombing in Oklahoma City, as he argued in a preceding statement that "it seems to us that it is individualism, and not equality, as Tocqueville thought, that has marched inexorably through our history. We are concerned that this individualism ... may be threatening the survival of freedom itself" (vii). While Bellah may disagree with my reference to a deindividuated postwar America, I think our differences are actually those of perception and emphasis: I see an anomic and alienated individualism taking reassurance in blind conformity as normative to the postwar mentality, with Americans for the most part engaging as individuals only when they perceive a threat to their moral beliefs (or an opportunity to act on them) *and only* when and where they believe they can have an impact as citizens. Bellah identified a fuller individualism of communitarian impulse and action in his interviews based on his participants' *habits of the heart,* the mores that remained privately held until the moment of their engagement as "concerned citizens." To my mind, the existence of privately held individualism does not deny an equally normative experience of public deindividuation—which is why I think we both take heart in finding the existence of cultural practices and traditions of public discourse.

27. Stanley Fish, *Is There a Text in This Class?* (Cambridge, Mass.: Harvard UP, 1980); Clifford Geertz, *The Interpretation of Cultures* (New York: Basic Books, 1973); Thomas Kuhn, *The Structure of Scientific Revolutions* (1962; Chicago: U of Chicago P, 1970).

28. The language of the informants is presented without change as it was transcribed from the taped interviews. Three interviews were conducted by telephone and were not tape-recorded: Justine Pas and Reverend Bradley Parsons of Albuquerque, N.M., and Reverend Wesley Crane of Calhoun County, Ala. In these cases, I took notes and copied key phrases as I listened. This gave me a

conversational sketch, which I then filled in immediately after ending the phone call, recalling verbatim as much of the conversation as possible.

Although my interviewees had the opportunity to review my use of their statements, were agreeable to their use, and were willing to have their names disclosed in my dissertation, I felt that in broader publication the use of their real identities served no particular purpose, and, on the unlikely chance of some unforeseen personal consequence, I decided to cloak their identities. I have done so by (1) referring to counties of place rather than the actual communities in California and Alabama, and to the general environs of Albuquerque rather than the actual community and school district involved; (2) in a very few places, slightly altering personal characteristics of interviewees without distorting culturally relevant information (presenting, in hypothetical example, a dairy delivery driver as a laundry service driver, or referring, as I did in fact, to positions of school superintendents, principals, and vice-principals as "senior school administrators") and in particular maintaining representation of gender, age, ethnicity, and class as well as referents of self-identification as given by my interviewees (i.e., "as a teacher, I felt"); and (3) providing pseudonyms. Pseudonyms were created from the names of several of my graduate students, and any similarity to any person in Calhoun County, Ala., Marin County, Calif., or Albuquerque, N.M., is purely coincidental. The ministerial title of "Reverend" has been retained in relation to the actual position and correct denomination of the interviewee: in all cases, several churches of the same denomination exist in the interview counties, so I felt that providing pseudonyms and changing the specific names of the churches involved to more generic names (i.e., *Marin County* Baptist) was sufficient. Beyond these alterations, I have neither fictionalized nor conflated individuals.

Chapter 1

1. I am indebted to Adam Moss's compilation of the publishing history of *Catcher* in "Catcher Comes of Age," *Esquire*, Dec. 1981, 56–57, and Michael Kenney's summary "Searching for Salinger," *Boston Globe*, 3 Sept. 1997, sect. C1. Some confusion crops up as to the initial copyright date for *Catcher*. Two incidents that appear in *Catcher* were published earlier as segments in two short stories by J. D. Salinger: "I'm Crazy" in *Collier's* (Dec. 1945), and "Slight Rebellion Off Madison" in the *New Yorker* (Dec. 1946). Nevertheless, the first date for the novel as a complete work is July 1951, published by Little, Brown and Co. (New York).

2. The television series are *Sixty Minutes* (CBS), air date 1 Nov. 1982; *Archie Bunker's Place* (CBS), air date 21 Feb. 1982; *Family Feud* (ABC), air date 19 Oct. 1983. The novels are Michael Bowen's *Can't Miss* (New York: Harper and Row, 1987), Erich Segal's *Oliver's Story* (New York: Harper and Row, 1977), W. P. Kinsella's *Shoeless Joe* (Boston: Houghton Mifflin, 1982), and Julie Smith's *New Orleans Beat* (New York: Ivy Books, 1994). These examples came to my attention

in the course of everyday experience rather than through an intentional survey—and many more were recounted to me that I did not formally verify.

3. *Family Feud,* host Richard Dawson. For a discussion of the assumed audience and intent of *Family Feud,* as well as its history as a highly successful television game show, see Mark Crispin Miller's essay "Family Feud" in *New Republic,* 18–25 July 1983, 23–27.

4. Bowen 202. In fact, the reference to *Catcher* here is so abbreviated that an unfamiliar reader would likely be more confused than drawn into further identification with Bowen's character: "She sounded like something out of *The Catcher in the Rye.* He gave her a benign smile. '*Phony* is a word I'm not particularly fond of, Rook.'"

5. Kinsella 72. See also 26–34, 51–60, 73–78, and 219–24. In the film version of the novel, *Field of Dreams* (1989), J. D. Salinger is dropped as a character; however, the play on "catcher" and the treatment of baseball as a Zen experience remains focal.

6. Smith 174–75.

7. Further evidence that *Catcher* is assumed to be a part of cultural knowledge exists in its inclusion in the popular 1980s board game Trivial Pursuit (copyright 1981 Horn-Abbot; distributed in the U.S. by Selchow and Righter, Co.). See the Genus edition, card no. 955, "Arts and Literature" category: Q. "What book does Holden Caulfield appear in?" A. "*The Catcher in the Rye.*"

8. Sanford Pinsker, "*The Catcher in the Rye* and All: Is the Age of Formative Books Over?" *Georgia Review* 1986 (40): 953–67. Of note, Pinsker identifies Kinsella's *Shoeless Joe* as a contemporary contender for "formative book" status.

9. Moss 56.

10. Interview with Monica Bullock, 10 Feb. 1986, Orange County, Calif.

11. Smith 175.

12. R. W. B. Lewis, *The American Adam* (Chicago: U of Chicago P, 1955), 1–2.

13. Ibid., 1. Lewis's reliance on a select body of literature for his analysis combined with his willingness to then generalize that analysis to "a native American mythology" of "our culture" reflects 1950s intellectual assumptions about cultural holism and the value of elite literature. Often referred to as the "myth-symbol-image" school of cultural analysis, this perspective has received just criticism since the late 1960s for its lack of distinction between dominant and subcultural realms of production, familiarity, and adoption of such a mythology. Rather than wholly discounting Lewis's work on the basis of these criticisms, I find *American Adam* to be instructive on two counts: as a primary source for understanding 1950s intellectuals and for his definition of the American Adam itself. Essentially, Lewis's analysis of the American Adam as both mythology and character type remains accurate, if needing a broader range of cultural materials for evidence. Similarly, Lewis's interpretation of that mythology is not so much inaccurate as lacking in address to the question of how such a mythology functions as an ideology, and for whom. Contemporary scholars

would perhaps not overlook broader sources nor fail to see the usefulness of the American Adam mythology in attempted justification of otherwise arbitrary, socially constructed inequalities in American life. I have little difficulty, for example, in recognizing the American Adam, alive if unwell, in the 1980s spate of *Rambo* films, literature, and consumer items, and could readily argue the ideological usage of the American Adam mythology in these materials. If Lewis suffered from the "intellectual blinders" of his own time of scholarship, it would be further nearsightedness to disavow what he did elucidate.

14. Lewis 9–10.

15. Ibid., 197, 198.

16. Ibid., 5, 111.

17. J. D. Salinger, *The Catcher in the Rye* (New York: Bantam Books, 1964), 1. Further citations appear parenthetically in the text.

18. Lewis 91.

19. See James Fenimore Cooper, *The Deerslayer* (1841; Albany: SUNY P, 1987), 124–29.

20. Lewis 104.

21. See Richard Slotkin, *Regeneration through Violence* (Middletown, Conn.: Wesleyan UP, 1973), and also Richard Drinnon, *Facing West: The Metaphysics of Indian-Hating and Empire-Building* (New York: New American Library, 1980).

22. Of note, this section of the novel is interpreted by Alan Nadel in *Containment Culture* as evidence that Holden Caulfield is a fictional McCarthyite: "Donning his red hunting hat, he attempts to become the good Red-hunter, ferreting out the phonies and subversives" (71). See my introductory discussion of my disagreement with Nadel's interpretation.

23. Lewis 55, 57.

24. Ibid., 100.

25. Necessary even to his limited consideration of post–World War II writers, this alteration of the classic mythos is what Lewis termed "the matter of Adam: the ritualistic trials of the young innocent, liberated from family and social history or bereft of them; advancing hopefully into a complex world he knows not of; radically affecting that world and radically affected by it; defeated, perhaps even destroyed . . . but leaving his mark upon the world, and a sign in which conquest may later become possible for survivors" (127).

26. Ihab Hassan, *Radical Innocence: Studies in the Contemporary American Novel* (Princeton, N.J.: Princeton UP, 1961).

27. Albert Camus, *The Myth of Sisyphus,* trans. Justin O'Brien (New York: Vintage Books, 1959), 90.

Chapter 2

1. Lewis 8–9. Whereas in the preceding chapter I made use of Lewis's text as a conceptual resource to help locate *Catcher* in a particular body of American literature, in this chapter I approach *American Adam* itself as a cultural artifact

and treat Lewis's arguments in the text as primary evidence in themselves of the immediate post–World War II intellectual environment in which they were constructed.

2. Ibid., 195.

3. *American Adam* was identified as an eloquent disclosure of the intellectual perspective of "beyond innocence" in Robert Skotheim's essay "'Innocence' and 'Beyond Innocence' in Recent American Scholarship," *American Quarterly* 13 (Spring 1961): 93–99. Skotheim responds to Henry May's *The End of American Innocence* and then demonstrates a corresponding concern with innocence in the scholarship of Leslie Fiedler, Cushing Strout, David Noble, Louis Hartz, Robert Osgood, and Arthur Schlesinger Jr. Skotheim speculates that "these younger writers see earlier America as an innocent America, and see themselves as beyond innocence" largely because they "matured during the Great Depression and the rise of totalitarianism" and hence "view American history differently from an older generation" (99). While I agree with Skotheim's contention that this preoccupation with the analysis of innocence disclosed a meaningful change in the outlook of American intellectuals, his explanation of the origins of this change is markedly insufficient; an insufficiency more than likely due to Skotheim's own participation in the same "scholarly climate" of nuclear fear—and denial. I remain indebted to Skotheim's essay for drawing my attention to the common concerns and themes of the 1949–59 body of American scholarship.

4. This controversy is documented in the rich and probing work of Paul Boyer in *By the Bomb's Early Light.*

5. Edward R. Murrow, *In Search of the Light: The Broadcasts of Edward R. Murrow, 1938–1961* (New York, 1967), 102; as qtd. in Boyer, *Bomb's Early Light* 7.

6. "The Atomic Bomb," *New York Herald Tribune,* 7 Aug. 1945, 22; as qtd. in Boyer, *Bomb's Early Light* 6.

7. "Man and the Atom," *Christian Century Magazine,* 22 Aug. 1945, 56; as qtd. in Boyer, *Bomb's Early Light* 6.

8. Donald Porter Geddes, *The Atomic Age Opens* (New York: Pocket Books, 1945), 38.

9. Kaltenborn broadcast transcript, 17 Aug. 1945; H. V. Kaltenborn Papers, State Historical Society of Wisconsin, Madison; as qtd. in Boyer, *Bomb's Early Light* 7.

10. Kaltenborn broadcast transcript, 6 Sept. 1945; as qtd. in Boyer, *Bomb's Early Light* 7.

11. Henry May (b. 1915), *The End of American Innocence* (New York: Alfred A. Knopf, 1959); see also Leslie Fiedler (b. 1917), *An End to Innocence* (Boston: Beacon P, 1955); Louis Hartz (b. 1919), *The Liberal Tradition in America* (New York: Harcourt, Brace and Co., 1955); R. W. B. Lewis (b. 1917), *The American Adam;* David Noble (b. 1925), *The Paradox of Progressive Thought* (Minneapolis: U of Minnesota P, 1958).

12. Alfred Kazin, *On Native Grounds* (1942; Garden City, N.Y.: Doubleday and Co., 1956), 411.

13. Hassan 3.

14. William Whyte Jr., *The Organization Man* (New York: Simon and Schuster, 1956), 7.

15. Ibid., 13–14.

16. Friedan 15.

17. Ibid., 15–16.

18. Ibid., 186–87.

19. Hassan 65.

20. Marcus Klein, *After Alienation: American Novels in Mid-Century* (Cleveland: World Publishing Co., Meridian Books, 1965), 21–22.

21. Ibid., 29, 29, 30.

22. Stephen J. Whitfield, "The 1950's: The Era of No Hard Feelings," *South Atlantic Quarterly* 76 (Autumn 1977): 554, 555.

23. Ibid., 551, 554.

24. Whitfield 557.

25. David Galloway, *The Absurd Hero in American Fiction* (Austin: U of Texas P, 1970), 12.

26. Klein 33.

27. Ibid., 14.

28. Jerome Klinkowitz, *Literary Disruptions: The Making of a Post-Modern Contemporary Fiction* (Chicago: U of Illinois P, 1975), 1–2.

29. Klein 14–15.

30. Kazin viii.

31. Paul Fussell, *The Great War and Modern Memory* (New York: Oxford UP, 1975), 74. Klinkowitz, also writing in 1975, argued this same point but highlighted the particular impact of the Vietnam War upon American literary forms, leading to the development of both journalistic "non-fiction novels" as well as "surfiction" of novelists such as Thomas Pynchon (1–32).

32. Fussell 321, 18, 320.

33. Hassan 62.

34. Klein 295.

35. John Clellon Holmes, "The Philosophy of the Beat Generation," *Esquire* 99 (June 1983): 158; reprinted from *Esquire* 1958 as part of *Esquire*'s 50th anniversary retrospective.

36. Ibid., 160.

37. Ibid., 162.

38. Frederick L. Gwynn and Joseph L. Blotner, *The Fiction of J. D. Salinger* (Pittsburgh: U of Pittsburgh P, 1958), 1.

Chapter 3

1. Clifton Fadiman as qtd. in Marvin Laser and Norman Fruman, *Studies in J. D. Salinger: Reviews, Essays, and Critiques of The Catcher in the Rye and Other Fiction* (New York: Odyssey P, 1963), 7.

2. See William Peden's discussion of the "*New Yorker* school" in "Esthetics of the Story," *Saturday Review* 36 (11 Apr. 1953): 43–44, in which he reviews *New Yorker* short fiction in general and specifically addresses the short stories of J. D. Salinger and John Cheever. See also David L. Stevenson's later review, "J. D. Salinger: The Mirror of Crisis," *Nation* 184 (9 Mar. 1957): 215–17.

3. "Backstage with Esquire," *Esquire* (October 1945): 34, editorial comment.

4. Laser and Fruman v.

5. The books of literary criticism devoted to Salinger and focusing on *Catcher* are (in order of publication) Frederick L. Gwynn and Joseph L. Blotner, *The Fiction of J. D. Salinger* (Pittsburgh: U of Pittsburgh P, 1958); William F. Belcher and James W. Lee, *J. D. Salinger and the Critics* (Belmont, Calif.: Wadsworth Publishing Co., 1962); Henry Anatole Grunwald, *Salinger: A Critical and Personal Portrait* (London: Peter Owen, 1962); Warren French, *J. D. Salinger* (Boston: Twayne Publishers, 1963); Laser and Fruman, *Studies in J. D. Salinger* (1963); Malcolm M. Marsden, *If You Really Want to Know: A Catcher Casebook* (Chicago: Scott, Foresman and Co., 1963); Harold P. Simonson and Philip E. Hager, *Salinger's "Catcher in the Rye": Clamor vs. Criticism* (Boston: D. C. Heath and Co., 1963); James E. Miller Jr., *J. D. Salinger,* University of Minnesota Pamphlets on American Writers 51 (Minneapolis: U of Minnesota P, 1965); Kenneth Hamilton, *J. D. Salinger: A Critical Essay,* Contemporary Writers in Christian Perspective Series (Grand Rapids, Mich.: W. B. Eerdmans Publishing Co., 1967); Warren French, *J. D. Salinger,* rev. ed. (1976); and James Lundquist, *J. D. Salinger* (New York: Frederick Ungar Publishing Co., 1979). A more recent collection of literary criticism including some cultural analysis is Jack Salzman, ed., *New Essays on* The Catcher in the Rye (New York: Cambridge UP, 1991). In his introduction to the essays, Salzman emphasizes that *Catcher* "remains one of the most popular, and more importantly, one of the most read, of all works of modern fiction" (2).

6. Robert Gutwillig, "Everybody's Caught *The Catcher in the Rye,*" *New York Times Book Review,* paperback section, 15 Jan. 1961, 38–39.

7. Harold L. Roth, "The Catcher in the Rye," *Library Journal,* July 1951, 1126.

8. "The Catcher in the Rye," *Booklist,* 15 July 1951, 401 (unsigned review).

9. Harrison Smith, "Manhattan Ulysses, Junior," *Saturday Review of Literature* 34 (14 July 1951): 12.

10. Ibid., 12–13.

11. Paul Engle, "Honest Tale of Distraught Adolescent," *Chicago Sunday Tribune Magazine of Books,* 15 July 1951, 3.

12. James Stern, "Aw, the World's a Crumby Place," *New York Times Book Review,* 15 July 1951, 5.

13. Ibid.

14. Virgilia Peterson, "Three Days in the Bewildering World of an Adolescent," *New York Herald Tribune Book Review,* 15 July 1951, 3.

15. Ibid.

16. "Problem Boy," *Newsweek,* 16 July 1951, 91–92; "With Love and 20-20

Vision," *Time,* 16 July 1951, 96–97. The *New Republic,* 16 July 1951, also published a review written by critic Anne Goodman. Titled "Mad About Children," Goodman's criticism echoed that of James Stern as she appreciated Salinger's skill in the characterization of Holden yet tired of the sustained immersion in the adolescent sensibility that such authenticity requires (21).

17. "With Love and 20-20 Vision," 96, 97.

18. T. Morris Longstreth, "Review of *The Catcher in the Rye,*" *Christian Science Monitor,* 19 July 1951, 7. Longstreth does not cite his source for Salinger's comment.

19. Ibid.

20. Harvey Breit, "Reader's Choice," *Atlantic* 188 (August 1951): 82.

21. Ibid.

22. S. N. Behrman, "The Catcher in the Rye" (review), *New Yorker,* 11 August 1951, 73–76.

23. American Book Publishers Council, *Bulletin,* (Nov. 1953–Nov. 1955); in December 1955 the *Bulletin*'s title was changed to *Censorship Bulletin*—see issues from Dec. 1955 through Dec. 1958. *Catcher* was one of the twenty books on the list of the Committee on Decent Literature and Crusaders for Decency in Literature which became part of National Organization for Decent Literature, established in 1938.

24. Laser and Fruman 21. *Nine Stories* was on the *New York Times* best-seller list for over three months.

25. Seymour Krill, review of *Nine Stories, Commonweal,* 24 Apr. 1953, 78; as qtd. in Laser and Fruman 21–22.

26. Stevenson 215.

27. Ibid.

28. Ibid., 215, 216.

29. Arthur Heiserman and James E. Miller Jr., "J. D. Salinger: Some Crazy Cliff," *Western Humanities Review* 10 (Spring 1956): 129–37. Discussion of *Catcher* can be found even earlier in Hugh Maclean's essay "Conservatism in Modern American Fiction," *College English* 15 (March 1954): 315–25; however, Heiserman and Miller's essay is the first to focus wholly on *Catcher.* Additionally, two other review articles on *Catcher* appeared in 1956: see James F. Matthews, "J. D. Salinger: An Appraisal," *University of Virginia Magazine* 1 (Spring 1956): 52–60, and Charles Kaplan's "Holden and Huck: The Odysseys of Youth," *College English* 18 (November 1956): 76–80.

30. Heiserman and Miller 129–30.

31. Ibid., 130, 130–31, 132, 137.

32. Edgar Branch, "Mark Twain and J. D. Salinger: A Study in Literary Continuity," *American Quarterly* 9 (Summer 1957): 144–58; quote on 145.

33. Ibid., 153, 157.

34. Gwynn and Blotner, *The Fiction of J. D. Salinger.*

35. George Steiner, "The Salinger Industry," *Nation* 189 (14 Nov. 1959): 360–63.

36. Gwynn and Blotner 360.

37. Ibid., 362.

38. Arthur Mizener, "The Love Song of J. D. Salinger," *Harper's Magazine* 218 (Feb. 1959): 83; Granville Hicks, "J. D. Salinger: Search for Wisdom," *Saturday Review* 42 (25 July 1959): 13. Both are quoted in Steiner's essay on p. 360.

39. Steiner 360.

40. Gutwillig 38.

41. Steiner 362.

42. Laser and Fruman v–vii.

43. Gutwillig 38.

44. See the listing of book-length studies on J. D. Salinger in n. 5 to this chapter. While the articles on Salinger in this period are too numerous to list here, excellent bibliographies of Salinger criticism in this period are located in the 1976 revised edition of Warren French's 1963 study of Salinger as well as in James Lundquist's 1979 book, *J. D. Salinger* (New York: Frederick Ungar Publishing). See also Ihab Hassan, *Radical Innocence: The Contemporary American Novel* (Princeton, N.J.: Princeton UP, 1961), and Marcus Klein, *After Alienation: American Novels in Mid-Century* (Cleveland, Ohio: The World Publishing Co., 1962).

45. Laser and Fruman v.

46. Mizener 83.

47. Joan Didion, "Finally (Fashionably) Spurious," *National Review* 11 (18 Nov. 1961): 341.

48. Ibid., 342.

49. Edward P. J. Corbett, "Raise High the Barriers, Censors," *America* 104 (7 Jan. 1961): 441.

50. Ibid., 443.

51. Ibid.

52. See p. 12 of this chapter for Salinger's statement as quoted by Longstreth.

53. This incident is recounted as rumor more than fact in Corbett's essay (p. 441). However, in my interviews with high school officials in Marin County, Calif., in 1983, the same incident was referenced twice as taking place at either San Francisco State College or City College some time between 1958 and 1960. I have not been able to further document its validity.

54. American Book Publishers Council, Inc., *Freedom-to-Read Bulletin* (previously the *Bulletin* and the *Censorship Bulletin*) 5, no. 1 (March 1962): 10.

55. See the summary citations from various newspapers, published in *Freedom-to-Read* 5–14 (Mar. 1962–Sept. 1965).

56. *Freedom-to-Read* 6, no. 1 (Fall 1963): 8.

57. *Freedom-to-Read* 13, no. 4 (July 1964): 42.

58. Miller Jr., *J. D. Salinger* (1965); Jonathan Baumbach, *The Landscape of Nightmare: Studies in the Contemporary American Novel* (New York: New York UP, 1965): see particularly "The Saint as a Young Man: *The Catcher in the Rye* by

J. D. Salinger," 56–67; and David P. Galloway, *The Absurd Hero in American Fiction*, rev. ed. (1966; Austin, Tx.: U of Texas P, 1970).

59. Hamilton, *J. D. Salinger* (1967). Grounds of censorship such as atheism will be discussed fully in the next chapter.

60. Mary Ely, "A Cup of Consecrated Chicken Soup," *The Catholic World* 202 (February 1966): 299.

61. Ibid., 298–99.

62. Ibid., 300.

63. Gutwillig 39.

64. Ely 301. The accidental discovery of such concrete reader response is in itself encouraging proof that voluntary reader evaluations exist and are accessible if sought.

65. Stanley Fish, *Is There a Text in This Class?* (Cambridge, Mass.: Harvard UP, 1980); Janice Radway, "American Studies, Reader Theory and the Literary Text: From the Study of Material Objects to the Study of Social Processes" (paper presented at the November 1983 Convention of the American Studies Association, Philadelphia, Penn.), 16. Radway's paper was a provocative hint of her fully developed argument in *Reading the Romance: Women, Patriarchy, and Popular Literature* (1984; Chapel Hill: U of North Carolina P, 1991). At roughly the same time, Frederic Jameson was making a similar semiotic argument (albeit regarding the historicity of cultural narrative as "a particular interpretive master code" rather than the greater complex of influences involved in the reader's membership in interpretive communities that Fish and Radway point to), writing that "we never really confront a text immediately, in all its freshness as a thing-in-itself. Rather texts come before us as the always-already-read; we apprehend them through sedimented layers of previous interpretations, or—if the text is brand new—through the sedimented reading habits and categories developed by those inherited interpretive traditions." See Frederic Jameson, *The Political Unconscious: Narrative as a Socially Symbolic Act* (Ithaca, N.Y.: Cornell UP, 1981), 9–10.

66. Fish 11.

67. Ibid., 14.

68. Radway 30.

Chapter 4

1. Richard Stayton, "Required Reading: Why Holden Caulfield Still Catches You," *Herald Examiner*, 12 Oct. 1985, 35.

2. Ibid.

3. Ibid.

4. Ian Hamilton, *In Search of J. D. Salinger* (New York: Random House, 1988). The biography was published against Salinger's will and material contained in the work was contested in court by Salinger.

5. Tracy Young, "People Are Talking about Books: Looking for Mr. Salinger," *Vogue* (August 1986): 196.

6. Donald Barr, "Should Holden Caulfield Read These Books?" *New York Times Book Review,* 4 May 1986, 1.

7. Ibid., 50.

8. Ibid.

9. Ibid., 51.

10. *Archie Bunker's Place* (CBS), 21 Feb. 1982.

11. Sandra Christenson, "On *The Catcher in the Rye*," student essay published in Fred B. Myers, *The Range of Literature: Nonfiction Prose,* Houghton Books in Literature (Boston: Houghton Mifflin, 1969), 40.

12. Ibid., 37, 38.

13. Ibid., 38.

14. Student essay excerpt published in Lois H. Blau, "The Novel in the High School Library: Censorship or Selection?" *Wisconsin Library Bulletin* 15 (May 1964): 178–181.

15. Christenson 39. Here Christenson gives unwitting evidence to David Riesman's understanding of the relationship between the masculine character of *Catcher*'s narrator (and his narrative) and its embrace by female adolescent readers as well as male readers. "There are no girls' stories comparable to *Catcher in the Rye*," Riesman wrote in his 1967 study *Conversations in Japan: Modernization, Politics, and Culture* (New York: Basic Books). "Yet girls can adapt themselves and identify with such a book, while a boy can't so easily identify with a girl." Qtd. in Stephen Whitfield's recent historical survey and critical evaluation of published response to Salinger's novel, "Cherished and Cursed: Toward a Social History of *The Catcher in the Rye*," *New England Quarterly* 4 (1997): 590.

16. Recounted in Alvin D. Alley's "Puritanism: Scourge of Education Today," *Clearinghouse* 38 (March 1964): 393–95.

17. All of the debate participants in the case studies were white and of broadly middle-class socioeconomic status. While actual demographics of the debate participants in other recorded incidents was not available, the concerns and ideological positions paralleled those in the case studies.

18. For extensive discussions of the middle-class origins and ideological base of American censorship, see Paul Boyer's *Purity in Print: The Vice Society Movement and Book Censorship in America* (New York: Scribners and Sons, 1968), and Evelyn Geller's *Forbidden Books in American Public Libraries, 1876–1939*. Regarding the expansive acceptance of middle-class ideology, I am here in agreement with Robert Bellah's assertion that "for the past hundred years or so, the middle class, in the modern sense of the term, has so dominated our culture that neither a genuinely upper-class nor a genuinely working-class culture has fully appeared. Everyone in the United States thinks largely in middle-class categories, even when they are inappropriate." See Bellah et al. viii.

19. In defense of the literary critics, the likelihood that more direct partici-pation on their part would have altered the discourse of the controversies is not very great, because their interests in and concerns regarding *The Catcher in the Rye* (as discussed in chapter 3) were different from those under debate in com-munities of place. It is also possible that literary critics were in fact involved as individuals but under primary membership in other communities of partici-pation—identifying themselves as English teachers, for example, or as parents. While I did not come across any participants—in print reports or in my case study interviews—who identified themselves as literary critics, it is possible that they were present but chose not to identify themselves as such because they were setting aside their professional cloak to emphasize that literary criticism was not their *primary* identification in this context.

20. The exceptions to this ordering are the parent participants who are included in this chapter in terms of their alliance with either the perspectives of the New Right participants or the educators.

21. As noted in the preceding chapter, the first ten censorship incidents that included *The Catcher in the Rye* are Marin County and Los Angeles County, Calif. (1954); Boston, Mass., Port Huron, Mich., Buffalo, N.Y., and Baltimore, Md. (1955); Fairmont, McMechan, and Wheeling, W.Va., and St. Louis, Mo. (1956). See the American Book Publishers Council (ABPC) *Bulletin* (Nov. 1953–Nov. 1955) and its superseding publication, the *Censorship Bulletin* (Dec. 1955–Dec. 1958).

22. Statement of the Episcopal Committee, National Organization for Decent Literature, as quoted in Msgr. Thomas J. Fitzgerald, "The Menace of Indecent Literature," *Ave Maria,* 22 Sept. 1956, 8.

23. As qtd. in the ABPC *Bulletin,* 27 Oct. 1953, 1.

24. As qtd. in the ABPC *Freedom-to-Read Bulletin,* 5.1 (Mar. 1962): 4.

25. Resolution of the National Council of Juvenile Court Judges, as qtd. in Fitzgerald 28.

26. As qtd. in Fitzgerald 9.

27. As qtd. in ABPC *Bulletin,* 12 Apr. 1954, 1.

28. As qtd. in Fitzgerald 28.

29. Ibid.

30. As qtd. in the ABPC *Bulletin,* May 1956, 3. Similarly, in his *Moral Stan-dard for the New Age* (New York: Vantage P, 1974), Christian author Majel Meyer responded to the threat of the Soviet's mind-conditioning appeal to American youth: "However, that is not likely to happen if our young people are aware that it can happen and if they are taught to condition their own minds in a way that counteracts Communist influence" (272).

31. Clarence Hall, "Poison in Print—And How to Get Rid of It," *Reader's Digest* (May 1964): 94.

32. That Keating was the founder of the CDL is identified in Hall's *Reader's Digest* article (ibid.); the year 1958 is identified as the founding date in the ABPC *Censorship Bulletin* 4 (June 1960): 1–4.

33. Hall 96.

34. Ibid., 94.

35. Ibid., 94, 96.

36. Jerry Falwell, as qtd. in J. Charles Park, "The Censorship War: Librarians at the Battlefront," *Newsletter on Intellectual Freedom* 30.6 (Nov. 1981): 180.

37. Gerald Larue, professor of biblical history and archaeology at the University of Southern California, has pointed out that "millions of Christians who belong to mainline churches affiliated with the National Council of Churches and who claim to have had born-again experiences are not associated with the MM [Moral Majority], nor are the millions of Roman Catholics and Eastern Orthodox Christians. Certainly millions of Jews and millions of non-church people who are deeply committed to moral and ethical positions are not members or affiliates of MM." See Gerald Larue, "The Moral Majority: An Immoral Minority," *Free Inquiry* 1.3 (Summer 1983): 18.

38. "Buncombe County, No. Carolina," *Newsletter on Intellectual Freedom* 30.3 (May 1981): 74.

39. Ibid.

40. Maxwell J. Lillenstein, "Books and Bookstores: The Moral Squeeze," *Newsletter on Intellectual Freedom* 30.6 (Nov. 1981): 159.

41. Qtd. in ibid.

42. Rev. H. Lamarr Mooneyham, as qtd. in "North Carolina Moral Majority Releases School Book Report," *Newsletter on Intellectual Freedom* 30.4 (July 1981): 112.

43. Richard A. Viguerie, *The New Right: We're Ready to Lead* (Fall's Church, Va.: Viguerie Co., 1981), introduction.

44. Ibid.

45. For a more complex discussion of the jeremiad tradition, see Sacvan Bercovitch's exhaustive text *The American Jeremiad* (Madison, Wisc.: U of Wisconsin P, 1978).

46. Ibid., xi.

47. Ibid., 57.

48. See David Reisman, *The Lonely Crowd* (New Haven, Conn.: Yale UP, 1950); William H. Whyte Jr., *The Organization Man* (New York: Simon and Schuster, 1956); and Betty Friedan, *The Feminine Mystique.*

49. Judith Krug, "Intellectual Freedom," *The ALA Yearbook* 6 (1981): 156.

50. Ibid.

51. Ibid., 157.

52. Melvil Dewey, as qtd. in Frances Clarke Sayers, "If the Trumpet Be Not Sounded," *Wilson Library Bulletin* 39 (Apr. 1965): 659.

53. As qtd. in ibid., 659.

54. As qtd. in ibid., 659.

55. Ibid., 662.

56. Ibid.

57. See the *Intellectual Freedom Manual*, edited by the ALA (Chicago: ALA, 1974), pt. 1, for both a discussion of the Library Bill of Rights and a reproduction of the bill in its 1967 form.

58. Geller 189.

59. Everett T. Moore, *Issues of Freedom in American Libraries* (Chicago, Ill.: ALA, 1964), 7.

60. ALA, "Declaration of Judith Krug," a deposition pursuant to 28 U.S.C.:1746 <www.ala.org/alanow/cda/krug.html>, 1996. Krug is director of the Office for Intellectual Freedom (OIF) of the ALA and executive director of the Freedom to Read Foundation (FTRF). Her declaration was on behalf of the ALA and the FTRF as plaintiffs seeking "relief against provisions of the Communications Decency Act of 1996" and contains both summary history and policy statements of the ALA's relation to the OIF and FTRF.

61. Arthur Anderson, *Problems in Intellectual Freedom and Censorship* (New York: R. R. Bowker Co., 1974).

62. ALA, *Intellectual Freedom Manual* (see n. 57). Published under the auspices of the ALA's Office for Intellectual Freedom.

63. ALA *Manual*, pt. 4, p. 12.

64. Dr. Charles J. Park, "The Censorship War: Librarians at the Battlefront," *Newsletter on Intellectual Freedom* 30.6 (Nov. 1981): 150.

65. Ibid.

66. John Robotham, *Freedom of Access to Library Materials* (New York: Neal-Schuman Publishers, 1982), iii.

67. "Survey Reports Rise in School Library Censorship," *Newsletter on Intellectual Freedom* 32.1 (Jan. 1983): 1, 18. This study also notes *The Catcher in the Rye* as the second most frequently censored book.

68. Information on "Banned Books Week" is taken from an undated direct mail letter to librarians, written by Judith F. Krug, Director of the OIF (ALA), and distributed in the summer of 1983.

69. "The Challenge of Censorship" [special theme issue], *Book Report* 1.3 (Nov.–Dec. 1982). The use of the word "challenge" here highlights an expansion in the ALA's lexicon for censorship. Where book "censorship" in the 1950s and 1960s was a term used as a broad past-tense reference to the removal or restriction of library materials, by the 1970s attempts to censor these materials were isolated and reframed (as discussed earlier) more optimistically as "requests for reconsideration," whereas "censorship" was reserved for a final disposition of restriction or removal. In the atmosphere of increasing confrontation in the 1980s, "requests for reconsideration" were phrased more defensively as "challenges." This shifting use of terms culminated in the ALA's issuance of a formal definition in their summary of "Challenged Books 1997." Under a headlined hypothetical question, "What's the difference between a challenge and a banning?" the ALA clarified: "A challenge is an attempt to remove or restrict

materials based upon the objections of a person or group. A banning is the removal of those materials" <www.ala.org/challe~1.htm>.

70. Alice Greene, "We Took Censorship to the Classroom," *Book Report* 1.3 (Nov.–Dec. 1982): 29–30; Judy M. Pitts, "Parent Power," in ibid., 331–32.

71. The "six steps" are contained in Gilbert Schwartz, "Policies and Procedures to Handle Complaints About School Library Materials," *Book Report* 1.3 (Nov.–Dec. 1982): 19–22. In this same issue, see also the reprinted letters to *Book Report,* in "Censorship Tips," 34–35; Beatrice Statz, "Preparing the School Staff for the Censor," 28, 30; Jane Wieman and Nancy Motomatsu, "Keeping Calm Under Pressure: Practical and Tested Strategies for Censorship Controversies," 14–18.

72. National Council of Teachers of English, *The Student's Right to Read* (Champaign, Ill.: NCTE Publications, 1962), 10.

73. "No Books—No Censorship, in Parts of the South," *Freedom to Read Bulletin* 6.1 (Fall 1963): 10.

74. "Censorship in the South," *Newsletter on Intellectual Freedom* 35.2 (Mar. 1986): 56.

75. Woods, *Decade of Censorship* 103.

76. Ibid., 106.

77. L. B. Woods and Claudia Perry-Holmes, "The Flak if We Had *The Joy of Sex* Here," *Library Journal* 107.16 (15 Sept. 1982): 1714.

78. Marilyn Knop, "I'm Totally Opposed to Censorship, But …," *Book Report* 1.3 (Nov.–Dec. 1982): 23.

79. Sara Aufdemberge, "Selection vs. Censorship: A Way to Cope," in ibid., 24–25.

80. Gary E. Joseph, "The Enemy Within," in ibid., 26.

81. John J. Farley, "Book Censorship in the Senior High School Libraries of Nassau Co., N.Y." (Ph.D. diss., New York U, 1964).

82. Robotham 72, 31, 32.

83. Ibid., 19.

84. Philippe Ariès, *Centuries of Childhood,* trans. Robert Baldick (New York: Random House, 1962); originally published as *L'Enfant et la vie familiale sous l'Ancien Régime* (Paris: Librairie Plon, 1960).

85. Stephen Kline, *Out of the Garden: Toys, TV, and Children's Culture in the Age of Marketing* (New York: Verso, 1993), 96.

86. Ibid., 89. See also pages 80–81 for Kline's discussion of Neil Postman's arguments regarding the emergence of modern childhood in *The Disappearance of Childhood* (New York: Dell, 1982).

87. Eric Quayle, *The Collector's Book of Children's Books* (London: Studio Vista, 1971), 87. As qtd. in Kline 94.

88. Kline 95. Kline notes that "by the 1980s over four thousand children's books were being published each year in the United States" (96).

89. Anne Scott MacLeod, "Censorship and Children's Literature," *Library Quarterly* 53.1 (1983): 33.

90. Ibid., 34.

91. MacLeod particularly noted the novels of writers Paul Zindel, John Donovan, Isabelle Holland, Sandra Scoppetone, Judy Blume, and Lois Duncan.

92. See Nyla Herber Ahrens, "Censorship and the Teacher of English: A Questionnaire Survey of a Selected Sample of Secondary School Teachers of English" (Ed.D. diss., Teachers College, Columbia Univ., 1965), particularly pp. 90–93.

93. Ibid., 94.

94. Ibid.

95. Edward Gordon, "Freedom to Teach and to Learn," *PTA Magazine* 58.2 (Oct. 1963): 4.

96. Ibid., 5, 7.

97. Hoke Norris, "Should We Censor What Adolescents Read?: Two Kinds of Censorship," *PTA Magazine* 59.7 (Mar. 1965): 10.

98. G. Robert Carlsen, *Books and the Teen-Age Reader* (New York: Harper and Row, 1967), 10.

99. Ibid., 11.

100. Ibid.

101. Ibid., 14

102. Ibid., 33.

103. Kenneth L. Donelson, "White Walls and High Windows: Some Contemporary Censorship Problems," *English Journal* 61 (Nov. 1972): 1191.

104. Ibid., 1192.

105. MacLeod 7.

106. Barr 51.

107. Donelson, "White Walls" 1992.

108. Kenneth L. Donelson, "Censorship in the 1970's: Some Ways to Handle It When It Comes (And It Will)," *English Journal* 63 (Feb. 1974): 48.

109. Ibid.

110. Ibid., 48–50.

111. Lee A. Burress Jr., "How Censorship Affects the School," *Wisconsin Teachers of English, Special Bulletin* 8 (Oct. 1963): 3.

112. Ibid., 5.

113. Ibid., 9.

114. Wayne C. Booth, "Censorship and the Values of Fiction," *English Journal* 53 (March, 1964): 157.

115. Ibid., 157–58.

116. Ibid., 155.

117. Donelson, "Censorship in the 1970's" 51.

118. Robert P. Doyle, ed., *Caution! A List of Books Some People Consider Dangerous* (Chicago: ALA, 1983). This listing of controversial titles was compiled by the American Booksellers Association.

119. The surveys conducted were as follows: 1961–62, high school librarians

in Nassau County, New York; 1963, high school English teachers in Utah; 1965, a national survey of high school English teachers and an Arizona survey of high school English teachers; 1971, ALA survey of censorship complaints published in the *Newsletter on Intellectual Freedom* in 1971; 1966–75, a survey of censorship complaints published in the *NIF* in this period; and in John Robotham's 1982 *Freedom of Access to Library Materials.* In respective order, these findings were presented in the following publications: John J. Farley, "Book Censorship in the Senior High School Libraries of Nassau Co., N.Y."; Utah Council of Teachers of English, "The Censorship Roundup in Utah," *Utah CTE Bulletin* 5 (30 Sept. 1963): 4–5; Retha K. Foster, "Censorship and Arizona High Schools," *Arizona English Bulletin* 8 (May 1966): 65–68; "1971 — The Battle of the Books," *Newsletter on Intellectual Freedom* 21.1 (Jan. 1972): 13; Woods, *Decade of Censorship* 13; Robotham 82.

120. "Footnotes," *Chronicle of Higher Education,* 29 Sept. 1982, 21.

121. For example, see the California State Board of Education, *Model Curriculum Standards, Grades Nine through Twelve* (Sacramento, Calif.: California State Dept. of Education, 1985), in which *The Catcher in the Rye* is listed as a "recommended reading for a core and extended literature program" (E-48) and specifically suggested as a core reading for curriculum "Theme D: Individuals and the Need for Acceptance" (E-58) and "Theme E: Passages and Transformations" (E-60).

122. ALA/Young Adult Library Services Association, *Outstanding Books for the College Bound: Choices for a Generation* (Chicago: ALA Editions, 1996).

123. Tracy Metz, "The New Crusaders of the USA," *Index on Censorship,* Jan. 1982, 20.

124. As cited in "Sideshow: Library Won't Throw Book during Amnesty," *Orange County Register,* 11 June 1985, sect. A2. The closest contender to *Catcher* on the Chicago "most-wanted" list of lost titles was George Orwell's *1984* at 206 missing copies.

Chapter 5

1. Please refer back to chapters 2 and 3 of this study for my discussion of the early "listing" of *Catcher.* Censorship challenges to the use of *The Catcher in the Rye* in high school classes have continued unabated throughout the 1990s, with *Catcher* ranking second on the fifteen-year listing of "Most Frequently Challenged Books" as surveyed by People for the American Way for the period 1982–96 <www.pfaw.org/attacks/96>. In annual surveys of challenged books conducted by the Office of Intellectual Freedom (OIF) of the American Library Association (ALA), *Catcher* ranked eighth in 1995 and moved up to sixth place in 1996. To give some perspective to this ranking, *Catcher*'s sixth-place ranking was determined out of a total of 664 challenges to books in public libraries, schools, and school libraries in 1996 that were reported to the OIF and/or

received media coverage sufficient to come to the attention of OIF staff. OIF research "suggests that for each challenge reported, there may be as many as four or five which remain unreported"; as qtd. under "1996 in Review" on the ALA's Web site, March 1997 <www.ala.org/alaorg/oif/actionnews_mar.html>.

2. Based on my survey of the *Newsletter on Intellectual Freedom* [hereafter *NIF*] (1960–82). My findings are in agreement with similar surveys reported in Woods, *Decade of Censorship,* and Symula, "Censorship of High School Literature."

3. All of the findings regarding the sixty cases of censorship of *The Catcher in the Rye* are based on my survey of reportage in the *NIF* (1960–82) and, again, are borne out by similar findings in the surveys by Woods and Symula (ibid.).

4. Parents were the complainant in twenty-six cases, a "citizen petition" in seventeen cases, ministers in fourteen cases, educators in eleven (nine were school administrators, two were librarians), and students in two cases. Furthermore, in seventeen cases the complainant was not identified.

5. Board of Trustees Meeting minutes, Marin County High School District, 19 Dec. 1960.

6. Interview with Michael Reed, 28 Apr. 1983, Marin County High School, California. The three additional books were *The Cruel Sea* by Nicholas Monsarrat, Carson McCullers's *Member of the Wedding,* and John Steinbeck's *Of Mice and Men.*

7. Interview with Shauna Butler (secretary in the Marin County School District since the early 1950s), 28 Apr. 1983, Marin County, California. See also the Marin County Board of Trustees Meeting minutes, September 13, 1954. Although we are able to hear Kristen Keefe's direct voice through her correspondence to the school board and board meeting minutes, I was unable to interview her, because she had died in the late 1970s.

8. Marin County District Board of Trustees minutes, 19 Dec. 1960. For local news coverage, see the *San Rafael Independent Journal* and the *San Francisco News-Call Bulletin,* Dec. 1960–Feb. 1961, both of which ran articles and updates on a weekly if not daily basis. Beginning 8 Dec. 1960, the controversy also received occasional attention in the *San Francisco Chronicle* in Herb Caen's regular column.

9. Marin County District Board of Trustees minutes, 19 Dec. 1960.

10. Reed interview, 28 Apr. 1983.

11. Butler interview, 28 Apr. 1983.

12. Reed interview, 28 Apr. 1983.

13. Ibid.

14. Ibid.

15. Butler interview, 28 Apr. 1983.

16. Marin County District Board of Trustees minutes, 19 Dec. 1960–6 Feb. 1961, and appended attendance sheets.

17. Interview with Kyle Russo, 28 Apr. 1983, Marin County High School, California.

18. Butler interview, 28 Apr. 1983.

19. In my review of school board minutes and across the numerous interviews I conducted in Marin County, Albuquerque, and Calhoun County as well as in my review of the reported controversies in the *NIF,* attendance at school board meetings during *Catcher* controversies ranged from 50 to 500 estimated "interested citizens," with 200–300 representing typical attendance. The school board members I interviewed in all three communities estimated average attendance at all other school board meetings to be between 3 to 15 "interested citizens," and occasionally 25–30 on particularly heated issues of finance or zoning changes.

20. Telephone interview with Rev. Bradley Parsons, 16 Aug. 1983, Albuquerque, New Mexico.

21. Interview with Kathleen Reynolds, 16 Aug. 1983, Albuquerque High School, New Mexico.

22. Parsons interview.

23. Ibid.

24. Interview with Bo Brackett, 19 Aug. 1983, Calhoun County, Alabama.

25. The other six books were Steinbeck's *The Grapes of Wrath* and *East of Eden, Doris Day: Her Own Story,* Anthony Burgess's *A Clockwork Orange,* Barbara Beasley Murphy's *No Place to Run,* and Francis Hanckel's *The Way of Love.* As reported in "Alabama," *NIF,* 32.1 (Jan. 1983): 7.

26. Brackett interview.

27. Ibid.

28. Central Complaint Committee Meeting minutes, 1 Nov. 1982, Calhoun County Board of Education.

29. Reynolds interview.

30. Butler interview.

31. Marin County Board of Trustees Meeting minutes, 19 Dec. 1960.

32. Interview with Jenny Thigpen, 19 Aug. 1983, Calhoun County, Alabama.

33. Jane Boutwell, "Parents' Protests Bring Removal of Alexandria Library Books," *The Calhoun County Star,* 6 Oct. 1982, sect. 3A.

34. Reed interview.

35. Ibid.

36. Ibid.

37. Parsons interview.

38. Dorothy Simpers, "I-J Reporter's Notebook," *San Rafael Independent Journal,* 29 Dec. 1960, sect. 1C.

39. Thigpen interview.

40. See Barbara Beasley Murphy's report to the Authors Guild, which supported her visit to Calhoun County: "Restricting Books in Alabama Schools: An Author Confronts Her Censors," *Authors Guild Bulletin,* Spring 1983, 5, 13–14.

41. Murphy 14.

42. "Camden, S.C.," *NIF* 19.5 (Sept. 1970): 73.

43. "Roselle, N.J.," *NIF* 20.2 (Mar. 1971): 34.

44. "Several Molalla High Library ...," *NIF* 14.1 (Jan. 1965): 5.

45. "Attacks on Books in U.S. Schools During 1961," *Freedom to Read Bulletin* 5.1 (Mar. 1962): 9.

46. See the earlier discussion in this chapter of Kristen Keefe's accounting and charting of offensive language in *Catcher* for the Marin County controversy. See also *NIF* issues, respectively: "Shawnee Mission, Kansas," 21.2 (Mar. 1972): 40; "Issaquah, Washington," 27.6 (Nov. 1978): 138; "Middlebury, Vermont," 31.2 (Mar. 1982): 48.

47. Marin County District Board of Trustees minutes, 19 Dec. 1960.

48. Reed interview.

49. Kristen Keefe, cover letter to Board of Trustees, Chairman of the Board, Marin County Unified High School District (16 Dec. 1960), 1. The referenced document itself has disappeared.

50. Parsons interview.

51. Brackett interview.

52. Donald P. Costello, as qtd. in Corbett 442.

53. Ibid.

54. Russo interview.

55. Reynolds interview.

56. Mary Lou Jennings, "Minister to Take Protest on Book to School Board," *Albuquerque Tribune*, 14 May 1968, 1.

57. Reynolds interview.

58. Jennings 1.

59. Interview with James Seckington, 18 Aug. 1983, Calhoun County Museum of Natural History, Alabama.

60. Brackett interview.

61. Central Complaint Committee Meeting minutes, 1 Nov. 1982.

62. Reynolds interview.

63. Reed interview.

64. Brackett interview.

65. Marin County Board of Trustees Meeting minutes, 6 Feb. 1961.

66. Keefe 1–2.

67. Russo interview.

68. "Issaquah, Washington," *NIF* 27.6 (Nov. 1978): 138.

69. Reed interview.

70. Ibid.

71. Marin County District Board of Trustees minutes, 19 Dec. 1960.

72. "A School without *Catcher in the Rye*," *NIF* 15.1 (Jan. 1966): 7.

73. Telephone interview with Justine Pas, 16 Aug. 1983, Albuquerque, New Mexico.

74. Marin County Board of Trustees Meeting minutes, 19 Dec. 1960. The parent was identified as Mrs. Clasby.

75. Reed interview.

76. Jennings 1.

77. Dorothy Simpers, "Tam Trustees again Refuse to Ban Books," *San Rafael Independent Journal,* 10 Jan. 1961, sect. 4A.

78. Ibid.

79. Based on my survey of the *Catcher* controversies as reported in the *NIF.*

80. Reed interview.

81. "Shawnee Mission, Kansas," *NIF* 21.2 (Mar. 1972): 40.

82. "Fort Myers, Florida," *NIF* 29.3 (May 1980): 50.

83. "Censorship at Mt. Pleasant," *NIF* 13.4 (July 1964): 50.

84. "Salinger Not Required," *NIF* 13.5 (Sept. 1964): 62.

85. "*The Catcher in the Rye,*" *NIF* 16.3 (May 1967): 34.

86. Marin County Board of Trustees Meeting minutes, 19 Feb. 1960. Recalling the reader response of Sandra Christenson (as discussed in chapter 4) as well as popular culture references such as Julie Smith's *New Orleans Beat* (as discussed in chapter 1), Hayakawa's gender distinction may simply reflect his own assumptions.

87. Ibid.

88. Butler interview.

89. Jennings 1.

90. *Albuquerque Tribune,* miscellaneous letters to the editor, 17–28 May 1968. Quoted phrase is from the 22 May letter written by Albuquerque resident Roz Oakley.

91. *Albuquerque Tribune,* editorial letter written by Luke Benz, 17 May 1968.

92. "Hinsdale, Ill.," *NIF* 20.3 (May 1971): 61.

93. "Middlebury, Vermont," *NIF* 31.2 (Mar. 1982): 48.

94. Keefe 2, 4.

95. Telephone interview with Reverend Wesley Crane, 18 Aug. 1983, Calhoun County, Alabama.

96. Keefe 2.

97. Reed interview.

98. Reverend Jonathon Menjivar, letter recorded in the Marin County Board of Trustees Meeting minutes, 19 Dec. 1960.

99. Seckington interview.

100. Reynolds interview.

101. "Still Alive: The Best of the Best, 1960–1974," *American Library Association* (Chicago). See particularly the plot summaries of the following eighteen novels: Maya Angelou, *I Know Why the Caged Bird Sings; Go Ask Alice;* Claude Brown, *Manchild in the Promised Land;* Alice Childress, *A Hero Ain't Nothin' but a Sandwich;* Richard Cormier, *The Chocolate War;* Blossom Elfman, *The Girls of Huntington House;* Robin Graham and Derek Gill, *Dove;* Hannah Green, *I Never*

Promised You a Rose Garden; Ann Head, *Mr. and Mrs. Bo Jo Jones;* S. E. Hinton, *The Outsiders* and *That Was Then, This Is Now;* Louise Meriweather, *Daddy Was a Number Runner;* John Neufeld, *Lisa Bright and Dark;* Robert Peck, *A Day No Pigs Would Die;* Chaim Potok, *The Chosen;* Gertrude Samuels, *Run, Shelley, Run!;* Sandra Scoppetone, *Trying Hard to Hear You;* Jean Thompson, *House of Tomorrow.*

102. The two "positive" novels and the plot summaries given in the ALA's "Still Alive" list are Robert Peck's *A Day No Pigs Would Die* ("Through his relationship with his hard-working father, 12-year-old Rob learns to cope with the harshness of Shaker life and emerges a mature individual") and Chaim Potok's *The Chosen* ("Two Jewish boys growing to manhood in Brooklyn discover that differences can strengthen friendship and understanding"). The final novel is Gertrude Samuel's *Run, Shelley, Run* ("Runaway Shelley, a victim of family neglect and juvenile injustice, finally gets the help she needs through the concern of a sympathetic judge and the intercession of a kindly neighbor").

103. As noted in Doyle, ed., "Caution! A List of Books Some People Consider Dangerous." The exceptions are *Dove* by Robin Graham and Derek Gill (largely an adventure and romance tale) and John Neufeld's *Lisa Bright and Dark* in which the "heroine" is recognized to be insane.

104. Reed interview.

Chapter 6

1. ALA, *Intellectual Freedom Manual* vii.

2. Even as *Catcher* was selected repeatedly over the past twenty-five years for the ALA's Young Adult Library Services Association (YALSA) annual listing of "Outstanding Books for the College Bound" (discussed in the preceding chapter), the question of exactly who should be reading *Catcher* appears to be unresolved even within the communities devoted to "young adult literature" and specifically within the YALSA itself. In a 1997 essay published in *Booklist* and then reproduced on the ALA's Web page "YA Talk," Marc Aronson (an editor and "vocal advocate of YA literature") attempted to define young adult (YA) literature as an independent genre. Acknowledging that YA literature might *overlap* other genres such as the "coming of age" novel, Aronson explained that YA novels are distinguished first and last by their intentional appeal to the audience of young readers. In a somewhat confusing expansion of this distinction, Aronson argued that "adult coming-of-age novels describe events or emotions that are part of the lives of adolescents, but they are not aimed at teen readership. . . . Works such as McCullers's *Member of the Wedding* and Salinger's *Catcher in the Rye* clearly speak to YAs, which is why they are assigned in classes and enjoy ongoing popularity. They certainly conform to the descriptive criteria of coming-of-age literature. They do not, however, fit within the specific genre called YA: that subset of books for young readers aimed at adolescents." See

Marc Aronson, "The Challenge and the Glory of Young Adult Literature," *Booklist* 93 (15 Apr. 1997): 1418–19. See also the "YA Talk" link on the ALA's Web site <www.ala.org/booklist/55YAT4~1.htm>.

3. Interview with Bo Brackett, 19 Aug. 1983, Calhoun County, Alabama.

4. Telephone interview with Justine Pas, 16 Aug. 1983, Albuquerque, New Mexico.

5. Board of Trustees Meeting minutes, 19 Dec. 1960, Marin County Union High School District.

6. Interview with Shauna Butler, 28 Apr. 1983, Marin County, California.

7. Kristen Keefe, letter to Board of Trustees, Chairman of the Board, Marin County Unified High School District, 16 Dec. 1960, 4.

8. Telephone interview with Reverend Bradley Parsons, 16 Aug. 1983, Albuquerque, New Mexico.

9. Telephone interview with Reverend Wesley Crane, 18 Aug. 1983, Calhoun County, Alabama.

10. Ibid.

11. Interview with James Seckington, 18 Aug. 1983, Calhoun County Museum of Natural History, Alabama.

12. Brackett interview.

13. Seckington interview.

14. Robotham 9.

15. Brackett interview.

16. Seckington interview.

17. Brackett interview.

18. Peter Goldman, "Living with the Bomb: The First Generation of the Atomic Age," *Newsweek*, 29 July 1985, 28.

19. In this segment, I am speaking in sweeping reference to the evidence and eloquent arguments of Betty Friedan in *The Feminine Mystique*, David Riesman in *The Lonely Crowd*, and William H. Whyte Jr. in *The Organization Man*, as well as Stephen Whitfield in his essay "The 1950's: The Era of No Hard Feelings."

20. Laurence Vesey, "Growing Up in America," in Leonard Dinnerstein and Kenneth Jackson, eds., *American Vistas: 1877 to the Present*, vol. 2 (New York: Oxford UP, 1979), 365.

21. Throughout the following section, I owe much to the scholarship and arguments of Daniel Bell in *The End of Ideology* (Garden City, N.Y.: Doubleday, 1964), William Chafe in *The Unfinished Journey: America since WWII* (New York: Oxford UP, 1986), Peter Clecak in *America's Quest for the Ideal Self* (New York: Oxford UP, 1983), Morris Dickstein in *Gates of Eden: American Culture in the '60's* (New York: Basic Books, 1977), Godfrey Hodgson in *America in Our Time* (Garden City, N.Y.: Doubleday, 1976), and William O'Neill in *Coming Apart* (New York: Times Books, 1971) as well as to Laurence Vesey for his essay "Growing Up in America."

22. And the list continues to develop even as this manuscript has: consider

the more recent revelations of 1980s Wall Street insider trading, banking failures and scandals, the Iran-Contra Congressional hearings as well as the 1990s "scandalgates" (from Whitewater to Monica Lewinsky) surrounding the Clinton presidency.

23. Sissela Bok, *Lying: Moral Choice in Public and Private Life* (New York: Pantheon Books, 1978), xvii.

24. Ibid., xviii. One would suspect that the percentiles expressing loss of confidence are at least as low in the late 1990s, if not lower.

25. Donald Warwick, "Social Scientists Ought to Stop Lying," *Psychology Today* 8 (Feb. 1975): 105.

26. Robotham 7.

27. Vesey 359–61.

28. Ibid., 361.

29. Lewis 111.

30. George F. Will, "Huck at a Hundred," *Newsweek,* 18 Feb. 1985, 92.

31. Ibid.

32. Lewis 129.

33. Ibid., 89.

34. David Madden, ed., *American Dreams, American Nightmares* (Carbondale and Edwardsville: Southern Illinois UP, 1970), 54.

35. I am here purposely ignoring the definition of the American Dream as a material construction of "the good life" that serves as a consumer prompt. Actually, I see this definition as an expression of the dual visions I outline above: our pursuit and provision of a symbolic "good life" is an attempt to maintain our faith in the dream in the face of doubtful realities — *if we live well, we must be doing something right.*

36. Frederic Jameson, *The Political Unconscious: Narrative as a Socially Symbolic Act* (Ithaca, N.Y.: Cornell UP, 1981), 13.

37. Bellah et al. 51, 282–83.

38. James Davison Hunter, *Culture Wars: The Struggle to Define America* (New York: Basic Books, 1991), 34, 42–43.

39. Unsurprisingly, several of the "culture wars" texts focus on censorship activity. Joan DelFatorre's *What Johnny Shouldn't Read: Textbook Censorship in America* (New Haven, Conn.: Yale UP, 1992) is an uneven polemic critiquing the beliefs of "fundamentalists" in opposition to those who favor "liberalized texts." By contrast, in James Moffat's *Storm in the Mountains: A Case Study of Censorship, Conflict, and Consciousness* (Carbondale: Southern Illinois UP, 1988), Moffat argues that text book censorship is the expression of "'the not-wanting-to-know' that I have called agnosis" and "far from being peculiar to fundamentalists or mountaineers or the uneducated, agnosis limits the thought and action of virtually everyone everywhere" (187).

40. George Lakoff, *Moral Politics: What Conservatives Know That Liberals Don't* (Chicago: U of Chicago P, 1996), xi, 12. Lakoff titles his chapter on educational systems "Culture Wars."

41. Ibid., 234–35.

42. Jane Tompkins, *Sensational Designs: The Cultural Work of American Fiction, 1790–1860* (New York: Oxford UP, 1985), xvii.

Afterword

1. Interview with Kyle Russo, 28 Apr. 1983, Marin County High School, California.

2. Interview with James Seckington, 18 Aug. 1983, Calhoun County Museum of Natural History, Alabama.

3. Board of Trustees Meeting Minutes, 6 Feb. 1961, Marin County Union High School District.

4. Whitfield 556–57.

5. Vesey 360.

6. Leonard Dinnerstein and Kenneth Jackson, eds., introduction to Vesey's "Growing Up in America," 358.

7. Irving Howe, *A World More Attractive: A View of Modern Literature and Politics* (New York: Horizon P, 1963), 85.

8. Dan Lacy, "The Prospects for the Future," in *The Future of General Adult Books and Reading in America,* ed. Peter S. Jennison and Robert Sheridan (Chicago: ALA, 1970), 144–45. All of the following quotations contained in this paragraph are from pp. 144–45.

9. Ibid.

10. Charles J. Park, "The Censorship War: Librarians at the Battlefront," *Newsletter on Intellectual Freedom* 30.6 (Nov. 1981): 150.

11. Spencer Weart, *Nuclear Fear: A History of Images* (Cambridge, Mass.: Harvard UP, 1988), xiii, 425. Picking up on Weart's argument, historian Peggy Rosenthal writes that "mushroom cloud images . . . glory in a sense of innocence that's classically American: they celebrate a bounty of mind and matter and energy infinitely resourceful at creating the ever-new. But the Mass Murderous Mushroom Cloud represents . . . something radically unfamiliar in the American cultural experience: a sense of sin. The Mass Murderous Mushroom Cloud is a huge gulp of remorse. It sees with a shudder that what we have created destroys. . . . Our resourcefulness has reached its limit, in ashes and radioactive dust." See Peggy Rosenthal, "The Nuclear Mushroom Cloud as Cultural Image," *American Literary History* 3.1 (Spring 1991): 83.

12. Boyer, *Bomb's Early Light* 5.

13. Ibid., 355.

14. Ibid., 357–58.

15. Ibid., 250.

16. Whitfield 553.

17. Christopher Lasch, *The Minimal Self: Psychic Survival in Troubled Times* (New York: W. W. Norton and Co., 1984), 16. See also Bellah et al.

18. A. Alvarez, "A Talk with Robert Lowell," *Encounter,* Feb. 1965, 39–46.

19. Hans Bethe, "The Hydrogen Bomb," *Bulletin of Atomic Science,* April 1950, 102.

20. The embrace of the bomb as a divine gift or a sign that God is "on our side" is best exemplified in President Truman's announcement of the bombing of Nagasaki (see chapter 1); widespread embrace of this notion is heavily documented in Paul Boyer's *Bomb's Early Light.*

In 1995, recognition of the fiftieth anniversary was split between (1) "commemoration" of the end of World War II, emphasizing the saving of American lives in parallel with the (implied) necessity of America's introduction of atomic warfare and (2) scholarly analyses of the decision to use atomic weaponry and consequences of the dropping of the atomic bombs—physical and psychic, for Japan and for America. This split response to the fiftieth anniversary was epitomized by the controversy over (and ultimately the cancellation of) the Smithsonian's planned exhibition at the National Air and Space Museum, "The Last Act: The Atomic Bomb and the End of the World," informally referred to as "the Enola Gay Exhibit." The historical advisory board for the exhibit produced a "cautious" accompanying script—so cautious that one historian serving on the board would later write that "the draft script offered only a glimpse into . . . documents that have compelled historians to rewrite the history of the atomic bomb project. . . . It appeared as if the curators were giving undue attention to established myths at the expense of historical research." Even so, the planned exhibit was protested by American military officers, veteran's groups, and members of both houses of Congress for its theme (*as understood)* "of American vengefulness and Japanese suffering in World War II." In the end, the Secretary of the Smithsonian canceled the original exhibit and its attempt at combining "historical commemoration with historical analysis" and announced that it would be replaced by a simplified display of the Enola Gay, an abbreviated statement of its mission and a videotape of its crew members.

For characteristic representation of the two opposing perspectives, see in particular Charles Krauthammer, "History Hijacked," *Time,* 13 Feb. 1995, 90, and Martin J. Sherwin, "The Assault on History: Forgetting the Bomb," *Nation,* 15 May 1995, 692–94. Commemorative articles range from Greg Mitchell's survey of television programs depicting "the bomb" in "Ground Zero: TV's Nuclear Ages" (*TV Guide,* 29 July–4 Aug. 1995, 16–17) to Suzanne Mantell's survey of recent titles addressing the bomb and its impact in "Fifty Years of the Nuclear Age" (*Publishers Weekly,* 31 July 1995, 23–24) to Paul Gray's retrospective account for *Time,* bleakly titled "Doomsdays" (7 Aug. 1995, 48–53). Scholarly perspectives were given the best anniversary representation in *Diplomatic History,* which devoted the entirety of the Spring 1995 journal issue to the atomic bombing of Japan. See in particular Paul Boyer's "Exotic Resonances: Hiroshima in American Memory" and J. Samuel Walker's "History, Collective Memory, and the Decision to Use the Bomb," both appearing in *Diplomatic History* 19.2 (Spring 1995): 297–318 and 319–28, respectively.

21. Peter Goldman, "Living with the Bomb: The First Generation of the Atomic Age," *Newsweek*, 29 July 1985, 28.

22. Ibid.

23. Norman Mailer, *Advertisements for Myself* (New York: Signet Books, 1960). As qtd. in Robert J. Lifton's *The Broken Connection: On Death and the Continuity of Life* (New York: Simon and Schuster, 1979), 347.

24. Lifton, *Broken Connection* 382.

25. Edgar Branch, "Mark Twain and J. D. Salinger: A Study in Literary Continuity," *American Quarterly* 9 (Summer 1957): 154.

26. Christenson in Myers 39. Additional sections of her essay are quoted and discussed in chapter 3.

27. Ibid., 39, 37.

28. Elizabeth Mehren, "An Updated 'Catcher' in Lotus Land," *Los Angeles Times*, 22 May 1985, pt. 5, p. 1.

29. Ibid., 13.

30. Ibid.

31. Ibid., 12.

32. Ibid., 13.

33. As qtd. in Kim Murphy, "Warning Signs of Massacre Were Hidden in Plain Sight," *Los Angeles Times*, 9 May 1999, sect. A1.

34. Ibid.

35. Lewis Mumford, "Social Effects," *Air Affairs*, March 1947, 370–82; as qtd. in Boyer, *Bomb's Early Light* 286.

36. Lifton 293.

37. Whitfield 563.

38. Michael J. Carey, "Psychological Fallout," *Bulletin of Atomic Science*, Jan. 1982, 24. See also JoAnne Brown's article "'A Is For Atom, B Is For Bomb.' Civil Defense in American Public Education, 1948–1963," *Journal of American History* 75.1 (June 1988): 68–90. Brown documents and analyzes civil defense programs in the 1950s, concluding that "children were taught that civil defense was just another 'precaution'—and atomic holocaust just another 'hazard'—of everyday life.... The school civil defense programs taught a generation to equate emotional maturity with an attitude of calm acceptance toward nuclear war. The anger, fear, and disillusionment that have followed as this generation grew to adulthood are in large measure the postponed cost of a mistaken alliance, of small and practical compromises that subverted education for national defense, traded away knowledge for security, and substituted banality for unmitigated horror."

39. Goldman 28.

40. "Depression," *Newsweek*, 4 May 1987, 48.

41. "Teen Suicide," *The Donahue Show* (NBC), 1987 (transcript no. 051270. I chose to use the suicide data presented on *The Donahue Show* for two reasons. Studies on teenage suicide vary depending upon the age of definition of "teenage," and the data on attempted suicide also varies due to definitional problems.

The figures used on *The Donahue Show* are midrange to conservative estimates. Furthermore, because of its presentation on a popular television program, this depiction of suicide is likely to be the most familiar to many Americans. For more scholarly discussion of teenage suicide in the postwar period see Herbert Hendin's survey text, *Suicide in America* (New York: W. W. Norton, 1984) and Donna Gaines's ethnographic study *Teenage Wasteland: Suburbia's Dead End Kids* (New York: Harper-Collins, 1990). Both Hendin's and Gaines's figures support *Donahue's* representation of teen suicide with one notable exception: Gaines raises the estimated number of attempted suicides (1980s) to 400,000.

42. *The Donahue Show* was a nationally televised daytime program in which host Phil Donahue led and mediated discussion between the studio audience and invited speakers. Speakers on this day were two mothers of suicide victims; a young woman who had attempted suicide; actress Heather Locklear, who lost two male relatives to suicide; and psychotherapist Karen Blaker, who specializes in work with suicidal teens. The eight "signs" are: (1) the recent suicide of a friend or relative; (2) expressing suicidal thoughts or lack of hope in the future; (3) change of personality, habits or appearance; (4) violent or rebellious behavior; (5) drug and/or alcohol abuse; (6) decline in schoolwork or athletic performance; (7) romantic breakup; (8) giving away prized or personal possessions.

43. "Teen Suicide," *Donahue Show.*

44. Christopher Lasch has stated, "Suicide becomes the ultimate form of self-defense in a world perceived — not just by writers but by ordinary men and women or at least those who instruct ordinary men and women in the everyday acts of survival — as a comfortable concentration camp." See *Minimal Self* 99.

45. One of the earliest works on "nuclear consciousness" is Jeff Nuttall's polemical *Bomb Culture* (New York: Delacorte P, 1968), in which he finds a distinction between pre- and postpuberty generations at the end of World War II as to whether they were able to conceive of a sense of a positive, realizable future or not: the prepuberty generation(s) were not able to. As to the "riskiness" of nuclear culture study, Spencer Weart makes a similar point, writing that "there is no final way to prove that nuclear fear, or any other combination of emotions and imagery, played a specific role in history. What can reliably be said, based on a large sample of writings, films, polls, and so forth, is that this closely knit structure of associated emotions and images did pervade Cold War and McCarthyist discourse" (Weart 127).

46. John E. Mack, "Psychosocial Trauma," in *The Final Epidemic: Physicians and Social Scientists on Nuclear War,* ed. Ruth Adams and Susan Cullen (Chicago: Educational Foundation for Nuclear Science, 1981), 21. John Mack has become somewhat of a controversial figure himself, given the notoriety received by his more recent book *Abduction: Human Encounters with Aliens* (1994). Disappointingly, Mack's earlier recognition of cultural and historical factors in his work on nuclear fear did not apparently lead to a similar recognition in

his interpretation of narratives of interplanetary contact. Even so, I value his primary data on nuclear fear in the imagery and statements of adolescents.

47. Ibid.

48. Ibid., 24–25.

49. Phyllis La Farge, "Learning to Live with the Bomb," *Parents' Magazine,* Mar. 1987, 125.

50. Boyer, *Bomb's Early Light* 16.

51. The interview with Hoffman appeared in *Time*'s 11 Jan. 1988 feature essay "1968," by Robert Ajemian, Anne Hopkins, and Dan Goodgame. Gerzon's meditative passage is in his 1982 book, *A Choice of Heroes: The Changing Faces of American Manhood* (Boston: Houghton Mifflin, 1982), 73.

52. Mack 26.

53. La Farge 122.

54. Ibid., 125.

55. The "scornful adolescent" is as quoted by Sibylle Escalona in her title essay, "Children and the Threat of Nuclear War," in the Child Study Association of America's *Children and the Threat of Nuclear War* (New York: Duell, Sloan and Pearce, 1964), 18–19, in which she argues that "*what* causes their [adolescents] distress is much the same for all—it is the fact that nuclear weapons might destroy much of the future they are counting on." The high school student speaking in the inset quote is as recorded in Mack 25.

56. La Farge 214.

57. Boyer, *Bomb's Early Light* 366.

58. Anna Gorman, Massie Ritch, and Matt Surman, "County Report: New Scrutiny for Goths," *Los Angeles Times, Ventura County Edition,* 2 May 1999, sect. B1.

59. See the Web site constructed in June 1999 "honoring" Harris and Klebold <www.maxpages.com/ericdylan>.

60. Gorman et al.

61. Terence Monmaney and Greg Krikorian, "Violent Culture, Media Share Blame, Experts Say," *Los Angeles Times,* 26 Mar. 1998, sect. A16.

62. Richard Serrano, "2 Gunmen Had Help, Police Fear," *Los Angeles Times,* 23 Apr. 1999, sect. A1.

63. Gorman et al. The school administrator quoted is Steve Myerchin.

64. Kim Murphy and Terry McDermott, "Shooter Kills 1, Injures 22 at Oregon School," *Los Angeles Times,* 22 May 1998, sect. A1.

65. Mike Downey, "Little Monsters, Gigantic Fears," *Los Angeles Times,* 2 May 1999, sect. A2. The resident quoted is Don Burkard.

66. Mike Males, "Who's Really Killing Our Schoolkids?" *Los Angeles Times,* 31 May 1998, sect. M1.

67. "Eric's Song," as originally posted on his (since removed) Web site and reposted on the memorial site cited in n. 59.

Bibliography

Primary Sources
The Primary Text

Salinger, Jerome David. *The Catcher in the Rye*. New York: Little, Brown and Co., 1951; reprint, New York: Bantam Books, 1964.

1951–59 Literary Reviews of The Catcher in the Rye

Behrman, S. N. "The Catcher in the Rye" [review]. *New Yorker*, 11 Aug. 1951, 73–76.

Branch, Edgar. "Mark Twain and J. D. Salinger: A Study in Literary Continuity." *American Quarterly* 9 (summer 1957): 144–58.

Breit, Harvey. "Reader's Choice." *Atlantic* 188 (August 1951): 82.

"The Catcher in the Rye" [unsigned review]. *Booklist*, July 1951, 401.

Engle, Paul. "Honest Tale of Distraught Adolescent." *Chicago Sun Tribune*, 15 July 1951, sec. 4, p. 3.

Goodman, Anne L. "Mad about Children." *New Republic* 125 (16 July 1951): 20–21.

Hassan, Ihab. "Rare Quixotic Gesture: The Fiction of J. D. Salinger." *Western Review* 21 (summer 1957): 261–80.

Heiserman, Arthur, and James E. Miller Jr. "J. D. Salinger: Some Crazy Cliff." *Western Humanities Review* 10 (spring 1956): 129–37.

Kaplan, Charles. "Holden and Huck: The Odysseys of Youth." *College English* 18 (Nov. 1956): 76–80.

Longstreth, T. Morris. "The Catcher in the Rye" [review]. *Christian Science Monitor*, 19 July 1951, 7.

Lowrey, Burling. "Salinger and the House of Glass" [letter to editor]. *New Republic* 141 (26 Oct. 1959): 23–24.

Mizener, Arthur. "The Love Song of J. D. Salinger." *Harper's Magazine* 218 (Feb. 1959): 83–90.

Peden, William. "Esthetics of the Story." *Saturday Review* 36 (4 Apr. 1953): 43–44.

Peterson, Virgilia. "Three Days in the Bewildering World of an Adolescent." *New York Herald-Tribune Book Review*, 15 July 1951, 3.

"Problem Boy." *Newsweek*, 16 July 1951, 91–92 [Portrait].

Roth, Harold L. "The Catcher in the Rye" [review]. *Library Journal,* July 1951, 1125–26.

Smith, Harrison. "Manhattan Ulysses, Junior." *Saturday Review of Literature* 34 (14 July 1951): 12–13.

Steiner, George. "The Salinger Industry." *Nation* 189 (14 Nov. 1959): 360–63.

Stern, James. "Aw, The World's A Crumby Place." *New York Times Book Review,* 15 July 1951, 5.

Stevenson, David L. "J. D. Salinger: The Mirror of Crisis." *Nation* 184 (9 Mar. 1957): 215–17.

Wiegand, William. "The Knighthood of J. D. Salinger." *New Republic* 141 (19 Oct. 1959): 19–21.

"With Love and 20-20 Vision" [Books section]. *Time,* 16 July 1951, 96–97.

Reports of Censorship of The Catcher in the Rye

American Book Publishers Council. *ABPC Bulletin,* 1953–55.

———. *Censorship Bulletin* [supersedes *ABPC Bulletin*].

  "The Freedom to Read—Abridged." 1.1 (Dec. 1955): 2.

  "NODL List Widely Used as Censorship Weapon." 1.1 (Dec. 1955): 3.

  "Books Banned by West Virginia Censors." 1.2 (Mar. 1956): 3.

  "Catholic Groups Scan Armed Services and Community Reading Matter." 1.5 (Sept. 1956): 2.

  "ACLU Challenges NODL Influence." 2.2 (July 1957): 5.

  "Censorship Debated at Catholic Library Association Meeting." 2.2 (July 1957): 6.

  "Churchmen's Committee for Decent Publications Formed." 2.2 (July 1957): 6.

  "Citizens for Decent Literature, Inc." 4.1–2 (June 1960): 2–5.

  "National Office for Decent Literature." 4.1–2 (June 1960): 5–7.

———. *Freedom-to-Read Bulletin* (supersedes the *Censorship Bulletin*).

  "Introduction." 5.1 (Mar. 1962): 1–2.

  "Attacks on Books in U.S. Schools during 1961." 5.1 (Mar. 1962): 2–12.

  "Catcher in the Rye—'I'd Burn It,' says Pennsylvania School Principal." 6.1 (fall 1963): 8–9.

  "No Books—No Censorship, in Parts of the South." 6.1 (fall 1963): 11.

American Library Association. "Catcher and Mice." *American Library Association Bulletin* 55 (Mar. 1961): 229–30.

———. "Threats to Books." *American Library Association Bulletin* 46 (Oct. 1952): 291–92.

———. *The American Library Association Yearbook* 6 (1981): 99, 156–59.

———. "1996 in Review." *Intellectual Freedom Action News,* Apr. 1997, 3–4.

———. *Newsletter on Intellectual Freedom.*

  "More on Nevada . . ." 4.4 (July 1956): 4.

  "Censors for Teens . . ." 9.1–2 (July 1960): 6.

"Borderline Books . . ." 10.1 (Mar. 1961): 3.

"Santa Ana, Calif." 10.2 (June 1961): 4.

"Specter over Texas." 11.2 (July 1962): 5.

"Miami Catches Catcher Fever." 11.2 (July 1962): 6.

"Student Attacks . . ." 11.2 (July 1962): 7.

"Textbooks under Fire." 12.1 (Jan. 1963): 13.

"From Anaheim to Eagle River." 12.3 (May 1963): 39–40.

"School Problems . . ." 12.4 (July 1963): 45, 49.

"Parents Conduct . . ." 12.4 (July 1963): 51, 54.

"Catcher Keeps Catching It." 13.1 (Jan. 1964)

"Salinger, Baldwin and Lee." 13.1 (Jan. 1964): 4.

"Tales out of School." 13.2 (Mar. 1964): 3.

"Where They Ban the Better." 13.2 (Mar. 1964): 35.

"Schools Score Two." 13.3 (May 1964): 35.

"Censorship at Mt. Pleasant." 13.4 (July 1964): 50–51.

"Rye and Sky in School." 13.4 (July 1964): 42.

"Salinger Not Required." 13.5 (Sept. 1964): 62, 64.

"Several Molalla High Library . . ." 14.1 (Jan. 1965): 5.

"Catcher Again and Again." 14.2 (Mar. 1965): 23.

"No Don Quixote." 14.3 (May 1965): 34.

"The Vestal Virgins of New York State." 14.3 (May 1965): 38.

"Restrictions in Richmond." 14.5 (Sept. 1965): 56.

"A School without Catcher in the Rye." 15.1 (Jan. 1966): 7.

"Pressure on Public Schools." 15.2 (Mar. 1966): 13.

"The Power of Anonymity." 15.3 (May 1966): 27.

"The Catcher in the Rye." 16.3 (May 1967): 34.

"Catcher Catches It in G.P." 17.1 (Jan. 1968): 7.

"Two from Missouri." 17.3 (May 1968): 30.

"Pastor Pledges Fight over Catcher." 17.5 (Sept. 1968): 57.

"Catcher in the Rye in Ohio." 18.2 (Mar. 1969): 32.

"Criterion: Filth." 18.4 (July 1969): 59.

"Rock County Librarians Unite." 18.4 (July 1969): 60.

"'Catcher' OK till Next Year." 19.2 (Mar. 1970): 27.

"Controversy at Glenwood . . ." 19.2 (Mar. 1970): 30.

"Camden, S.C." 19.5 (Sept. 1970): 73.

"Yorktown, NY." 20.1 (Jan. 1971): 8.

"Roselle, N.J." 20.2 (Mar. 1971): 34.

"Troy, NY." 20.2 (Mar. 1971): 35.

"Yorktown, NY." 20.2 (Mar. 1971): 52.

"Hinsdale, IL." 20.3 (May 1971): 61.

"Naperville, IL." 20.3 (May 1971): 61.

"The Battle of the Books: 1971." 21.1 (Jan. 1972): 13.

"Hinsdale, IL." 21.1 (Jan. 1972): 31.

"Worcester, MA." 21.1 (Jan. 1972): 18.

"Shawnee Mission, Kan." 21.2 (Mar. 1972): 40.

"'Catcher' Catches It ... Again." 21.3 (May 1972): 88.

"Clinton, Tenn." 21.3 (May 1972): 72.

"Dallas, Tex." 21.4 (July 1972): 105.

"Hermon, NY." 21.4 (July 1972): 103.

"Hollidaysburg, Pa." 21.4 (July 1972): 105.

"Salem, N.J." 27.1 (Jan. 1978): 8.

"If School Is Open, Can Censorship Be Far Behind?" 27.6 (Nov. 1978): 133, 146.

"Issaquah, Washington." 27.6 (Nov. 1978): 138, 144.

"Omak, Washington." 28.4 (July 1979): 75–76.

"Fort Myers, Florida." 29.1 (Jan. 1980): 6.

"Middleville, Michigan." 29.1 (Jan. 1980): 7.

"Westfield, Indiana." 29.1 (Jan. 1980): 6.

"Fort Myers, Florida." 29.3 (May 1980): 50.

"North Jackson, Ohio." 29.3 (May 1980): 51.

"Lee County, Florida." 29.4 (July 1980): 76.

"Southeastern Greene, Pa." 29.5 (Sept. 1980): 100.

"Buncombe County, No. Carolina." 30.3 (May 1981): 74.

"Brodsheadsville, Pa." 30.4 (July 1981): 93.

"North Carolina Moral Majority Releases School Book Report." 30.4 (July 1981): 85, 112–13.

"AAP/ALA/ASCD Study Cites Censorship Increase." 30.5 (Sept. 1981): 117, 141.

"Livermore, CA." 31.1 (Jan. 1982): 8.

"Farmville, No. Carolina." 31.2 (Mar. 1982): 48.

"Middlebury, Vermont." 31.2 (Mar. 1982): 48.

"Atlantic, Iowa." 31.3 (May 1982): 82.

"Anniston, AL." 32.1 (Jan. 1983): 7.

"Survey Reports Rise in School Library Censorship." 32.1 (Jan. 1983):1, 18.

"Anniston, AL." 32.2 (Mar. 1983): 37.

"Morris, Manitoba." 32.2 (Mar. 1983): 38.

"Censorship in the South." 35.2 (Mar. 1986): 56.

Doyle, Robert P. "Caution! A List of Books Some People Consider Dangerous" [pamphlet]. Chicago: American Library Association, 1983.

Edwards, Tamala M. "What Johnny Can't Read." *Time*, 21 Dec. 1998, 46–47.

Internet Web Sites Reporting Censorship Challenges

American Library Association, Office of Intellectual Freedom: <www.ala.org/alaorg/oif>.

People for the American Way: <www.pfaw.org/attacks>.

Later Reviews and Literary Responses to
Censorship of The Catcher in the Rye

Barr, Donald. "Should Holden Caulfield Read These Books?" *New York Times Book Review,* 4 May 1986, 1, 50–51.

"The Catcher on the Hill." *Newsweek,* 18 Nov. 1974, 17 [Portrait].

Chester, Alfred. "Salinger: How to Live without Love." *Commentary* 35 (June 1963): 467–74.

Christenson, Sandra. "On *The Catcher in the Rye,*" in Fred B. Myers, *The Range of Literature: Nonfiction Prose.* Houghton Books in Literature. Boston: Houghton Mifflin, 1969.

Costello, Donald. "Salinger and His Critics." *Commonweal* 79 (25 Oct. 1963): 132–35.

Didion, Joan. "Finally (Fashionably) Spurious." *National Review* 11 (18 Nov. 1961): 341–42.

"The Dodger in the Rye." *Newsweek,* 30 July 1979, 11 [Portrait].

Ely, Mary. "A Cup of Consecrated Chicken Soup." *Catholic World* 202 (Feb. 1966): 298–301.

"Footnotes." *Chronicle of Higher Education,* 29 Sept. 1982, 21.

Gutwillig, Robert. "Everybody's Caught *The Catcher in the Rye.*" *New York Times Book Review,* 15 Jan. 1961, 38–39.

———. "J. D. Salinger: 'He Touches Something Deep in Us.'" *Horizon* 4 (May 1962): 100–107.

Harper's 225 (Dec. 1962): 12 [miscellaneous letters to editor].

"In Place of the New, A Reissue of the Old." *Newsweek,* 28 Jan. 1963, 90–91 [Books].

Kenney, Michael. "Searching for Salinger." *Boston Globe,* 3 Sept. 1997, sect. C1.

McCarthy, Mary. "J. D. Salinger's Closed Circuit." *Harper's* 225 (Oct. 1962): 46–48.

Mehren, Elizabeth. "An Updated 'Catcher' in Lotusland." *Los Angeles Times,* 22 May 1985, pt. 5, pp. 1, 12.

Moss, Adam. "Catcher Comes of Age." *Esquire* 96 (Dec. 1981): 56–58.

"The Mysterious J. D. Salinger . . ." *Newsweek,* 30 May 1960, 92 [Portrait].

Parrish, Michael E. "Seymour: A Postscript." *Commentary* 36 (November 1963): 350.

Pinsker, Sanford. "*The Catcher in the Rye* and All: Is the Age of Formative Books Over?" *Georgia Review* 40 (1986): 953–67.

Stayton, Richard. "Why Holden Caulfield Still Catches You." *Herald Examiner,* 12 Oct. 1985, 35.

Trowbridge, Clinton W. "Hamlet and Holden." *English Journal* 57.1 (Jan. 1968): 26–29.

Young, Tracy. "People Are Talking About Books: Looking for Mr. Salinger." *Vogue Magazine,* Aug. 1986, 196.

Case Study Interviews and
Related Community Commentary

Albuquerque, New Mexico

Four interview meetings and one telephone interview were conducted on 16–17 August 1983.

Albuquerque Tribune, 17–28 May 1968 [miscellaneous letters to the editor].

Jennings, Mary Lou. "Minister to Take Protest on Book to School Board." *Albuquerque Tribune,* 14 May 1968, 1.

Calhoun County, Alabama

Five interview meetings and one telephone interview were conducted on 18–19 August 1983.

Boutwell, Jane. "Parents' Protests Bring Removal of Alexandria Library Books." *Anniston Star,* 6 Oct. 1982, sects. 1A, 3A.

Calhoun County Board of Education. Central Complaint Committee Meeting Minutes. 1 Nov. 1982.

Murphy, Barbara Beasley. "Restricting Books in Alabama Schools: An Author Confronts Her Censors." *Authors Guild Bulletin* (spring 1983): 5, 13–14.

Marin County, California

Three interview meetings were conducted on 28 April 1983.

Simpers, Dorothy. "I-J Reporter's Notebook." *San Rafael Independent Journal,* 29 Dec. 1960, sect. 1C.

———. "Tam Trustees Again Refuse to Ban Books." *San Rafael Independent Journal,* 10 Jan. 1961, sects. 1A, 4A.

Smart, Anne. Letter to the Board of Trustees, Tamalpais Unified High School District, Marin County, Calif., 16 Dec. 1960.

Tamalpais Union High School District. Board of Trustees Meeting Minutes. 19 Dec. 1960–6 Feb. 1961.

English Teachers, Librarians, and Censorship

American Library Association. "Still Alive: The Best of the Best 1960–1974." Chicago: ALA, 1976.

———. "Best Books for Young Adults." Chicago: ALA, 1982.

———. "Outstanding Fiction for the College Bound." Chicago: ALA, 1982.

———. "Best Books for Young Adults." Chicago: ALA, 1983.

American Library Association, Office for Intellectual Freedom. *Intellectual Freedom Manual.* Chicago: ALA, 1974.

American Library Association, Young Adult Library Services Association. *Outstanding Books for the College Bound: Choices for a Generation.* Chicago: ALA/ALA Editions, 1996.

Aronson, Marc. "The Challenge and the Glory of Young Adult Literature." *Booklist* 93 (Apr. 1997): 1418–19.

Blau, Lois H. "The Novel in the High School Library: Censorship or Selection?" *Wisconsin Library Bulletin* 15 (May 1964): 178–81.

Boaz, Martha. "ALA's Intellectual Freedom Committee." *Wilson Library Bulletin* 39 (Apr. 1965): 651.

Bob, Murray C. "The Case for Quality Book Selection." *Library Journal* 107.16 (15 Sept. 1982): 1707–10.

Booth, Wayne C. "Censorship and the Values of Fiction." *The English Journal* 53.3 (March 1964): 155–164.

Burress, Lee A., Jr. "How Censorship Affects the School." Stevens Point, WI: *Wisconsin Council of Teachers of English*, Special Bulletin #8 (October 1963).

Carlsen, G. Robert. *Books and the Teen-Age Reader.* New York: Harper and Row, 1967.

"The Challenge of Censorship" [special theme issue]. *Book Report* 1.3 (Nov.–Dec. 1982).

"Classics You Ought to Keep." *The U*N*A*B*A*S*H*E*D* Librarian* 42 (1982): 19, 25.

Corbett, Edward: J. "Raise High the Barriers, Censors." *America,* 7 Jan. 1961, 441–44.

Crosthwait, Charles. "Censorship and the School Library." *Wilson Library Bulletin* 39 (Apr. 1965): 670–72.

Crowell, Robert L. "A Little Bit of Censoring." *Wilson Library Bulletin* 39 (Apr. 1965): 652–57.

Donelson, Kenneth L. "White Walls and High Windows: Some Contemporary Censorship Problems." *English Journal* 61 (Nov. 1972): 1191–98.

———. "Censorship in the 1970's: Some Ways to Handle It When It Comes (And It Will)." *English Journal* 63 (Feb. 1974): 47–51.

Edwards, June. "Censorship in the Schools: What's Moral About *The Catcher in the Rye*?" *English Journal* 72 (Apr. 1983): 39–42.

Ernst, Morris L. "Some Aspects of Censorship." *Wilson Library Bulletin* 39 (Apr. 1965): 668–69.

Foran, Donald, J.S.J. "A Doubletake on Holden Caulfield." *English Journal* 57.7 (Oct. 1968): 977–79.

Foster, Retha K. "Censorship and Arizona High Schools." *Arizona English Bulletin* 8 (May 1966): 65–68.

Kirsch, Robert R. "Custodians, Eunuchs, and Lovers." *Wilson Library Bulletin* 39 (Apr. 1965): 647–50.

Krug, Judith F. Undated letter to librarians regarding Banned Books Week, 1983. Chicago: American Library Association, Office of Intellectual Freedom.

Library Journal 108.9 (May 1983), cover artwork.

Lillinstein, Maxwell J. "Books and Bookstores: The Moral Squeeze." *Newsletter on Intellectual Freedom* 30.6 (Nov. 1981): 159, 184–85.

MacLeod, Anne Scott. "Censorship and Children's Literature." *Library Quarterly* 53.1 (1983): 26–38.

Moon, Eric. "The Benefit of Doubt." *Wilson Library Bulletin* 39 (Apr. 1965): 663–67.

National Council of Teachers of English. *The Student's Right to Read.* Champaign, Ill.: NCTE Publications, 1962.

Park, Charles J. "The Censorship War: Librarians at the Battlefront." *Newsletter on Intellectual Freedom* 30.6 (Nov. 1981): 150, 178–81.

Perry-Holmes, Claudia, and L. B. Woods. "The Flak if We Had The Joy of Sex Here." *Library Journal* 107.16 (15 Sept. 1982): 1711–15.

Sayers, Frances Clarke. "If the Trumpet Be Not Sounded." *Wilson Library Bulletin* 39 (Apr. 1965): 659–62, 684.

"Sideshow: Library Won't Throw Book During Amnesty." *Orange County Register,* 11 June 1985, sect. A2.

Utah Council of Teachers of English. "The Censorship Roundup in Utah." *Utah C.T.E. Bulletin* 5 (30 Sept. 1963): 4–5.

Censorship: School Boards, Parents, and Religious Leadership

Alley, Alvin D. "Puritanism: Scourge of Education Today." *Clearinghouse* 38 (Mar. 1964): 393–95.

Bowen, Robert O. "The Salinger Syndrome: Charity Against Whom?" *Ramparts* 1 (May 1962): 52–60.

Brown, Robert McAfee. "Listen, Jerry Falwell!" *Christianity and Crisis* 40 (22 Dec. 1980): 360–64.

Bull, Barry L. "The Constitution, Liberal Theory, and Textbook Bias." *Educational Forum* 44.2 (Jan. 1980): 147–62.

CIBC Racism and Sexism Research Center for Educators. *Human and Anti-Human Values in Children's Books: A Content Rating Instrument for Educators and Concerned Parents.* New York: Council of Interracial Books for Children, 1976.

Denier, Greg. "A Shift Toward the Right? Or a Failure on the Left?" *Christianity and Crisis* 40 (22 Dec. 1980): 355–60.

Fitzgerald, Thomas J., Msgr. "The Menace of Indecent Literature." *Ave Maria,* 22 Sept. 1956, 8–9, 28–30.

Gordon, Edward. "Freedom to Teach and to Learn." *PTA Magazine* 58.2 (Oct. 1963): 4–7.

Hall, Clarence W. "Poison in Print—And How to Get Rid of It." *Reader's Digest,* May 1964, 94–98.

Hogan, Robert F., and James R. Squire. "Should We Censor What Adolescents Read?: Where is the Danger?" *PTA Magazine* 59.7 (Mar. 1965): 12.

Hook, Sidney. "The Ground We Stand On: Democratic Humanism." *Free Inquiry* 1.1 (winter 1980–81): 8–10.

Hove, John. *Meeting Censorship in the School: A Series of Case Studies.* Champaign, Ill.: National Council of Teachers of English, 1967.

Kurtz, Paul. "A Secular Humanist Declaration." *Free Inquiry* 1.1 (winter 1980–81): 3–7.

Larue, Gerald. "The Moral Majority: An Immoral Minority." *Free Inquiry* 1.3 (summer 1983): 18.

Metz, Tracy. "The New Crusaders of the USA." *Index on Censorship,* Jan. 1982, 20–21.

Meyer, Majel. *Moral Standard for the New Age.* New York: Vantage P, 1974.

Norris, Hoke. "Should We Censor What Adolescents Read?: Two Kinds of Censorship." *PTA Magazine* 59.7 (Mar. 1965): 10–12.

North, William D. "Pico and the Challenge to Books in Schools." *Newsletter on Intellectual Freedom* 31.6 (Nov. 1982): 195, 221–25.

Rich, R. Bruce. "The Supreme Court's Decision in Island Trees." *Newsletter on Intellectual Freedom* 31.5 (Sept. 1982): 166, 173–81.

Ryan, William. "The Fundamentalist Right: Its Attack on Secular Humanism." *Free Inquiry* 1.1 (winter 1980–81): 16–21.

———. "The New Book Burners." *Free Inquiry* 1.3 (summer 1983): 14–18.

"Salinger: An Introduction." *Christian Century: An Ecumenical Weekly* 80 (27 Feb. 1963): 287.

Viguerie, Richard A. *The New Right: We're Ready to Lead.* Fall's Church, Va.: Viguerie Co., 1981.

Warwick, Donald. "Social Scientists Ought to Stop Lying." *Psychology Today* 8 (Feb. 1975): 38–49, 105–6.

Popular Culture Representations of Catcher *and Related Censorship*

Archie Bunker's Place. CBS Television Network. Episode aired 21 Feb. 1982.

Bowen, Michael. *Can't Miss.* New York: Harper and Row, 1987.

Family Feud. ABC Television Network. Episode aired 19 Oct. 1983.

Kinsella, W. P. *Shoeless Joe.* Boston, MA: Houghton-Mifflin, 1982.

Segal, Erich. *Oliver's Story.* New York: Harper and Row, 1977.

Sixty Minutes. CBS Television Network. Episode aired 1 Nov. 1981.

Smith, Julie. *New Orleans Beat.* New York: Ivy Books, 1994.

"Teen Suicide." *The Donahue Show.* Transcript no. 05127. NBC Television Network. 1987.

Nuclear Consciousness

Adams, Ruth, and Susan Cullen, eds. *The Final Epidemic: Physicians and Scientists on Nuclear War.* Chicago: Educational Foundation for Nuclear Science, 1981.

Alvarez, A. "A Talk with Robert Lowell." *Encounter,* Feb. 1965, 39–46.

Bethe, Hans. "The Hydrogen Bomb." *Bulletin of the Atomic Scientists,* Apr. 1950, 102.

Carey, Michael J. "Psychological Fallout." *Bulletin of the Atomic Scientists,* Jan. 1982, 20–24.

Child Study Association of America. *Children and the Threat of Nuclear War.* New York: Duell, Sloan and Pearce, 1964.

"Depression." *Newsweek,* 4 May 1987, 48.

Elias, Richard. "Facts of Life in the Nuclear Age." *School Library Journal,* Apr. 1985, 42–43.

Geddes, Donald Porter. *The Atomic Age Opens.* New York: Pocket Books, 1945.

Goldman, Peter. "Living with the Bomb: The First Generation of the Atomic Age." *Newsweek,* 29 July 1985, 28–50.

Gray, Paul. "Doomsdays." *Time,* 7 Aug. 1995, 48–53.

Krauthammer, Charles. "History Hijacked." *Time,* 13 Feb. 1995, 90.

LaFarge, Phyllis. "Learning to Live with the Bomb." *Parent's,* Mar. 1987, 122–25, 214.

Lane, Howard A. "What Are We Doing to Our Children?" *National Elementary Principal* 30 (June 1951): 4–8.

Mantell, Suzanne. "Fifty Years of the Nuclear Age." *Publishers Weekly,* 31 July 1995, 23–24.

Mitchell, Greg. "Ground Zero: TV's Nuclear Ages." *TV Guide,* 29 July–4 Aug. 1995, 16–17.

Rosenthal, Peggy. "The Nuclear Mushroom Cloud as Cultural Image." *American Literary History* 3.1 (spring 1991): 63–92.

Sherwin, Martin J. "The Assault on History: Forgetting the Bomb." *Nation,* 15 May 1995, 692–94.

References

Ahrens, Nyla Herber. "Censorship and the Teacher of English: A Questionnaire Survey of a Selected Sample of Secondary School Teachers of English." Ed.D. diss., Teachers College, Columbia Univ., 1965.

Ajemian, Robert; Anne Hopkins and Dan Goodgame. "1968." *Time,* 11 Jan. 1988, 16–27.

Anderson, Arthur James. *Problems in Intellectual Freedom and Censorship.* New York: R. R. Bowker Company, 1974.

Ariès, Philippe. *Centuries of Childhood.* Trans. Robert Baldick. New York: Random House, 1962. [Originally published under the title *L'Enfant et la vie familiale sous l'Ancien Régime.* Paris: Librairie Plon, 1960.]

Aronowitz, Stanley, and Henry Giroux. *Postmodern Education.* Minneapolis: U of Minnesota P, 1991.

Baumbach, Jonathan. *The Landscape of Nightmare: Studies in the Contemporary American Novel.* New York: New York UP, 1965.

Belcher, William, and James Lee. *J. D. Salinger and the Critics*. Belmont, Calif.: Wadsworth Publishing, 1962.

Bell, Daniel. *The End Of Ideology: On the Exhaustion of Political Ideas in the Fifties*. Garden City, N.Y.: Doubleday, 1964.

Bellah, Robert, et al. *Habits of the Heart: Individualism and Commitment in American Life*. Berkeley: U of California P, 1985.

Bennett, William J. *The De-Valuing of America: The Fight for Our Culture and Our Children*. New York: Simon and Schuster, 1992.

Bercovitch, Sacvan. *The American Jeremiad*. Madison: U of Wisconsin P, 1978.

Bok, Sissela. *Lying: Moral Choice in Public and Private Life*. New York: Pantheon Books, 1974.

Boyer, Paul. *Purity in Print: The Vice Society Movement and Book Censorship in America*. New York: Scribner's and Sons, 1968.

———. *By The Bomb's Early Light*. New York: Pantheon Books, 1985.

———. "Exotic Resonances: Hiroshima in American Memory." *Diplomatic History* 19.2 (spring 1995): 297–318.

Bradbury, Ray. *Farenheit 451*. New York: Ballantine Books, 1953.

Brown, JoAnne. "'A Is For Atom, B Is For Bomb': Civil Defense in American Public Education, 1948–1963." *Journal of American History* 75.1 (June 1988): 68–90.

Camus, Albert. *The Myth of Sisyphus*. Trans. Justin O'Brien. New York: Vintage Books, 1959.

Chafe, William. *The Unfinished Journey: America Since World War II*. New York: Oxford UP, 1986.

Clecak, Peter. *America's Quest for the Ideal Self*. New York: Oxford UP, 1983.

Coles, Robert. *The Moral Life of Children*. New York: Atlantic Monthly P, 1986.

Conroy, Frank. "The Fifties: America in a Trance." *Esquire* 99 (June 1983): 115–16.

Cooper, James Fenimore. *The Deerslayer*. 1841. Albany: State U of New York P, 1987.

Craig, Alec. *Suppressed Books*. New York: World Publishing Co., 1963.

DelFattore, Joan. *What Johnny Shouldn't Read: Textbook Censorship in America*. New Haven, N.J.: Yale UP, 1992.

Dickstein, Morris. *Gates of Eden: American Culture in the Sixties*. New York: Basic Books, 1977.

Didion, Joan. *Slouching towards Bethlehem*. New York: Farrar P, 1968.

Dinnerstein, Leonard, and Kenneth T. Jackson, eds. *American Vistas: 1877 to the Present,* vol. 2. 1971. New York: Oxford UP, 1979.

Drinnon, Richard. *Facing West: The Metaphysics of Indian-Hating and Empire-Building*. New York: New American Library, 1980.

Durkheim, Emile. *The Elementary Forms of Religious Life*. Trans. Joseph Ward Swain. 1915. New York: Free P/Macmillan Publishing, 1965.

Eco, Umberto. *A Theory of Semiotics*. Bloomington: Indiana UP, 1976.

———. *The Role of the Reader: Explorations in the Semiotics of Texts*. Bloomington: Indiana UP, 1979.

Emerson, Ralph Waldo. *Journals and Miscellaneous Notebooks of Ralph Waldo Emerson*, vol. 1, 1819–22. Cambridge, Mass.: Harvard UP, 1960.

Engelhardt, Tom. *The End of Victory Culture: Cold War America and the Disillusioning of a Generation*. New York: Basic Books, 1995.

Escarpit, Robert. *The Book Revolution*. London, Toronto, Paris: Unesco, 1966.

Farley, John J. "Book Censorship in the Senior High School Libraries of Nassau Co., N.Y." Ph.D. diss., New York Univ., 1964.

Fiedler, Leslie. *An End to Innocence*. Boston: Beacon P, 1955.

Filene, Peter. *Him/Her/Self*. New York: New American Library, 1974.

Firth, Raymond. *Symbols: Public and Private*. Ithaca, N.Y.: Cornell UP, 1975.

Fish, Stanley. *Is There a Text in This Class?* Cambridge, Mass.: Harvard UP, 1980.

FitzGerald, Frances. *America Revised: History Schoolbooks in the Twentieth Century*. Boston: Little, Brown and Co., 1979.

Fleishman, Stanley. "Witchcraft and Obscenity: Twin Superstitions." *Wilson Library Bulletin* 39 (Apr. 1965): 640–46.

French, Warren, ed. *The Fifties: Fiction, Poetry, Drama*. Deland, Fla.: Everett/Edwards, 1970.

———. *J. D. Salinger*. 1963. Rev. ed. Boston: Twayne Publishers, 1976.

———. *J.D. Salinger, Revisited*. Boston: Twayne Publishers, 1988.

Friedan, Betty. *The Feminine Mystique*. New York: W. W. Norton, 1963; reprint, New York: Dell Publishing, 1974.

Fruman, Norman and Marvin Laser, eds. *Studies in J. D. Salinger*. New York: Odyssey P, 1963.

Fussell, Paul. *The Great War and Modern Memory*. New York: Oxford UP, 1975.

Gaines, Donna. *Teenage Wasteland: Suburbia's Dead End Kids*. New York: Harper-Collins, 1990.

Galloway, David. *The Absurd Hero in American Fiction*. 1966. Austin: U of Texas P, 1970.

Geertz, Clifford. *The Interpretation of Cultures*. New York: Basic Books, 1973.

Geller, Evelyn. *Forbidden Books in American Public Libraries, 1876–1939: A Study in Cultural Change*. Westport, Conn.: Greenwood P, 1984.

Gerzon, Mark. *A Choice of Heroes: The Changing Faces of American Manhood*. Boston: Houghton Mifflin, 1982.

Graebner, William. "Coming of Age in Buffalo: The Ideology of Maturity in Postwar America." *Radical Historical Review* 34 (1986): 53–74.

Grunwald, Henry Anatole, ed. *Salinger: A Critical and Personal Portrait*. London: Peter Owen, 1964.

Gwynn, Frederick L., and Joseph L. Blotner. *The Fiction of J. D. Salinger*. Pittsburgh: U of Pittsburgh P, 1958.

Hamilton, Kenneth. *J. D. Salinger*. Grand Rapids, Mich.: W. B. Eerdmans Publishing, 1967.

Hassan, Ihab. *Radical Innocence: Studies in the Contemporary American Novel.* Princeton, N.J.: Princeton UP, 1961.

Hillocks, George Jr. "Books and Bombs: Ideological Conflict and the Schools— A Case Study of the Kanawha County Book Protest." *School Review* 86 (Aug. 1978): 632–54.

Hodgson, Godfrey. *America in Our Time.* Garden City, N.Y.: Doubleday, 1976.

Hoffman, Abbie. *Soon to Be a Major Motion Picture.* New York: G. Putnam's Sons, 1980.

Howe, Irving. *A World More Attractive: A View of Modern Literature and Politics.* New York: Horizon P, 1963.

Hunter, James Davison. *Culture Wars: The Struggle to Define America.* New York: Basic Books, 1991.

James, Henry. *The American Essays.* Ed. Leon Edel. New York: Vintage Books, 1956.

Jameson, Frederic. *The Political Unconscious: Narrative as a Socially Symbolic Act.* Ithaca, N.Y.: Cornell UP, 1981.

Jansen, Sue Curry. *Censorship: The Knot That Binds Power and Knowledge.* New York: Oxford UP, 1988.

Jennison, Peter S., and Robert N. Sheridan. *The Future of General Adult Books and Reading in America.* Chicago: American Library Association, 1970.

Kazin, Alfred. *On Native Grounds.* 1942. Garden City, N.J.: Doubleday, 1956.

Klein, Marcus. *After Alienation: American Novels in Mid-Century.* Cleveland: World Publishing/Meridian Books, 1965.

Kline, Stephen. *Out of the Garden: Toys, TV, and Children's Culture in the Age of Marketing.* New York: Verso, 1993.

Klinkowitz, Jerome. *Literary Disruptions: The Making of a Post-Contemporary Fiction.* Chicago: U of Illinois P, 1975.

Kuhn, Thomas S. *The Structure of Scientific Revolutions.* 1962. Chicago: U of Chicago P, 1970.

Lakoff, George. *Moral Politics: What Conservatives Know That Liberals Don't.* Chicago: U of Chicago P, 1996.

Langer, Suzanne. *Philosophy in a New Key.* Cambridge, Mass.: Harvard UP, 1942.
———. *Reflections on Art.* Baltimore, Md.: Johns Hopkins UP, 1942.

Lasch, Christopher. *The Minimal Self: Psychic Survival in Troubled Times.* New York: W. W. Norton, 1984.

Lewis, R. W. B. *The American Adam: Innocence, Tragedy, and Tradition in the Nineteenth Century.* 1955. Chicago: U of Chicago P, 1975.

Lifton, Robert Jay. *The Broken Connection: On Death and the Continuity of Life.* New York: Simon and Schuster, 1979.

Long, Elizabeth. "Designing Reader Studies: Towards the Empirical Investigation of Theories of the Text." Paper presented at the 1981 Biennial Convention of the American Studies Association, Memphis, Tenn.

Lukacs, Georg. *The Theory of the Novel.* Trans. Anna Bostock. Cambridge, Mass: MIT P, 1971. [First published by Cassirer (Berlin) 1920.]

Lundquist, James. *J. D. Salinger.* New York: Frederick Ungar Publishing, 1979.

Madden, David, ed. *American Dreams, American Nightmares.* Carbondale and Edwardsville: Southern Illinois UP, 1970.

Marsden, Malcolm. *If You Really Want to Know: A Catcher Casebook.* Chicago: Scott, Foresman, 1963.

Matthiessen, F. O. *American Renaissance: Art and Expression in the Age of Emerson and Whitman.* New York: Oxford UP, 1941.

Miller, Mark Crispin. "Family Feud." *New Republic* (18–25 July 1983): 23–27.

Moffett, James. *Storm in the Mountains: A Case Study of Censorship, Conflict, and Consciousness.* Carbondale: Southern Illinois UP, 1988.

Moore, Everett T. *Issues of Freedom in American Libraries.* Chicago: American Library Assoc., 1964.

Nadel, Alan. *Containment Culture: American Narratives, Postmodernism, and the Atomic Age.* Durham, N.C.: Duke UP, 1995.

Neibuhr, Reinhold. *The Irony of American History.* New York: Charles Scribners' Sons, 1952.

Nelson, Jack, and Gene Roberts Jr. *The Censors and the Schools.* Boston: Little, Brown, and Co., 1963.

Nuttall, Jeff. *Bomb Culture.* New York: Delacorte P, 1968.

O'Neill, William. *Coming Apart: An Informal History of America in the 1960's.* New York: Times Books, 1971.

Palladino, Grace. *Teenagers: An American History.* New York: Basic Books, 1996.

Postman, Neil. *The Disappearance of Childhood.* New York: Delacorte, 1982.

Radway, Janice A. "American Studies, Reader Theory, and the Literary Text: From the Study of Material Objects to the Study of Social Processes." Paper presented at the 1983 Biennial Convention of the American Studies Association, Philadelphia, Penn.

———. *Reading the Romance: Women, Patriarchy, and Popular Literature.* 1984. Chapel Hill: U of North Carolina P, 1991.

Riesman, David. *The Lonely Crowd.* New Haven, Conn.: Yale UP, 1950.

Robotham, John. *Freedom of Access to Library Materials.* New York: Neal-Schuman Publishers, 1982.

Root, E. Merrill. *Brainwashing in the High Schools.* New York: Devin-Adair, 1958.

Rosen, Gerald. "A Retrospective Look at *The Catcher in the Rye.*" *American Quarterly* 29 (winter 1977): 547–62.

Rudman, Marsha Kabakow. *Children's Literature: An Issues Approach.* Indianapolis, Ind.: Heath, 1976.

Sadker, David Miller, and Myra Pollack Sadker. *Now Upon a Time: A Contemporary View of Children's Literature.* New York: Harper and Row, 1977.

Salzman, Jack, ed. *New Essays on "The Catcher in the Rye."* New York: Cambridge UP, 1991.

Santayana, George. *Character and Opinion in the United States.* New York: George Braziller P, 1955.

Schell, Jonathan. *The Fate of the Earth.* New York: Alfred A. Knopf, 1982.

Simonson, Harold, and Philip E. Hager, eds. *Salinger's "Catcher in the Rye": Clamor vs. Criticism.* Lexington, Mass.: Heath, 1963.

Skotheim, Robert Allen. "'Innocence' and 'Beyond Innocence' in Recent American Scholarship." *American Quarterly* 13 (spring 1961): 93–99.

Slotkin, Richard. *Regeneration Through Violence.* Middletown, Conn.: Wesleyan UP, 1973.

Sochen, June. "On Writing Cultural History." *American Studies Association Newsletter,* June 1985, 3–4.

Solomon, J. Fisher. *Discourse and Reference in the Nuclear Age.* Norman: U of Oklahoma P, 1988.

Spacks, Patricia Meyer. *The Adolescent Idea: Myths of Youth and the Adult Imagination.* New York: Basic Books, 1981.

Symula, James Francis. "Censorship of High School Literature: A Study of the Incidents of Censorship Involving J.D. Salinger's *Catcher in the Rye.*" Ed.D. diss., State Univ. of New York, Buffalo, 1969.

Thaxton, Carlton J. "An Analysis of the Twenty-Four Novels Published Between 1947 and 1957 Which Were Reported ... Banned or Blacklisted in the United States in the Years 1956 or 1957." Master's thesis, Florida State Univ., 1958.

Tompkins, Jane. *Sensational Designs: The Cultural Work of American Fiction, 1790–1860.* New York: Oxford UP, 1985.

Turner, Victor. *Dramas, Fields, and Metaphors: Symbolic Action in Human Society.* Ithaca, N.Y.: Cornell UP, 1974.

Vonnegut, Kurt. "Two Letters." *Index on Censorship,* June 1981, 19–21.

Walker, J. Samuel. "History, Collective Memory, and the Decision to Use the Bomb." *Diplomatic History* 19.2 (spring 1995): 319–28.

Weart, Spencer R. *Nuclear Fear: A History of Images.* Cambridge, Mass.: Harvard UP, 1988.

West, Mark I. *Children, Culture, and Controversy.* Hamden, Conn.: Archon Books, 1988.

Whitfield, Stephen J. "The 1950's: The Era of No Hard Feelings." *South Atlantic Quarterly* 76 (autumn 1977): 550–68.

————. "Cherished and Cursed: Toward a Social History of *The Catcher in the Rye.*" *New England Quarterly* 70.4 (1997): 567–600.

Whyte, William H., Jr. *The Organization Man.* New York: Simon and Schuster, 1956.

Will, George F. "Huck at a Hundred." *Newsweek,* 18 Feb. 1985, 92.

Wise, Gene. "'Paradigm Dramas' in American Studies: A Cultural and Institutional History of the Movement." *American Quarterly* 31 [bibliography issue] (1987): 291–337.

Woods, L. B. *A Decade of Censorship in America: The Threat to Classrooms and Libraries, 1966–1975.* Metuchen, N.J.: Scarecrow P, 1979.

Index